SOCIETY AND CULTURE IN EAST-CENTRAL EUROPE
General Editors: Irena Grudzinska-Gross and Jan T. Gross

THE DYNAMICS OF THE BREAKTHROUGH IN EASTERN EUROPE

The Polish Experience

JADWIGA STANISZKIS

TRANSLATED BY CHESTER A. KISIEL
FOREWORD BY IVAN SZELENYI

UNIVERSITY OF CALIFORNIA PRESS
BERKELEY   LOS ANGELES   OXFORD

University of California Press
Berkeley and Los Angeles, California

University of California Press
Oxford, England

Copyright © 1991 by The Regents of the University of California

Library of Congress Cataloging-in-Publication Data

Staniszkis, Jadwiga.
   The dynamics of the breakthrough in Eastern Europe / Jadwiga
Staniszkis : translated [from the Polish] by Chester A. Kisiel.
      p.   cm.—(Societies and culture in East-Central Europe : 6)
   Includes bibliographical references and index.
   ISBN 0-520-07218-9
      1. Communism—Europe, Eastern—History.   2. Europe,
Eastern—Economic Conditions—1989–   3. Europe, Eastern—Politics and
government—1989–   I. Title.   II. Series.
HX238.5.S73   1991
320.5'323'0947—dc20   90-23848
                                                                     CIP

Contents

Foreword

Poland's Self-limiting Revolution

Jadwiga Staniszkis is one of the most original and influential Polish sociologists of our times.

She became widely known in the United States when her book *Poland's Self-limiting Revolution* was published in 1984. Jadwiga Staniszkis was one of the seven advisers of Solidarity during the strikes of August 1980 in the Gdansk Shipyard. In her first book she gave an empirically well-documented, theoretically complex, though politically detached and often quite critical account of the birth of the Solidarity movement.

The current book resembles in many ways the first one. Like *Poland's Self-limiting Revolution, The Dynamics of the Breakthrough in Eastern Europe* is an ongoing, theoretically informed commentary of revolutionary events by a "participant observer." This time the events are the breakdown of socialism in Eastern Europe with an emphasis on Poland between 1989–1990. Her style and methodology make the book particularly exciting allowing us not only to observe how history unfolds but also to follow the evolution of the thinking of the author. *The Dynamics of the Breakthrough in Eastern Europe* is a collection of essays written immediately after major events took place. These essays were not altered significantly, thus allowing the reader to check how accurate Staniszkis's assessments were, how well her predictions about alternative futures stood the test of time. One could hardly think of a more risky task for a sociologist to undertake, for during the years 1989–1990 history seems to have progressed at an extraordinarily fast pace. Like the first book, the current one is also distinguished by the even-handedness, the thoughtful, detached character of the analysis. Though Jadwiga Staniszkis in these years was once again an adviser—this time she helped the presidential campaign of Lech Walesa during the late autumn of 1990—she is far from an advocate of the views of the pro-Walesa wing of Solidarity. She keeps as much analytical distance from Walesa's populism as the kept from the politics of the Solidarity movement in her first book. In both books she presents herself as a trustworthy commentator, a sociologist who practices her profession as a vocation in the best traditions of our trade.

The Ontology of Socialism

Before the dramatic events of 1989–1990 Staniszkis completed a new manuscript, *The Ontology of Socialism*, which was published in Polish in 1989. The *The Ontology of Socialism* Staniszkis spots contradictions in three spheres: in politics, the economy, and international relations. Politically socialism is threatened by the contradiction between the claim of the vanguard to represent the "objective laws of history" and and the actual "subjectivism and anarchy" in the social system. Economically socialist systems pretend to be stable and tightly controlled, whereas in reality, due to the absence of market and the resulting lack of information, the economic processes are quite chaotic. Internationally socialist countries are caught in dual dependency: they are dependent on the capitalist world system and also on the "Empire," the U.S.S.R. and the socialist world system.

Whereas *The Ontology of Socialism* was an analysis of systemic contradictions within socialism, *The Dynamics of the Breakthrough in Eastern Europe* looks at those historically unique factors, conjunctures, or "chance events," which were present during the end of the 1980s and thus contributed to the collapse of socialism. The book also analyzes the new contradictions, which are the products of the breakdown of the socialist system and the emergence of postsocialist socioeconomic order. Thus Staniszkis argues that although the systemic contradictions were grave enough, in themselves they may not have led to the breakdown of socialism. It was chance events that deepened the crisis produced by such systemic contradictions. Among such chance events Staniszkis names the rise of Mikhail Gorbachev to power, with the corresponding changes in the elite in the U.S.S.R. These new elites were the "globalists," that technocratic fraction of the *nomenklatura* which looks "at things from the perspective of the world system." The globalists believe in the necessity for the U.S.S.R. to adapt to the logic of advanced capitalism, and they are ready to go a long way on the road of pragmatic reform—they are even ready to give up Eastern Europe—to achieve this.

The Transition from Socialism to Capitalism

Such an interplay of systemic contradictions and chance events created the conditions of what Staniszkis calls "ontological opening": a change in the mode of production, a change in property rights, a transition from socialism into capitalism.

Collective ownership under socialism was an "ontological barrier," its function was to prevent the penetration of capitalism while interacting with the capitalist world system. However this ontological barrier resulted in "dependent socialism": the influx of innovation from the capitalist world economy was blocked but the socialist economies of Eastern Europe were still affected by the fluctuations of Western capitalism. Thus "socialist dependence" according to Staniszkis was purely "negative." With the current breakthrough, with the transition from socialism to capitalism, Eastern Europe will retain its peripheral and dependent status in the world, but from the "negative" socialist dependence it may move towards captitalist "dependent development." Socialist dependence resulted in the development of underdevelopment: Staniszkis now anticipates Eastern Europe to experience some development, even if it will be of a dependent nature.

The essence of the breakthrough that took place in Eastern Europe in 1989–1990 is the breakdown of this ontological barrier. It is an ontological opening, or convergence, and privatization is the major mechanism of such an ontological convergence.

According to Staniszkis ontological opening usually takes the form of "political capitalism." The economy in the epoch of tran-

sition is segmented into two sectors: first, there is the traditional private sector, composed of the new entrepreneurs who emerge
from what used to be the second economy; and second, there is the
state sector, which is now being privatized, and which becomes the
private property of the former *nomenklatura*.

The traditional private sector is not particularly dynamic, it may
even be shrinking as a result of postsocialist economic policies,
which cut into the real incomes of small entrepreneurs. The second
economy in the past coexisted with the statist sector, it was de-
fended against free competition from the world market, its inputs
were subsidized.

Political capitalism evolves in the second sector, as political authority is being converted into economic power, or private property. The growth of capitalism takes place almost exclusively in this
sector. The privatization of the public sector, the strategy of "making owners of the *nomenklatura*," gained momentum, particularly
since this was a strategy to change the foundation of the dominant
position of the ruling apparatus without disturbing the system of
domination. It won the *nomenklatura* over, made them supporters, rather than opponents, of the transition from socialism to
capitalism. According to Staniszkis, by mid-1990 about 10 to 20
percent of all fixed capital was privately owned by the former
nomenklatura in Poland.

In the first part of the book Staniszkis makes a major contribution to the study of the postcommunist transition in Eastern
Europe: I find her description of the current East European evolution as political capitalism insightful and sobering. She also has
formulated the most stimulating, most provocative sociological
hypothesis so far about changes of social structure: the former
nomenklatura may not be the victims of the transition, but many if
not most of them may be able to convert their political authority
into private wealth. Staniszkis is concerned about the prospects of
political capitalism and the bourgeoisification of the *nomenklatura*. She sees that this may actually strengthen monopolies in the
economy, rather than create competitive markets. She is afraid
that the new *nomenklatura* bourgeoisie may be in a good position
to pass some of their costs successfully over to the state and tax-
payers. Political capitalism is likely to be rather corrupt and may
discredit the idea of privatization. In may hurt traditional capital-

ists, genuine entrepreneurs who cannot compete with the thus created monopolies. Staniszkis is also aware of the political opposition to such developments. However on the whole, as an analyst, she accepts political capitalism as the most likely scenario for postcommunist transition.

The major problem of this transition is to reconcile two contradictory imperatives: those of stabilization and transformation. The major puzzle new elites in Eastern Europe have to solve today is how to demonstrate to their constituencies that sufficient and deep enough change has taken place, but that stability is also maintained. Political capitalism and *nomenklatura* bourgeoisification is transformation and stability at the same time.

The Nature of the New State: Standestaat

The second part of the book discusses the politics of the transition.

It gives an empirically detailed overview of the struggles within the former Communist party, between the old apparatus and the "New Center." The New Center itself was segmented into a "globalist" and "populist" wing. The globalists were ready to move more radically toward the West, to integrate the economy into the capitalist world system, to conduct far-reaching privatization, and to accept the multiparty system. The populist wing of the former Communist party focused more on internal contradiction, such as changes in leadership, and hoped to reform the party and institute self-management. In Eastern Europe the New Center won but soon after its victory it collapsed both in Poland and Hungary.

The most stimulating sections of the second part of the book deal with the nature of the new political system, which emerged after the collapse of the New Center. In common parlance one refers to the recent political transformation in Eastern Europe as "transition from totalitarianism to democracy." Staniszkis, however, subjects the nature of the emergent East European state to theoretical scrutiny.

In her view states like those of contemporary Poland or Hungary are not quite democratic yet. One can best describe them as *Standestaat*. The concept of Standestaat was used in Germany during the last phases of feudalism. The Standestaat is segmented into several "estates" that represent different group ethos, and they are certainly not "clearly defined groups with specific economic interests." Under such circumstances political struggles center mainly around symbols; political battles are not fought over economic interests. This, according to Staniszkis, corresponds to the relative backwardness of civil society. Indeed, civil society cannot come into existence without the "ontological opening," thus without the emergence of private property and the corresponding emergence of class cleavages. The economic bases of civil society does not yet exist.

Politics in Standestaat is quite peculiar. Since political struggles are primarily "symbolic," parties do not have clearly defined constituencies. Political actors are campaigning for each others' constituencies. One unanticipated consequence is massive demobilization of the population. Low electoral turnout is an indication of this: in June 1989 at the Polish elections only 62 percent of the eligible voters cast their vote. Younger people and the working class—those who were driving forces of the Solidarity movement in 1980–1981—were especially unlikely to vote. Membership of Solidarity is down from 80 percent in 1980 (when it was risky to join the union) to 10 to 30 percent today (when it is not only safe, but may even be advantageous to be in Solidarity).

The period 1989–1990 in Eastern Europe was a revolution from above, and it could not have been otherwise since there was no organized social force to conduct its own revolution. Staniszkis notes that this revolution from above was conducted out of "theoretical interests." She quotes the Polish Minister of Industry, who stated before the Seym (the Polish Parliament): "I represent interests that do not exist yet." There is an astonishing similarity between this liberal, precapitalist stand and the Leninist view of history. The bolsheviks conducted a proletarian revolution in a peasant country without a proletariat in order to create a proletariat. The East European intelligentsia is conducting a bourgeois revolution in a society without a bourgeoisie in order to create the bourgeoisie.

This is a formidable, powerful book. Staniszkis's conclusions about socioeconomic and political consequences of the postcommunist transition are thoughtful and thought-provoking. This is not an easy book to read. It assumes the reader to have some familiarity with East European societies and European social thought.

But it is worth the investment of time and effort, since Staniszkis poses the hypotheses that are likely to guide social research on postcommunist transitions for years to come.

Ivan Szelenyi

Chapter One

History and Chance:

The Dynamics of the Breakthrough in the Eastern Bloc

> *The logic of previous (descending) formation is unable to explain fully the manner and pace of its passage to a new formation. For this change is not merely the cumulation of a sequence of evolutionary transformations but is something that is taking place by leaps. Chance and a special tangle of historical circumstances are just as important here as the dynamics of the contradictions of the waning formation.*
>
> —J. Staniszkis,
> *The Ontology of Socialism*

February 1990

The above remarks were written about the passage from feudalism to capitalism, but they apply to the present transformation in Eastern bloc countries.[1] The breakthrough in the Eastern bloc can be seen as a sequence of three moments: systemic contradictions within socialism, unique historical circumstances and chance phenomena, and the new contradictions within the emerging system. I wrote extensively about the contradictions within socialism in my previous book, *The Ontology of Socialism* (Oxford University Press, in preparation). The aim of this book is to grasp the second and third components in the sequence.

I ended *Ontology* with a description of the moment of the exhaustion of real socialism—in other words, the moment when it was no longer possible to resolve the crisis within the existing system on account of the lack of material and symbolic reserves and of institutional freedom of maneuver. At that point, the measures that could reduce tensions go beyond the existing system and violate its identity (e.g., sharing power and responsibility with the previous opposition).

Contradictions within Socialism

The contradictions of real socialism, which destroys itself in successive series of crises, appeared in Eastern Europe in three spheres.

First, in the sphere of domination. This was the contradiction between the Communist authorities' claims to be an "avant-garde" and to represent the "objective laws of history," on the one hand, and the subjectivism and anarchy inexorably resulting from such a formula, on the other. In laying claim to the role of the substitute for the "real [vulgarizing Hegel] subjects of history," the Communist leadership rejected the idea of "representation." The anarchy toward which the system of domination in real socialism moved was also associated with the lack of a civil society. In this situation political crises were first and foremost attempts of the atomized society to form itself into an entity of collective action. Owing to the absence of a number of key economic interests in the state-controlled economy, the crystallization of this collective entity took place either with the use of national slogans or with the help of the "added value" of the myth of moral right, as in Solidarity's case. (The Communist party used the myth of the "avant-garde.") Politics and mediation were made difficult in this situation. As we can see from the example of Poland of 1988 through 1990, the passage to the phase of politics and "revolution from above" became possible only after the corrosion and dismantling of the fundamentalist myths expressed by workers' Solidarity of 1980 and 1981. Rationalization of the political identity of the sides, which made it possible for the breakthrough in the system to get under way, was combined with a rejection of their previous ideological identity. This process concerned both sides, the Communist party and the opposition, and was equally painful for the "base" of both.

The second sphere was the similar ontological contradiction that appeared in the economy. The formula of state ownership destroyed a number of economic interests and mechanisms and led to unavoidable attempts to replace them by the state. This changed the economy into a structure of controls. On one hand, stability/control became the main principle according to which the authorities conducted redistributive activity. On the other hand, with the absence of a market (which cannot come into being when only one owner exists, the state) neither did there exist crucial information to make economic sense of actions. In this situation real control of the economic process was impossible. And so here, as in the sphere of domination, we observe inexorable anarchization and regulation solely through exceptional actions undertaken in crisis situations.

The third sphere in which a systemic contradiction appeared was the special colonial situation in Eastern Europe. This involved dependency of two degrees, so to speak: first, the bloc as a whole on the world capitalist system, and second, politically imposed economic co-dependency within the bloc (COMECON, the Council for Mutual Economic Assistance). This council had the goal of reducing the tensions generated by the first type of dependency. The production and trade specializations and forced transfers and investments imposed on individual countries of the region were supposed to serve this end. Without this it would not have been possible to build the military (and political) power of the empire. Today, however, the costs of maintaining the COMECON (chiefly structural costs) exceed the benefits for all of its participants (including the U.S.S.R.). And so the previous form of the adaptation of real socialism to its systemic (resulting from the type of ownership) "subarticulation" to world capitalism exhausted itself in the Eastern bloc. The complexity of this situation was due to the fact that a return to the structures of the world division of labor is a socially painful and costly process. It requires privatization and moving to market rules of the game. The system of production based on state ownership made the East European economies noncompetitive in world markets, and the branch structure of production imposed by the COMECON deepens this isolation even more. In this situation redefinition of the relation of the Eastern bloc to the world system (and this is how the present systemic transformations in Eastern Europe can be interpreted) does not do away with the peripheral status of this region, but only bases this peripheral status on different principles. This new form of dependency (between the European Economic Community, Japanese banks, and Moscow) can have implications just as dramatic as the earlier dependency within the empire.

Causes of Breakthrough in the Socialist System

The sources of the incipient breakthrough in the socialist system lie in the dynamics of the above contradictions, on one hand, and in the dynamics of the colonial situation within the empire, on the other. Ontological contradictions in the spheres of domination and the economy have the effect of creating anarchy in both these spheres. Until recently, however, instruments were available for overcoming this anarchy—temporarily at least—and restoring the disturbed wholeness. The novelty of the present situation is that contradictions continue to create anarchy in the system, whereas the techniques for overcoming anarchy have been almost completely exhausted.

Foremost among these techniques was the mechanism of regulation through crisis,[2] when during periodically recurring economic crises corrections were made in investment plans and investments in progress and inputs were shifted to industries working for the market—thereby temporarily reducing the tensions accompanying extreme economic disequilibrium and the evident uncontrollability of the system (in which normal procedures were unable to ensure fulfillment of planned tasks.) Those countries in which severe economic crisis did not break out also made corrections in their plans. They observed the troubles of their neighbors and anticipated similar tensions at home (if only because in all the socialist countries, investment cycles, most often interrupted by crisis in the self-choking, unbalanced economy, were associated, inter alia, with obligations to the COMECON and the Warsaw Pact). Also, paradoxically, the political crises were a singular factor restoring wholeness, because they laid bare the phenomenon of a "lifeless structure." It became apparent that even a radical rejection of the system (e.g., in moral categories) would not necessarily bring about a change in it. On the contrary, in every crisis a factor that reproduced the underlying structure of the system recurred (as when wage demands revived the redistribution activity of the state in the economy, while the politics of identity—that is, the efforts of the atomized society to form itself into an entity of collective action—made use of the added value of the myth, recalling in its very reasoning the ideological thinking of the Communist party).

Today, however, the nature of the mechanisms described above has changed. Regulation through crisis in the material sphere, consisting in using an exceptional procedure for the allocation of funds, is much more difficult than before because obligations within the empire are more strictly monitored than before. The Soviet center of the empire is itself feeling the costs of subarticulation more strongly (and must burden its colonies with part of them), while Mikhail Gorbachev's reforms require a relatively favorable market (which in a period of smaller revenues from the sale of crude oil can be ensured only by specialization and trade imposed on the East European countries by political methods and often in competition with their domestic needs). Thus the freedom to maneuver production factors is limited, the more so as we have been observing a so-called equilibrium gap since the end of the 1970s in the countries of real socialism.[3] This means that the reserves of extensive development have become exhausted, but the excessive use of energy and raw materials per unit of national income in comparison with the capitalist countries does not constitute a reserve:[4] it cannot be tapped because it forms a link in the local system of equilibrium. The stabilizing effect of the inert structure has also diminished considerably. For instance, the decentralization of wage decisions in the course of the reform efforts (which are unable to restore the interests and mechanisms eliminated by the act of nationalization) to the enterprise level caused an immediate increase in wages to the highest possible level in a given enterprise. Therefore, in the face of new tasks the only reserve turned out to be taxes paid to the state and regarded by it as rent due to it by virtue of ownership. Hence it was no accident that in May 1988 striking workers raised the problem of ownership and the right of the state to siphon off the depreciation fund and other deductions from the enterprise.[5] Consequently, the same wage demands, which in the past had the effect of invoking the same role of the state in the economy, began to lead to questions about this role (and the entire formula of state ownership).

In 1987, during the first stage of "breakthrough" (yet before the "round table"), new interests were appearing that were already beginning to infringe upon the critical mass of the structure, described above, both in its dimension of ownership and in the system of prerogative domination. These interests were coupled with a reformulated rationale of control and with the needs of the Communist state itself. What was more, purely economic interests were increasing in importance as changes accelerated and as groups and classes appeared that were materially interested in continuing the changes. A similar sequence of events took place during the separation of exclusive ownership from the structure of divided rights in the passage from feudalism to capitalism.[6] It is in the interest of the power elite to create additional gratifications for its executives (*nomenklatura*) by enabling them to become an economic class, in addition to their status as a political class.

Another example was the desire of the power elite to reshape workers' identity by allowing them to acquire ownership shares in enterprises. The aim was to bring about a more pragmatic, deconcentrated articulation of possible protests and to direct protests against the administration in place of fundamentalist criticism articulated in moral terms directed against the Communist party. Another reason for the state's interest in ownership changes was that such changes released at least some of the locked-up production factors.[7] The state also expected that ownership changes would make possible real control over production. It had finally been understood that such control is possible only when there is a full range of economic interests and objective economic information flowing from the economy and verified by the market.

Finally, the state was the channel for signals and pressures from the Soviet center of control. The Soviets, though unwilling (and unable in the Soviet conditions of the equilibrium gap, the very strongly felt tensions of subarticulation, and the complicated process of domestic reforms) to modify obligations within the COMECON, consented to and even pressed for economic reforms in the East European countries. For the Soviet center wanted compensation—through better economic performance achieved through reforms—for the burdens it bore for the dependent countries, and it hoped thereby to increase the political stability of the empire. The matter was further complicated in so far as the same

dual dependency increased the consent of the Soviet center to reforms, and—at the same time—made these reforms highly difficult (owing to the imposed integration in COMECON and to the
allocation of a considerable part of production factors in accordance with obligations in the imperial cluster). The colonial situation was conducive to reforms not only from the viewpoint of the
interest of the Soviets; those Eastern bloc countries that were the
most developed and were saddled with the greatest burdens of
forced redistribution (to distribute the costs of subarticulation
evenly) were also interested in reforms. They pushed for the
assignment of ownership and a more precise definition of financial
obligations with the empire—in order to perceive obligations
more clearly and to be able to conduct political negotiations with
the Soviets.[8]

This stage (1987 through early 1988) can be labeled as a phase
of "libertization," not "democratization." At this stage political
reforms were treated by the Communist power center as unavoidable because of their role in economic reforms. They understood
that economic changes must be followed by political changes. This
was not a question of political reforms in the name of values (e.g.,
human rights), but of changes indispensable for promoting and
consolidating ownership reforms. First and foremost, a change
was necessary in the philosophy of prerogative domination, with
guarantees for the permanence of ownership rights (including
new property rights for the *nomenklatura*). Legal guarantees are
nothing without a change in the relation between the political leadership and society and in the principles for recruiting the power
apparatus. It is also necessary to abandon the formula of monolithic domination in favor of Montesquieu's tripartite division of
powers. This sequence of events—obviously, spread over time—
seems probable because it is functionally indispensable for the success of ownership reforms, which in turn are indispensable for the
stability of the empire.

The severity of the crisis and its long duration were also conducive to political reforms, which, inter alia, were connected with
recognition by the leadership of the right of independent subjects
to be present in the political arena. The ruling group was expressing more and more willingness to share the responsibility of
government. It was well aware that the simple co-optation of a

few independent persons would not solve the problem but would only destroy the authority of those persons. Thus of necessity it consented to more universal rules (e.g., political rights for associations to put forward their candidates to the new second chamber, the Senate, in Poland). From the point of view of the leadership, this last solution had the advantage of somewhat curbing competition with the Communist party. This search by the leadership for greater legitimation (in official language called expanding the base of government) visibly galvanized the other parties in the official coalition, which until then had been largely a facade. The obvious efforts in Poland to make this coalition a real one (e.g., the pronouncement by the head of the Democratic party that the entire coalition should have a majority in the Seym—and not necessarily the Communist party [PUWP] alone—while the role of a specific party should depend on the attractiveness of its program) showed that the likely first step in political reforms would be to breathe life into the facade, thereby considerably restricting and indirectly formalizing the leading role of the Communist party. At this stage the opposition (Solidarity) was more a detonator than a participant in the pluralization process, which was limited to the subjects in the political arena that were officially recognized by the Communists.

Characteristics of Breakthrough

The first phase of the breakthrough described above (1987 through early 1988, before the "round table") exploited to the maximum an instrument characteristic of the system that was itself the object of reform efforts. For instance, the creation of an economic class from the present political class took place by exploiting the legislative amorphousness (and the concept of legality) characteristic of the prerogative state. An example of this was the first stage of the assignment of ownership from the previous homogeneous state ownership. The key element of this stage was the dual ownership status (which could not be legalized as such) of fixed assets in the state sector: sometimes these assets were regarded as being in assigned group ownership; at other times they were considered part of state property.[9] As this phase proceeded, however, it became necessary—if only to create legal guarantees (without which capital will not flow in)—to call the process of assigning ownership rights and their formalization by name. That stage was reminiscent of the period of feudal divided ownership (when different subjects had the informal right of ownership to the same thing). The next phase, which would compel the rejection of the existing philosophy of law, would be that of defining exclusive rights.

A fascinating problem in studying the breakthrough in the socialist system is the continuity in change. The actions that disturb the critical mass of the system are often a more radical pursuit of some goals specific to this system (e.g., adaptation to systemic subarticulation). Sometimes these actions make use of instruments characteristic of the system itself. This is especially apparent in the first phase of changes, which are greatly facilitated by the underformalized or, more broadly, the prerogative nature of domination (e.g., the dual, not fully legalized status of fixed assets in joint stock companies formed on the basis of state enterprises, or the role of the *nomenklatura* principle in transforming the political class into an economic class). These instruments, however, which create a population with new interests, set in motion events that—independently of the original intentions—bring about changes in the system (e.g., the new class looks for legal guarantees of the permanence of its status and presses for transformations in the philosophy of prerogative domination). The most surrealistic example of continuity in change at this stage of breakthrough is the return during ideological debate inside the Communist elite to certain dilemmas that were perceived at the very establishment of the system. Thus the plans to sell ownership shares to workers in order to transform this class into a mythologized proletariat go back directly to discussions in the 1920s, though certain solutions accepted at that time (the Communist party as a substitute for the proletariat) are rejected today. The study of continuity in change facilitates understanding of the logic of changes from above—when the leadership attempts to limit itself but rejects social control in this respect and does not (or perhaps cannot) give any guarantees of the permanence of this process.

Breakthrough rather than Internal Reforms

Why do I speak of a breakthrough in the political system of the countries of real socialism rather than of internal systemic reforms? It seems to me that the dynamics of structural contradic-

tions and the dilemmas of the position of the empire reached a
point in the mid 80s at which interests appeared (including among
the leadership) that encroached on the critical mass of the system,
which hitherto had been reproduced only through partial changes
or regulation through crisis. In any event, this change is not
directed from one center. Rather, it is a tangle of processes, in
many cases local adaptive behavior that in an unplanned way take
on broader meaning. Even if guided, the intentions of these movements would be not a breakthrough but reproduction of the system of domination (and even a radical return to the ideology). The
outcome was the opposite. I am interested in the outcomes and not
in the intentions, however. And the crucial point of the breakthrough is changes in the web of interests and an increase in the
number of people interested in change as it continues. This creation of a population with new interests (spontaneously or planned)
and the evolution from theoretical to real interests[10] are specific to
the breakthrough in real socialism, which at the beginning of this
process was lacking a number of crucial interests and a civil
society.

Chance and Special Circumstances

The acceleration of changes observed recently in Eastern Europe,
however, is not due solely to the intensification of the above contradictions; also important here is a series of chance events. What
are they?

First, finding (through trials and errors made in conditions of
the severe crisis of 1988 and 1989) *a new model of the conflict* in
the economy. This new model gives a certain "breather" to the
state even before a new systemic quality has appeared in the economy. In other words, before privatization of the state sector (that
is, before the nature of the contradiction has changed). As it
moved away from setting prices and subsidizing the economy, the
state simultaneously withdrew from the scene of the conflict. In
the previous model of the conflict the state was rejected in moral
categories, but at the same time it was referred to as the administrative distributor of money. Today (1989–1990) the conflict
gives the impression that it is taking place within the society alone
and for the time being remains on the threshold of political arti-

culation. An example: the dramatic conflict over the formation of capital taking place today in Poland in conditions of a severe recession. This is a conflict between state-owned industry, private companies built into that structure (and benefiting from the possibility of throwing some of their costs onto it), and private farming. The state (or rather the Central Bank and the Treasury) set the rules of the capital formation game (and thus the chances in this conflict of the individual segments of the economy), but this is power more of the structural than relational type[11] and is not commonly perceived. This difficulty of articulating the new map of conflicts (deepened by the fact that the government—constituted with the participation of solidarity—is perceived as "ours") gives the state the aforementioned "breather." And so a peculiar protective niche has appeared in the boundary wall between real socialism and the new, not yet existing, system. This new structuralization of the conflict, characteristic of the phase after the 1989 parliamentary elections, is now being initiated in other countries of Eastern Europe, but the precursor was Poland.

The second historical accident is the appearance, once again in Poland, in recent years (as a result of the struggle of authentic social forces) of *a unique formula of communication*, the so-called "round table," which is somewhat similar to the process of "transition through transactions" during democratization in Latin America. The "round table" talks (February–March 1989) were talks between Solidarity leaders and the Communist elite, initiated by the latter after being proposed by Interior Minister Czeslaw Kiszczak in August 1988 after a violent wave of strikes. This unique formula evolved from a process of trials and errors over several years, exploiting Poland's characteristic symbolic political culture and unique role of the Church, characteristics that do not exist in other countries of Eastern Europe. As a result, a singular innovation appeared in the techniques of control, one that became useful for the entire bloc, in which it is being successfully imitated today. It is also imitated in countries where, as in Bulgaria or Mongolia, there is less opposition than chairs at the table. Symbolic "turning points," the developed (and imitated) repertoire of demands, and finally, the unmistakableness of the ritualized moment of the breakthrough make it possible to work out (and popularize via TV) a characteristic canon of the process of changes. This is true even in countries where only the seeds of an opposition exist; using the unique "round table" communication, such countries can imitate the Polish process. This also makes the entire process more predictable. It gives the regime elite a feeling of safety and allows the previous power elite to reorient itself at the right moment.[12] A good example is Czechoslovakia. This invention of "television revolutions" makes it possible to ritualize (and control) the process of changes. For the present transformation in Eastern Europe it is just as important as the invention of printing or the passage from extensive to intensive techniques of power in late feudalism.[13] Only Romania broke away from this ritualization on account of the sharp domestic conflict between the pro-Gorbachev and pro-Ceauşescu (authoritarian-national) elites and the social tensions that had built up for years. Nor was there the phase of ritualization of repression in Romania, which in all the other countries preceded the phase of ritualization of changes. To emphasize once again: the changes are deep and real, but their vehicle was the ritualized ceremony of communication at the "round table," after which part of the opposition was co-opted to the political leadership. In the U.S.S.R. the changes are taking a different course. Centrifugal nationalistic pressures and the lack of a set of similarly experienced symbols common to the entire country make such ritualization impossible. Paradoxically, the only common symbol is the negatively experienced Communist party, which is the initiator of the reforms. In the German Democratic Republic, in turn, where in the first phase of the changes an attempt also was made to use the ritual of the "round table," the situation got out of control. The reason lies in the extent of the corruption of the old-regime authorities which came to light. This exposure of corruption completely shattered the characteristic "Prussian" legitimacy of the G.D.R.'s communist state (as the expressor of the spirit of the "German character"),[14] in contrast to "Americanized" West Germany. In this situation the government side at the "round table" disintegrated, and social demands became more radical. Confidence in any form of "reformed socialism" was dashed. There also was a decline of social confidence in the activists of the Forum, many of whom resembled the "revisionists" of October 1956, in Poland. Demands for the unification of Germany became more insistent, for arguments in favor of pre-

serving two German states had collapsed along with the disintegration of the illusion of the "Prussian" legitimacy of the German Democratic Republic.

A third series of historical accidents, like the previous ones, cannot be explained by the dynamics of the contradictions of real
socialism; namely, *the special composition of the present elite in
Moscow* (chiefly the segment responsible for relations within the
bloc and with the world). In the sixties many of its members either
had rubbed shoulders with Otto Kuusinen's circle[15] (with his vision of controlled pluralism as politically more effective than
monocentrism) or with the Prague editors of "Problems of Peace
and Socialism" and participants in the Prague Spring.[16] These people, who had been shunted aside by Leonid Brezhnev, resurfaced
after his death, during the Yuri Andropov regime. Common to
them was the perception of the crisis of real socialism in the perspective of the world system and also a thorough knowledge of the
real dependency of the bloc on world capitalism. This dependency,
we might add, can be reduced (or changed into a situation of "dependent development") only by—paradoxically—moving struc-
turally closer to capitalism. From this comes the vision of making
"owners" of the *nomenklatura*—a way to privatize yet retain
control—and of using an opposition figure in the office of president (while maintaining control through other offices and agencies) to guarantee stability and as a symbol the West understands.
This vision had circulated among the elites of Eastern Europe long
before the "round table."[17] This *perception shock* as to the nature
of the crisis (seen today in the perspective of the world system and
not—as until recently[18]—as a manifestation of the inadequate
translation of the idea into practice) radically changed the vision
of the necessary remedies—necessary if the Eastern bloc was to
retain any chance at all in the political (and especially military)
rivalry with the West. Remember, however, that this not the only
vision of reforms. Another option appeared at the February Plenum of the Communist Party of the Soviet Union (Moscow, 5–7
February 1990). It concerns not so much the role of the Communist party as relations between particular institutions of the state
(including particular segments of the KGB) and relations of the
state with the society (especially with the nations demanding their
independence). Such notions as "order" (and charges against the

faction of "globalists" who look at things from the perspective of the world system that they had destroyed the protective buffer zone in Eastern Europe) appeared at this Plenum more often than ideological slogans connected with communism or the party. It should be borne in mind that the political system in the U.S.S.R. has not passed through such radical changes as the rest of the countries of the bloc. For the time being one can speak of three processes in the U.S.S.R.:

• a characteristic "reformation" in the Communist party, in which Gorbachev played the role of Luther.[19] The Communist party was stripped of its mythological status and "secularized." The ideology was replaced by a pragmatic reform of procedures (which had the aim of strengthening the faction of globalists) and competition between individuals and programs;

• "relativization"[20] of the role of the Communist party of the Soviet Union by strengthening the role of the state, and especially the structures of the KGB, which, besides the army, is the only semipolitical organization of national scope (suprarepublic). This is highly important after the repeal of Article 6 of the Constitution concerning the leading role of the Communist party. For it must be remembered that in the U.S.S.R. there is no other party of national scope. In this situation only the KGB (or the army) can replace the weakened Communist party as the coordinator of actions on the scale of the entire state. This is why, paradoxically, there was only one vote (Boris Yeltsin's) against repealing Article 6. The other participants of the Plenum were more interested in which faction of the broadly understood KGB (A. Yakovlev's globalists or Kru-iczkov's people oriented toward "order" and domestic relations) would impose its line, and neither faction felt threatened, for the repeal of Article 6 had even strengthened their material structure. Only Yeltsin and J. Afanasyev attempted to found a new party of nationwide scope (also gathering the Interrepublican Parliamentary Forum). For they were aware that with the lack of such a party, the weakening of the Communist party would benefit structures even more exempt from social control and take its place as the coordinator on the state scale;

• the establishment of new institutions in the center of power, of which the politburo is now only one. Clearly emerging here is the rivalry between the highly politicized army and KGB and the differences among their individual sections.

The cost (from the point of view of the Communist party) of all of these changes is the breakup of political and ideological identity. For example, recently the classical conception held by Andropov has revived, which is in competition with the vision of the globalists (Yakovlev, G. Shevardadze, Gorbachev). Andropov's continuators seem to be Kruiczkov and Nicolai Ryzhkev. Their suggested response[21] to bureaucratic anarchy and the surfacing through party channels of national aspirations (as in Lithuania) was to fuse more strongly party structures with cadres of the KGB and army (that is, a reversal of the process taking place in Poland and Czechoslovakia),[22] to centralize the Communist party, to limit democracy in the republic parties (in order to reduce the inflow of local national elites), and finally to react with force to national upheavals and to limit the flow of information on this subject. The above strategies are also having an effect on the profile of reorganizing parties of the "left" in Eastern Europe. For example, in Poland the Social-Democratic Party of the Republic, which after the breakup of the Communist party was founded with more than half of the votes at the founding congress, demanded restoration of the presence of the party in the army and civic militia[23] (which brings it close to Vorotnikov's line). In contrast, Jaruzelski, Kiszczak, and Orzechowski (head of the Parliamentary Club of the former Communist party) have generally remained outside the new parties. They seem to represent a line closer to the Soviet "globalists."

Two additional unique historical accidents that are influencing the systemic changes in Eastern Europe are *the approaching unification of Germany* and *deeper than expected anarchy in the Soviet Union*. With unification, East Germany will consume most of the capital available from West Germany. Soviet anarchy is rooted in both economic chaos and the not fully controlled shift from formal to informal empire. Even if the actual ambiguity was introduced to the power structure of the Soviet Union consciously (with a triangle of three parallel control networks operating with different rules: Gorbachev's presidency, the Communist party hierarchy, and Yeltsin's new federation based on bilateral economic agreements), it only adds to the invisible anarchy and makes the economic destiny of the Soviet Union less predictable.

Naturally, all these accidents and unique coincidences (which, like the "round table," later become precedents to be followed or objective limits) cannot be traced back to the dynamics of the con-

tradictions of real socialism. What is more, these accidents show
how important *the time factor* is in politics. For if the tensions on
the political scene in the U.S.S.R. (with visible politicization of the
army) had occurred earlier, the "round table" might not have
taken place and changes in Eastern Europe would have been more
difficult.[24] Had the pace of changes been slower and the "critical
mass" of the old regime been destroyed later, the probability of
attempts by Moscow to block these changes would have been
greater.[25]

Increasing social tensions are obviously in the background of all
of these unique coincidences. Without them the old regime elite
surely would not have decided to take the risk of "revolution from
above." These tensions are accompanied by growing awareness of
the necessity for a radical change, for these tensions no longer can
be reduced within the framework of the old system.

Eastern Europe today is in a real transition period. The future of
the countries of this region may be decided by a new series of
chance events. With the loosening stays of the old ideology and
imposed economic and political solutions, the chance for diversity
is returning in Eastern Europe. Each country is returning to its
own tradition and political culture. Will this be—as in the case of
Poland—"authoritarianism with authority," as in the twenties
after the establishment of the Second Republic? An example is the
legally unsettled role of a strong leader (Lech Wałęsa) in the role of
a balancing factor. There are also similar tendencies to form supraparty political blocs based on foggy symbolic references and not
on clear programs. This makes it harder to articulate the entire
complexity of the interests of the society and increases social
apathy, with the exception of periods of mobilization during elections. In the opinion of the new "avant-garde of the establishment" that was formed after the "round table," this model makes
necessary the demobilization of the society, which has been too
much activated around fundamentalist ideals. Only after such demobilization will the elite be able to "play politics." This demobilization from above is taking place in conditions of a sweeping
revolution (also from above). This paradox lies behind the phenomenon of the "joyless victory" that so surprised Western observers.[26] Czechoslovakia, in turn, where the economic crisis is not as
severe, the society less mobilized, but the traditions of democratic

institutions stronger, rejects the plebiscitary model of democracy (e.g., the referendum formula), though even there the temptations to act in supraparty blocs are strong, for this helps to consolidate the new configuration of forces. The differentiation of economic models in individual countries also is increasing: today the chances of becoming part of the Western division of labor are decided both by unique political situation (G.D.R.) and the model of dependency applied in the past by Moscow.[27] In this respect the chances of Czechoslovakia and Hungary are much better than Poland's. A series of accidents also may have some effect on the future economic model. For instance, in Poland the sequence of reformatory measures and the fact that the stabilization plan came before the privatization and demonopolization of economic structures might turn out to be important. This in turn was determined by the makeup of political forces.[28]

New Contradictions in the System during Transition

To an ever greater degree new contradictions also are starting to influence the dynamics of the breakthrough in the system. They can be called *contradictions of the transitory period.*

The process of transformation in Eastern Europe can be presented as a tangle of three groups of overlapping mechanisms:

• systemic contradictions of real socialism which have "used up" this system and brought it to a stage that made change necessary. These contradictions still do not determine the direction and pace of these changes;

• a series of chance events concerning both innovations in the sphere of control and in the unique personal configuration in Moscow (and following this, in the other capitals of Eastern Europe). This new configuration in turn is coupled with a new perception of the nature of the crisis and the reforms required;

• new contradictions that are mounting with the advancement of systemic changes, which can be called contradictions of the transitory period.

As the changes move forward, the systemic contradictions of real socialism become less important. Their dynamics play themselves out, for the structures generating these contradictions (e.g., one-party rule) are in a state of collapse. Simultaneously there is an increase in the role of unique elements of the tradition and culture of individual countries and of new contradictions. The latter have their sources in the process of the breakthrough itself. This book is about the intensification and manifestation of these new contradictions. The systemic contradictions that led to the exhaustion of the system and initiated the breakthrough were described in my last book (*The Ontology of Socialism*). New political and economic subjects are coming into being, and new conflicts and dependencies are appearing. The latter are connected with the process of change itself and no longer can be explained by the logic of these systemic contradictions. Finally, the importance of the new economic relations of Eastern Europe with the West is growing, as is the importance of the new model of the peripheral status of Eastern Europe connected with these changes.

These contradictions of the transitionary period (or rather, of its first phase) are of two kinds.

Conflict between Stabilization and Transformation

The first contradiction is the conflict between the requirements of stabilization (both economic and political) and transformation (understood as sweeping ownership changes and evolution toward pluralism). On the economic plane this contradiction appears in the collision between the government anti-inflation policy (expensive credit, high taxes, a wage freeze, and import duties, in order to support the rate of the internal convertability of the złoty to the dollar in conditions of very limited foreign currency reserves) and its effects in the form of a deep recession and the intended privatization of the state sector. The devaluation of savings, a considerable decline of real wages,[29] and limiting the activities of the small private sector,[30] reduce the chances of future privatization if it is to be based on domestic capital and commercial principles, for this capital is shrinking at an alarming rate. The more so as the requirements of political stabilization (specifically, the wish to channel social frustrations connected with the durability of old hierachies and arrangements) have intensified attacks from above on new owners from the *nomenklatura*.[31] Regardless of the moral aspects of this economic process, it did speed up the formation of capital in private hands (at the cost of the state sector). This capital could be used for further—now rational and controlled—privatization, but after the political attacks much of it has been leaving the country (via foreign banks) and not appearing on the local scene. Without domestic capital, eventual privatization (the first step is currently being debated in Poland in the Seym) might take the form of state capitalism (companies jointly financed by the Treasury and foreign capital). Other countries of Eastern Europe (Hungary and Czechoslovakia) are relying less on monetary methods of fighting inflation and are also seeking reserves elsewhere (trade within the COMECON,[32] the branch structure of the economy).[33] In these conditions the model of future privatization there might be different, for the recession (and the shrinkage of domestic capital) will not be as deep as in Poland. The model of privatization also will influence the future model of dependency of individual countries of Eastern Europe on the world economy. The radical nature of the stabilization plan (as in Poland) also is beginning to create psychological barriers to a radical transformation of property rights in the state sector. Populistic attitudes are spreading rapidly and are finding their political expression.[34] Both populist pressures operant in "political capitalism" and systemic weakness of the economy (such as Polish agriculture) cause a lack of structure where capital formation would appear. And the described features of the stabilization policy lead to reduction of people's savings. This creates serious dilemmas for slowly emerging capitalism.

In the political dimension the contradiction between the requirements of stabilization (consolidation) of the new leadership and transformation is expressing itself on two planes.

● First, there is a strong temptation to apply the model of *exclusionary corporatism* (the mobilization of voters in supraparty blocs, thereby camouflaging divisions within the society and making more difficult the articulation of interests). Such a consolidation also makes it easier to win elections (as in the Polish experience of June 1989). Similar tendencies are appearing today in most of Eastern Europe. In Poland as well there is a strong tendency to repeat this formula in local elections (May 1990), as the new establishment tries to stabilize its power position. In historical perspective, however, exclusionary corporatism does not promote a deep transformation of relations between the political leadership and the society. On the contrary, it gives rise to political apathy,[35] and political parties, deprived of room to really compete in elections, become stunted (turning toward the politics of symbols) or come together into similar blocs, thereby losing their identity.[36] Since they do not have to compete openly (voting of the plebiscitary type is based on loyalty and hazy ethoses), the opposition is in no hurry to state clearly its programs and the role of contingency factor is very high. This increases the uncertainty of the entire reform process. For example, it is hard to say whether opposition leaders are for or against radical privatization, and that discourages potential Western investors. This overlaps a deeper phenomenon connected with the transitional period of this phase of changes. The old mechanisms are no longer working; though the new rules of the game are clear (monetary rigor), they leave no room for individual and group adaptation strategies. The chances of survival depend on factors no one can control: the former place in trade with the U.S.S.R.,[37] dependence on imports that are presently very costly, the cost of bank credit, and the pace at which demand barriers appear in the group of goods produced. Former strategies of survival (pressure on the state for funds) no longer work, and new ones have not yet been developed. The inability of economic subjects to adapt (the recession) is an integral part of the program. This increases still further the tensions and frustrations of this phase, which even without this are considerable owing to the difficulty of articulating group and individual interests.

• Second, political stabilization in this phase of changes is coupled with attempts to restore the authority (and power) of the state. In the past the power of the state had been sapped by bureaucratic anarchy and lack of respect for the law and the idea of a contract. A contract was impossible in the socialist relations of production, while law in the "state of higher necessity" was used as an instrument of day-to-day politics. Though such temptations are returning today,[38] as a rule emphasis is put on the "revolution in the majesty of the law" (a cliché from the rhetoric of the new establishment, meaning evolutionary changes). This often collides with strong pressures from below on substantive—but not formal—justice. One can see this, for instance, in the wave of "provincial revolutions," which consist in the occupation of buildings formerly used by the disintegrating Communist party.[39] The government strongly opposes such actions, using both force[40] and arguments that today the state is a "common good" that was taken away from the *nomenklatura*. This, however, does not calm the public feeling nor prevent "local revolutions," which have a logic of their own.[41] For in spite of changes in central institutions, local power structures are very durable; they often change only the form and foundations of domination (from political to economic).[42] The evolutionary tactics of the new government also reinforce the impression of continuity. The government wants to ward off the anarchy of the transitionary period (and the sabotage of its decisions by executive organs) by giving these bodies a feeling of security and continuity of employment.[43] Yet this in turn increases tensions in the society, which expects a dismantling of the hierarchy, at least symbolically. Thus there are more and more attacks from below on managing directors and displaced acts of aggression: People are frustrated by the difficult economic situation, and it does not seem right to them to attack their own government. The displacement of aggression can be seen from the fact that today, after the start of the painful maneuver of economic stabilization, there are more attacks on the executive level of power (for the most part on people still in jobs that they held before the old government fell) than immediately after the elections. The level of confidence in the government has remained almost unchanged during this period, though it is declining in strategic groups: young people, farmers, private producers.

Today each of the countries of Eastern Europe is entering such a phase of provincial revolutions, which are not wanted by the central authorities (including ex-opposition leaders, now in government). These actions from below are often met by a sharp reaction on the part of the forces of law and order, which accelerates even more the spiral of tensions and frustrations. The new authorities are convinced that the "society is not ripe for democracy" and that their tactics of "exclusionary corporatism" are correct. As one can see from the above, over the long run the requirements of stabilization (e.g., the evolutionary and not "revolutionary" tactics in relation to the old executive apparatus) can hinder the transformation toward a pluralist model of democracy.

The Intensified Identity Crisis of
New Leaders

The second contradiction of the transitionary period is the intensification of the identity crisis of the "avant-garde of the new
establishment" (the reformed elite of the old regime and part of
the former opposition, now in power). For the elite of the old regime, this identity crisis as the reforms progress is coupled with the
inexorable breakup of the Communist party, in spite of the fact
that it was the initiator of the reforms or gave its consent to them. The
defeat of the Communist party reformers at the polls is the second
reason for frustration (e.g., the election results in Poland in June
1989; the results of the referendum in Hungary in January 1990).
For the former opposition, the crisis of identity comes with legalization and taking on part of the responsibility (and all of it as the
Communist party disintegrates) for the future of the country.
These phenomena are interrelated. For as the old opponent (the
Communist party) disintegrates, it becomes more and more difficult for the new authorities to justify plebiscitary methods (e.g.,
a majority and not proportional election law).[44] What is more,
part of the old power elite has retained its influences, but today is
using them differently. Paradoxically, it is even making use of the
market rules introduced by the new authorities. Today the Social-
Democratic Party of the Polish Republic, numbering several
thousand members, heirs of the former Communist party, is the
owner of the press concern RSW and controls a majority (nine-
teen) of the provincial newspapers. Personnel changes in them are
not possible without the consent of RSW (which is owned on the
principle of "organizational property"—see chapter 2). Recalcit-
rant newspapers are punished by turning the financial screws,
which threatens them with bankruptcy. A similar situation exists
in the hierarchy of agricultural cooperatives, where people who in
the past ruled over rural communes through *nomenklatura* positions in the cooperative apparatus today have formed private companies and also control areas crucial for the commune. What is
more, as in the first case, they are beyond the reach of the political
mechanism, and this new power configuration will not change
much (even in Poland after the Citizen's Committees of Solidarity
win the elections to local offices). The above phenomena corrode

the legitimacy of the new authorities in two ways. First, disintegration of the Communist party undermines the justifications for exclusionary corporatism, (which was also used to eliminate the other factions of the opposition from power). Second, the strange phenomenon of the survival of the old power elite on the local level (with the new base of domination) strengthens the charges that the new authorities are powerless to break up the old arrangements. The very idea of "revolution in the majesty of the law" in such situations is also under attack. In this situation the new authorities are faced with a dilemma (see, for instance, Wałęsa's conflict with Tadeusz Mazowiecki, summer of 1990) known to all political arrangements in the phase of consolidation: to expand the base of rule (by including political forces which were absent at the "round table") or to inveigh against the opponent, which would justify further pressures for loyalty and exclusionary techniques. For example, such a demonized opponent might be a "nationalistic right" (which obviously does not exclude the possibility of the intensification of nationalisms but, paradoxically, such demon apponents sometimes are an effect of precisely such exclusionary tactics).[45] Another source of the strange "legitimacy vacuum" beginning to plague the new authorities is the difficulty of achieving rapid economic successes in such a deep crisis. This vacuum in turn increases the frustration of the new authorities and their oversensitivity to criticism. And this gives rise to altercations over drafts of bills on censorship: The government wants the law to protect the state, while the deputies demand freedom of expression for the society. All of this adds to social frustrations (and charges of continuity) on one hand and to the isolation of the new authorities on the other. For the new political leadership has broad symbolic support, but it has no clear social base in the form of distinct groups whose interest it represents. In this phase of the breakthrough it chiefly represents the "theoretical" interest of the society at large; its task is to find the way out of real socialism at the lowest possible costs. Those who have a concrete economic interest in elements of the government's program (e.g., privatization) will appear later.

What is more, we can observe two new phenomena on the common consciousness level, which can also lead to corrosion of the ex-opposition–based government's legitimacy.

First, there is the clash between two visions of the "revolution." On one hand it is "revolution from above" presenting itself as an "evolution" (for tactical reasons and in spite of introducing basic changes in structural terms). It calls itself "legal revolution," rejecting both mass participation (with the technique of "exclusionary corporatism") and rapid changes in the old executive apparatus of power (especially at middle and low levels). On the other hand it is the popular vision of "revolution" as the elevation of those who are "powerless," with strong elements of status politics, destruction of old hierarchies, and dramatic change of relationship between state and society. Moments of "culture revolution" are perceived as more essential than slow, legal reforms (which are boring and do not give the taste of "victory" to be had from throwing out the old elite).

Second, there is conflict between two types of economic rationality: macro and micro (with strong undertones of "ethical economy"). The elegance and logic of the government "stabilization plan" (fighting inflation with the help of so-called corrective inflation and induced recession) is not widely understood. The popular vision is to fight inflation with more "entrepreneurship" and an increase of productivity. The new mechanisms (tight credit, high taxes in order to reduce the budget deficit) not only make creation of new businesses more difficult (for example, the black market for hard currency ends when "internal convertibility" is instituted) but lead to the pattern of bankruptcy that is seen by the average person as irrational. Adjustment on both the individual and the collective level is difficult when nearly all conditions are out of control. And the concept of "demand barrier" (the main instrument reducing inflation in the government program) is seen as "immoral" when basic social needs are not met and real incomes fall by 25 percent and are frozen. What is more, the reduction of prices through reduction of costs is difficult due to old technologies and high fixed costs (dividends paid to the state, taxes, credit interests).

Conclusion

A complicated web of old and new contradictions (as well as unique historical circumstances) is responsible for the complex pattern of transformation in the Eastern bloc, and it leads to more general theoretical questions:

- What is the relationship between real socialism's ontology (with its inner dynamics and contradictions) and the transition of real socialism toward the ontologically new system (formation)?
- What is the status of unique circumstances ("chance") that cannot be explained by contradictions of real socialism? Are they "chance" phenomena only from the point of view of socialism's ontology, or from the history of Eastern Europe as well? Or maybe we should (in order to understand the present processes in this region) not only look into the theory describing contradictions on the ontological level (which "wear off" that formation) but also elaborate a theory of "chance phenomena"?

These and other dilemmas of the first phase of the breakthrough in the Eastern bloc are the subject of this book. It describes events taking place in Poland, though most of them are also appearing (or will appear as the process of changes advances) in the other countries of Eastern Europe and in the Soviet Union. This is still an open phase: the impression of making history is unavoidably interwoven with the awareness of various determinants and limited freedom of maneuver. This accounts for the waves of euphoria interlaced with skepticism and fears. One of the sources of ambiguity in the present stage of transformation is the role of society. Society is visibly different in each set of mechanisms that put into motion the whole process; society's tissue changes as well. During the last stage of real socialism (mid 70s–mid 80s) (with cyclically repeated crises, serving as peculiar regulation), society is highly mobilized. Yet its pattern of political articulation can be labeled as non-transformative:[46] the radical rejection of the system in moral terms in followed by the simultaneous invoking of state redistribution in the economy. This stage of social self-organization can be labeled as "politics of identity" when an atomization caused by collective property rights and totalitarian legacy is overcome with the help of "value added" fundamentalist myths of moral rightness—or by reinforcement of nationalism. The paradox is that the very same articulation has to be demobilized in order to make possible the second stage: "revolution from above" (the "round table" process). Until now we could not speak about the creation of civil society, if the latter is understood in the Hegelian way as the peculiar pattern of socialization, when both inner differences and conflicts in society are recognized as legitimated and the state is perceived as a necessary regulatory appendix. Only now are Eastern European societies entering the stage of painful efforts to create such a pattern of socialization. It will demand the destruction of the fundamentalist myth of social unity, evolution from substantive to formal concepts of law and justice, as well as the end of the paternalistic concept of the state. Privatization (which has just begun in Eastern Europe) is a precondition for creating an ontological base for the genuine civil society. Division of labor is only an illusory substitute for such a base: it creates only multiplicity of theoretical interests[47] and visions. As the result, we observe—as today in Eastern Europe—pluralism of elites in an atomized society (or, society unified around nationalism or fundamentalist myth). A new concept of legality and law (as well as creation of mediating institutions and contractual relationships) in some societies cannot be built without some elements of cultural Westernization. This is the reason for the recent wave of Christianization in the Far East soceities that are in the process of going out of real socialism: the concept of individuality and legal, formal rationality, necessary in civil society, is absent there because of not only real socialism's legacy but the deeper, cultural tradition as well.

As we see, the creation of a civil society is a much more complex process than mere political liberalization: it demands both property rights reform and deep cultural change. It is painful, just as is the creation of new politics occurring now in the Eastern bloc. Not only the old, facade institutions are activated (thus is usually the first step, before new institutions are created and oppositions recognized) but both the old and the new elites have to resist the temptations of unlimited power. The evolution from the situation when only society (not the ruling elite) is bound by rules to the legal structure limiting all actors is not completed yet in the Eastern bloc: oppositional reformers as well as "revolutionaries from above" of the old establishment demonstrate temptation to use techniques (and philosophy) of the prerogative state in the name of reform.

This book was written as the events and processes unfolded. I have given the dates when chapters were finished: For some read-ers it might be interesting to follow what subsequent events have proved to be my prognostic and analytical slips. They show the difficulties a sociologist faces when grappling with rapidly changing reality; the sociologist attempts to grapple by finding concepts and names for ostensibly chaotic processes and phenomena. Sometimes such labeling is the only, though deceptive, way society can gain control of these processes. For no one is fully coordinating the changes in Eastern Europe, which are processes running on many levels, undertaken in the name of various (often contradictory) intentions and interests. Neither is anyone able to control all the unexpected effects complicating the dynamics of change. The peculiar ideology of this "revolution from above" (undertaken due to fear of mounting tensions and real "revolution from below") is the lack of programmatic ideology. A vision of general direction (pluralism, privatization) is mixed up with the continuous adjustment to challenges linked not only to crisis but to transition as well.

Part One

Privatization in Eastern Europe from the World-System Perspective

Introduction

The Logic of Privatization in the State Sector

The hinge of the economic reforms in some of the countries of Eastern Europe (Poland, Hungary, and to a lesser degree the U.S.S.R. and Bulgaria) seems to be the maneuver of "ontological opening."[1] Privatization in the state sector (which, as I will show, takes very different forms) is its practical result. This is real "ontological opening" (that is, changing the mode of production in such a way as to allow the economy to be penetrated by the logic of the capitalist system, with its specific rationality) and not, as in the previous reforms, the appearance of opening (e.g., through forced export of products that were in demand domestically, or the reaching for Western credits that were subsequently distributed through bureaucratic horse trading).

It is worth remembering that wherever it was introduced in a conscious way (Russia,[2] China[3]) and not imposed (Eastern Europe), collective (state) ownership was regarded as a specific kind of "ontological barrier." This barrier had the intention of protecting the economy from the penetration of capital and the status of dependent capitalism. The result, however, was *dependent socialism*, which was sensitive to the fluctuations of the Western capital market but incapable of having an influence on how it functions, determined by the capitalist world system and the inefficiency of dependent socialism's labor in relation to worldwide labor efficiency. And finally, dependent socialism was imitative of the capitalist form of organization of production and exchange but without its ontological underpinnings in private ownership.

Thus dependent socialism had superficial resemblances to the market but was unsteerable as a system. The dependence (subarticulation) of socialism on capitalism is linked additionally with the shrinking in capacity of the former to reproduce its own foundations (on account of the lack of innovativeness and key economic interests).[4] This increases the dependency of socialism on Western credits and technological borrowings.

Thus the dependency of the countries of real socialism on the world capitalist system is a purely negative one. The countries of this region are "punished" in two ways, so to speak: for beginning industrialization later and, on account of ownership relations, for being incapable of applying the logic of the market: the lack of a market greatly reduces the rationality of decisions concerning production and the allocation of productive factors). Furthermore, within the socialist bloc itself this situation creates the "ontological compulsion of dependency" (combined with the imposition by the empire of transfers and production specialties regardless of their costs in individual countries). This is the way in which the socialist bloc adapts to its subarticulation in relation to the capitalist world, while at the same time engaging in political rivalry with this world.

Privatization in the state sector has the aim of removing this "ontological blockade" and creating conditions for the penetration of capital from the West. In other words, reconstituting missing economic interests and the market. The goal is to enable the system to pass from the present, purely negative dependency to *dependent development* (that is, to capitalist situations or to something close to the capitalism of Third World countries in the economy, while continuing political and military rivalry between the blocs). Ontological convergence in ownership relations is regarded as a way of increasing the chances of the socialist bloc in this rivalry. This is why, as I will show, privatization in the state sector often takes the form of "political capitalism," in which the state/empire is the major client and people connected with the power structures are the operatives.

In this situation the political reforms (taking various forms in individual countries, depending on local conditions)[5] have the aim of creating an arrangement of forces and institutions that could guarantee the continuity of the above reforms (also vis-à-vis the

West, which is the second element of this "opening") and also of ensuring social stability (this seems to be the motivation behind co-optation of part of the opposition elite, who can administer the mechanisms of self-control and demobilization more efficiently and "elegantly" than can those of the apparatus of compulsion).

This scenario of economic reform is based on segmentation of the economy in two stages. The first stage is the separation by administrative means of that part of the state sector in which privatization is allowed and of that part which will be more closely integrated—again by administrative methods[6]—with the economic structures of the empire through direct ties at the production level. The former (privatized part) is supposed to allow a more rational adaptation to the subarticulation of the system in relation to capitalism, a dependency that cannot be eliminated fully and all at once. The second stage of segmentation will take place within this reprivatized part of the economy, for two types of private sector will arise which operate in different markets according to different principles and have different sources of accumulation and expansion possibilities.

Such a maneuver of limited, controlled "ontological opening" was seen as the first in a sequence of three steps. The next step is the formation of a market, or rather markets, for segmentation of the economy and two forms of private sector ("political capitalism" along with the expansion of traditional private sector) in the first phase result in further segmentation and not in the development of economic relations that embrace the entire economy. The objective of this stage is to create conditions for the penetration of Western capital and passage to the phase of dependent development.

There is awareness that the maneuver to transform the system will not overcome the peripheral status of the countries of the socialist bloc in the world system. For rather than a change of the role of this bloc in the world division of labor (the export of raw materials, energy, food; the import of technologies), there will be an increase in the efficiency of carrying out this role. This peripheral status (though with a somewhat higher GNP on account of greater efficiency) may even be strengthened, since the opening maneuver will eliminate goods that are produced today expensively and archaically for reasons of prestige and to keep up the appearances of modernity (e.g., the production of automobiles or computers). This new form of peripheral status also will be linked to a differently shaped social structure and to a new distribution of incomes. Some groups will gain from "opening," others will lose. The principles of political dependency also will change with the loosening of Eastern European ties with Moscow and increased ties with Bonn and Tokyo and with continuing—though in a new form—political rivalry between the present military-political blocs. The COMECON will probably be dissolved,[7] while adaptation of the remaining portion of the system to subarticulation will take place through new institutions (the integration of production through the joint ownership of enterprises; the use of private companies and banks, foundations, etc.). The problem of the fictional sovereignty of the small countries of Eastern Europe will persist, but owing to different mechanisms it will not have the same form. The creation of "guarantees" (through the ownership of buildings and land) for Western investors or joint ownership and erasing the obstacles to the flow of productive factors and goods through "frontier trade" in the East (while continuing to enforce obligations stemming from the political rivalry between the blocs) will further erode the control of the state over resources in its own territory. This model of the eradication of sovereignty, however, will be closer to the European model of integration than the present situation. Thus after the "opening" maneuver the present dualism (the developed countries of Western Europe and the East European periphery) will not disappear, but this will be dualism on new principles, with hopes for "dependent development" (e.g., the East will be a market for technologies that have become obsolete in the West, technologies that are no longer useful there for deepening development but are more modern than what the East now has).

One can also imagine a different variant, when after the "ontological opening" (reprivatization in the state sector in order to enable Western penetration) such penetration does not occur. The reason might be fear of social destabilization in Eastern Europe (the shock of the June 89 events in China), when transformation takes place in conditions of a deep crisis, or the internal considerations of the capitalist world (recession in capitalist countries, or other, more attractive areas of investment, such as the U.S.S.R.). It seems that the maneuver of privatization from above (when it started in 1987) was being carried out in Eastern Europe with the possibility of absence of eventual penetration in mind. For the form of "political capitalism" dominant at this stage in the privatization process of the state sector would make it possible to hook up private companies with a highly centralized command economy operating on the basis of government orders. Even today the major customers of companies of this type are the COMECON, Warsaw Pact, and the state sector (including its "sensitive segments," those connected to military production). Privatization in the state sector in Eastern Europe is not a result of the expansion of the traditional private sector; on the contrary, the dominant form is a peculiar linkage of political power and capital, changing the foundations of the dominant position of part of the ruling apparatus, but not disturbing the system of domination. Here it is worth asking why the countries of real socialism are not attempting the methods of passage to "dependent development" used by some of the Third World countries (e.g., India). This method consists in restructuralization of the economy and the undertaking of production to reduce dependency on imports from the developed countries, increasing exports to these countries, and finally, accelerating development through expansion of the consumer goods market (when the increase of wages prods consumption, demand, and growth of production, which enables further wage increases). On the surface such a path seems less costly to the power elite of real socialism, for it does not lead to such radical changes in the system as privatization in the state sector. Yet to the power elite of Eastern Europe the maneuver of "making owners of the *nomenklatura*" seems easier: no investment outlays for restructuralization are required (as in India). Also, this maneuver takes place in an "ownership vacuum" (and resistance to privatization is chiefly instrumental—it is seen as a way of defining one's own political identity and not seen as defense of well-defined economic interests), whereas restructuralization would require breaking the resistance of branch interest groups. And finally, the variant of "political capitalism" accepted in Eastern Europe in the privatization process does not require a reorientation toward consumption; on the contrary, it allows a better satisfaction of the interests of the state and the empire. At the same time, material reserves are set in motion and more efficient use is made of productive factors. And in fact, the main barriers to growth in Eastern Europe are material, in spite of hidden reserves. What is more, the variant of "political capitalism" makes it easy to return to the centralized economy (without disturbing the newly acquired economic status of the *nomenklatura*).

This background leads up to chapter 2, which will

• analyze the forms making up the model of "political capitalism" (I want to underline that evaluation is very difficult here. The same form of political capitalism that is seen as "corrupted" (shifting some costs to the state sector) can be treated as an efficient mechanism for capital formation and redeployment of assets from the state to a private branch of the economy);

• show other variants of privatization in the state sector;

• present research findings on social opinions about privatization and analyze other possible sources of resistance (organizational interest in the case of workers' councils, the search for identity in the case of factions in the party elite and the opposition);

• ponder the implications of various forms of privatization for economic policy and the evolution of the crisis.

Before analyzing "political capitalism," I once again want to emphasize that it is the result of actions from above initiated by the Communist power elite and not an expression of the economic expansion of the traditional private sector. The goal of this elite is to carry out the "ontological opening" safely (in a controlled way) and in a manner that keeps open the possibility of returning to the centralized economy (if the interests of the empire so require or if the penetration by Western capital does not take place). Political and organizational interests and values, not economic ones, are the source of resistance to this maneuver. The aim of the maneuver of "ontological opening" is to put an end to the period of discontinuous development of the system; in other words, to bring back onto the stage actors, interests, and mechanisms that were intentionally eliminated during the period of setting up the "ontological blockade." This discontinuity is so deep, however, that today there are no economic interests that could propel the transformation of ownership. The state-controlled economy left in place only the wage interests of hired workers and organizational interests.[8] Economic interests in the continuation of changes appear only *after* the changes have been initiated. This unfortunately means that there must be a "revolution from above" connected with reformulating the rationality of control of the political leadership itself. It would be utopian to expect a stampede to buy shares and a fast spread of "people's capitalism." Privatization does not all at once result in the formation of a universal, open market; on the contrary, in the first phase the market becomes even more segmented, and some of the features of the changed mode of production (e.g., monopolistic tendencies) are even strengthened. The role of the state in the economy also changes during the privatization process (though in the first phase it hardly declines); the way of reasoning and sources of profit of the actors on the economic stage also become different. This is and will be accompanied by paroxysms caused not only by resistance to changes, but also by fear of the political costs of opening (as in the case of China: the operation of the army against "colonialization" and a return to the rhetoric of the 1940s on "dependent capitalism").[9] Another potential source of upheavals in Eastern Europe may be a new distribution of the costs of peripheral status that are no longer cushioned by administrative redistribution in individual countries and the bloc as a whole (e.g., in the COMECON by different obligations and subsidies).

Chapter Two

Political Capitalism and Other Patterns of Privatization

Political Capitalism

The most spectacular version of privatization in the state sector taking place in both Poland and Hungary[1] and beginning to appear in the U.S.S.R. is what is called "making owners of the *nomenklatura*."[2] Both in trade, where they are dislodging state-owned trade enterprises, and in production, companies are being set up with various combinations of power and capital. In some cases administrative or economic power is even assigned a monetary value in the basic capital of the company.[3]

In Trade

The role of these companies in trade is to link capital and markets of various kinds which otherwise would not come into contact because of the rules of the game or which are still isolated from one another by a buffer zone and thus can be approached only by these companies because the authorities regard such mediation as beneficial. An example of linking markets of various kinds (or rather, a market with a quasi-market) is the organization and mobilization of traditional small private farms in provinces lying along the frontier with the U.S.S.R. by companies belonging to farmers' associations (in fact, the machinery of government). These companies engage in the "frontier trade" (often in kind) of agricultural products with their counterparts in the U.S.S.R.[4]

Another example of the linking of different markets is private companies acting as brokers in the export of products of state enterprises to capitalist markets, thereby replacing state foreign trade offices. These private brokers often are people who work in the state foreign trade offices. Now they work for themselves, however, and make use of the information and contacts acquired in their state jobs.[5] They work more efficiently and quickly, and in the eyes of Western competitors they reduce the danger of dumping (selling below production costs by state foreign trade offices was one of the main charges raised by the European Common Market countries and is an obstacle to the entry of Eastern European producers to the Western market). Western partners are unable to understand that even when a private exporter has big profits, the producer may be selling below production costs and be subsidized by the state (especially if the exporter belongs to the *nomenklatura*) in order to get hard currency. They do not understand that in Eastern Europe hard currency is regarded as a commodity that must be acquired at all cost—including dumping if necessary—in order to be able to start up branches of industry based on cooperative import. Thus the private form of brokerage in export based on the principle of profit does not necessarily rationalize the sphere of production, but it certainly is more aggressive. Even more radical privatization (when the agent also becomes the owner of the most profitable departments of an exporting enterprise) still does not mean rationalization because the costs are shifted to the other departments of the state enterprise which begin to require even greater state subsidies than before (which is why it is so important for the new owners to remain in the state company's administration). Benefits of these subsidies now flow to private hands and not, as before, to the organization, which enabled it to survive without much effort.

A third example of the linking of various types of markets (which, without this brokerage, could not come into contact with one another) is the computer market in Eastern Europe. Cooperatives (belonging to state organizations) or openly private companies set up by groups of people from the *nomenklatura* buy from private persons high-class Western computers (even those under embargo, which state enterprises cannot purchase) and resell them at a profit to state industry, the army, or the state administration.[6] Private computer companies (run by "people from the street") do not have access to this market; being in the *nomenklatura* (not necessarily in the Communist party) is necessary, for through the computer and software market one has access to the heart of sensitive areas, such as the military and inner security.

Yet another example of the linkage of various types of capital in trade are small cooperative companies set up ad hoc to act as middlemen between state enterprises and the traditional private sector. This is most often fictional activity, because the agent does not even come into contact with the commodity, which is sent directly from the producer to the customer. This fiction, however, makes it possible for the customer (who offically buys from a "cooperative," which is a social form of ownership) to avoid the high turnover tax[7] (paid when a state enterprise buys from a private supplier). Even after this tax was abolished in 1988 this practice continued because it enables the management of a state enterprise to avoid the charge that it had a personal interest in the transaction,[8] that it jacked up the price (to the disadvantage of the enterprise) and shared the profit with the private supplier. Recently this form has been developing intensively in the U.S.S.R. (it is derivative of shortages and cooperative difficulties on one hand and of the heating up of the anticorruption campaign on the other). In Poland it has attained such a scale that the administration is trying to limit it. In this situation an additional source of profit for cooperatives set up earlier is to resell their names for fictional branches, which in fact work for their own profit rather than the cooperatives'. The real function of these cooperatives, especially in the U.S.S.R, is to substitute for the market: the artificial freezing of prices (for political reasons) blocks adaptation processes (the movement of goods) between republics. Only people employed in state trade (and who have access to accurate information) and those with means of transporation (people in managerial positions) can exploit this situation for their own profit: this is nothing more than a "sanctioned" (by the participants close to centers of political power) form of what recently was called speculation.

The aim of all of the above forms of brokerage in the "buffer zone" between various markets and various forms of capital is

- to replace state structures and to operate in the same area, but more efficiently (although this still does not mean more rational production processes). These structures operated by trusted people control the presence of the traditional private sector in foreign markets; or
- to fill in the gaps both in the East and in the West created by absurd tax regulations that discourage direct dealings between state enterprises and private producers. These companies make a profit out of the situation of permanent shortages (with simultaneous, unutilized reserves). The hope of big profits makes people of the *nomenklatura* who are in the state sector and simultaneously running the kinds of companies described above willing to put part of these reserves (about which only they know) into circulation. This is one of the basic motives behind the consent of the power elite to the setting up of such companies—in the U.S.S.R. as well as Eastern bloc countries—and also why this elite admits that the official structures of the economic administration are absolutely unsteerable, and that commands, appeals, and controls are ineffective. In this brokerage activity the "basic capital" is access to information and means of transportation; being in the *nomenklatura* affords both.

Eventual abuses cannot be controlled. For example, a manager might lower the efficiency of the state enterprise he or she runs by using its trucks for the private company in which he or she is a shareholder. Whether these trucks are used by the private company or the state enterprise at a given moment or not is decided by the same people who benefit from working on their own account.[9] Lowering the efficiency of the state enterprise in this way and saddling it with part of the costs of private business activity also affects the state budget, for it increases the number of unprofitable enterprises that require subsidies. At the same time, however, it increases the utilization of equipment and the number of services rendered (because the manager operating privately can act more freely, unrestricted by rules imposed on the state firm), though the profits from this flow go into private pockets. Thus such activity has not only a redistributive effect but also positive material benefits. It should be emphasized once again that the redistributive effects (e.g., making profits from "privatized" means of transportation, which sometimes are purchased well below their true value, since the withdrawal of equipment from use by the state enterprise is decided by persons who are simultaneously shareholders of a private company and managers of a state enterprise) affect not only the employees of the state enterprise, but also the Treasury. An example: Eastern bloc companies trading in food in the frontier area use equipment that belongs to farmers' associations (theoretically for services to agriculture, but actually engaging in trade in kind, e.g., potatoes for television sets) and make profits from shortages in both markets. In the bargain (at the official exchange rate of the ruble-złoty) they may be able to record bookkeeping losses and receive subsidies from the Treasury for the export of food (since the export of food to the Soviet market is subsidized).

In Production

In the sphere of production, we will examine six forms of the combination of power and capital in turn.

The first form consists of a *dual status of fixed capital* on the premises of the formally state-owned enterprise.[10] In periods when the enterprise is unable to use this fixed capital (caused by shortage of labor or the funds to pay workers or by lack of foreign currency for cooperative import) it can be put to use by companies set up by the managerial cadre of this enterprise. The benefit for the state is the production of goods in short supply (making possible in turn the utilization of idle productive capacity). These machines are better cared for, and labor is used more efficiently. A sort of auxiliary operation to the state enterprise is set up that enables business to be done outside the regulations constraining the state enterprise (e.g., avoiding the tax on above-standard wages), makes better use of productive factors, and lowers the tensions and frustrations of the managerial cadre—without changing the formal ownership status of the enterprise. The state has unregulated ownership power (including the power to change arbitrary financial obligations and deductions, which are regarded as the owner's rent and not tax in the Western sense). For the managerial cadre the private company is not only a source of income but also an additional instrument of control over employees. The right to work in the private company is treated as a financial privilege, and managers select conformist, not trouble-making employees, for this privilege.

The high profits of the managerial cadre organizing additional production (and during this time treating machines as its de facto property) are not taxed, whereas some of the costs (e.g., overhauls, transport, insurance of employees) are borne by the state enterprise. The managers themselves decide when the machines "are not needed by the state enterprise" and channel the most profitable production of the enterprise (e.g., for export) to the private company. The purchase of foreign currency in the free market facilitates cooperative import from the West (these imports are modest, yet their lack can be a bottleneck), which often generates inordinately high profits. The latter work to raise the price of the dollar in the free market, and this fuels inflation in a double way. On one hand it increases the amount of złotys in the hands of sellers of foreign currency, and on the other, the "cost" of the dollar enters into the price of the company's products. The price of the dollar also is reflected in the prices of the products of state enterprises that require a "foreign currency input." It is impossible to formalize this type of "ownership" (which is called "managerial experiments").[11] From the point of view of the *nomenklatura* it is precisely this undefined legal status and the dual status of fixed capital and its new "owners" (making it possible to manipulate costs) that determine profitability. The state presumably also prefers such an undefined legal status. It still remains the formal owner, and at the same time productive factors are used in a way that could not be achieved with administrative methods.

The second form is *spinning off certain functions of the enterprise* (e.g., computer programming and design) and having them done by a *private company* set up by the managerial cadre and some of the employees.[12] This company works both for the enterprise from which it was separated and—what is new—also for other customers. Continuing to hold managerial positions in the state enterprise and taking advantage of its often monopoly position give the owners of the company an edge in the fight for markets. Customers are pressured to sign linked contracts: we—as a state enterprise—won't sell you our product if you don't order a design (or some service) from our private company. The producer's market and the overall situation of shortages facilitate such a practice. The advantage of the private companies is that they perform their services more quickly and often more cheaply (in comparison with what the enterprise paid before for the same services), even though the wages of specialists are much higher, for there are no deductions for the state as owner. The disadvantage (especially as regards data processing) is that often entirely superfluous work is done (e.g., the reports on details of operations that the enterprise must prepare anyway are never analyzed).[13] This leasing out of selected functions of the enterprise in the sphere of control is the managerial version of "workers' brigades" that handle selected production services for the enterprise and for their own profit.

These two forms appear in Poland and Hungary[14] and in the U.S.S.R. Managers' private companies, however, do not always promote more rational decisions concerning production in the state enterprise or in the separated operation. Very often the private company engages in the same fictional activity as the state enterprise (e.g., a computer center that produces data that is never used), though this time for the private profits of the owners of these companies. This form may even solidify this fiction and also strengthen monopoly tendencies in the state sector, for these companies exploit the monopoly position of the parent enterprise in the fight for segmentation and monopolization of the market for their own benefit.

The third form is connected with the *selective leasing out of picked departments of the state enterprise* to private companies in which persons associated with the managerial staff of this enterprise often have shares.[15] This makes it possible to lease out the most modern departments and, once again, to throw some of the costs onto the pared-down state enterprise.

Such a possibility of manipulating costs recalls to some extent the operations of multinational corporations, especially in the Third World, where they exploit tax loopholes and differences in the economic policy of individual countries to shift profits—through bookkeeping operations—to countries where they will pay the lowest tax.

The imprecise formal status of this and earlier forms of ownership by the *nomenklatura* makes it impossible for outsiders to control this shifting of costs. The workers' council and the crew are often bought off by wage increases that are paid regardless of the financial performance of the enterprise and covered by subsidies from the state budget. Here as well the positive effects are a somewhat better use of fixed capital and an increase in the company's production. The outflow of money, however, seems to eat up these production increases.

Companies owned by private persons and the Treasury are the fourth form. The contribution of the private persons is often symbolic, since as a rule such companies arise from the bankruptcy of state enterprises (arranged by fiscal or even political methods).[16] Very often the persons playing the role of representatives of the Treasury are selected in such a way that they are a sort of protective umbrella that makes the company untouchable (e.g., the company may destroy the natural environment with impunity).[17] Contacts with top-ranking political leaders also make it easier to get supplies and subsidies, lower taxes, and so on.

The fifth form is the *participation of the managerial cadre of state enterprises or the regional administration in private companies* with foreign capital operating in exceptionally favorable financial conditions in comparison with other private companies and the state sector.[18] The contribution of the joint owner-managers sometimes boils down to putting the company on the list of customers allowed to buy a semi-product in short supply and manufactured in the state enterprise run by this owner-manager.

Finally, the sixth form is so-called *organizational ownership*: that is, the possession by political parties,[19] trade unions,[20] and social organizations[21] of productive assets. The employment of these assets and the division of the profits are decided by boards appointed by (and most often made up of) the higher functionaries of these organizations. The benefits to these persons are that they can arbitrarily set their own wages and also have cheaper access for themselves and other functionaries of the organization to attractive services (construction, remodeling, travel),[22] which enable them to attain a high level of consumption legally. This form of ownership, which only in exceptional cases of ownership by the *nomenklatura* has fixed legal status,[23] is an additional way of disciplining and winning over the members of the organization, for the organization now becomes an attractive employer or provider of services. This form, now seen in Poland, is also developing in

Hungary[24] and the U.S.S.R. Thus productive or service enterprises belonging to social organizations have two variants: they are either separate (which makes it harder for the apparatus to use in an uncontrolled way the state subsidies granted to the organization for purposes that will give apparatchiks an immediate profit), or they are hidden within the organization (as departments for recreation, overhaul, etc.). The latter form makes outside control impossible and is more convenient for the apparatus. That is why the horse trading often ends by including in the private companies members of the state administration who decide about the structure of organizations (departments of internal affairs of national councils) or by putting them on the lists of persons benefiting from attractive services at lower cost. These bargainings concern not only the amount of the subsidy but also organizational arrangements. Organizational ownership sometimes is transformed into private shareholders' companies when the functionaries of the organization, after purchasing the property from the state (as a social organization, for peanuts), make the next decision to change into a company and distribute the shares among themselves. Ownership by social organizations is the most parasitical and—with a few exceptions (where the organization cannot count on subsidies)[25]—most economically inefficient form of ownership. To be sure, one can also conceive of efficient forms, e.g., the economic operations of some foundations, insurance companies, and commercial banks created after the Solidarity government's stabilizing policy was introduced (Balcerowicz Plan, January–November 1989).

Features of Political Capitalism

The above forms of the linkage of power and capital (including various forms of turning power over goods in short supply into capital with a definite market value) can be given the common name *political capitalism* (somewhat reminiscent of the nineteenth-century version of this mechanism).[26] Its basic features are
  • the linkage of power over people and things in industry and the state administration with activity geared toward profit for certain individuals in a private company;
  • the fact that the main customer of these companies is not the

consumer market, but state industry and the structures of the empire in the broad sense. This form also maintains consumption by members of the apparatus as a social group on a relatively high level (such as, the exchange of favors between the apparatchiks of various departments; services for their own use);

• the derivation of profits from the exclusive access reserved for "owners of companies" who have dual status to attractive markets and capital, decision-making centers, information, goods in short supply—that is, influence connected with a monopoly position in state industry.

Political capitalism is already becoming legitimized (through the practice of the power elite, but not in the law) by the creation of new foundations of the privileged status of the *nomenklatura*. This form of ownership should be distinguished from individual, formalized, inheritable, and disposable private ownership. Its incomplete nature and lack of any guarantee of permanence[27] (which are partially due to the political climate around this form of ownership) only increase its predatoriness. Some people look for the roots of this form in Tibor Liski's 1963 idea of "personalized social ownership,"[28] when the private leasing of state property obtained through competition (and guaranteeing the most efficient use) was regarded as the structural basis of the market reform. Simultaneously holding a managerial position in a state enterprise along with a position in a private company guarantees efficiency because only the managerial cadre of the state enterprise knows the reserves that can be tapped by the private company set up within this enterprise.

Political capitalism as a form of privatization within the state sector promotes the further segmentation of the market. Two separate private sectors come into being (a traditional one and one controlled by the *nomenklatura*), and each of them operates in a different market, according to different principles and with different chances of expansion (the big deals in contacts with the world, the empire, and the state sector are reserved for owners from the *nomenklatura*). Such a form of privatization gives the political elite the illusion of control. The actual control is over the expansion of the traditional private sector, which is limited to operating in the consumer market and excluded from the maneuver of "ontological opening" and privatization of the state sector.

The main disadvantages of political capitalism are

• a further erosion of the law and, inevitably, a delay of legislative reforms, for legal ambiguities and loopholes are exploited in this form as a source of profit;

• a strengthening of monopoly tendencies in the state sector, which help the companies built around monopolies to acquire no less a monopoly status and a certain segment of the market as their property, so to speak;

• that with this form (at least in the initial stage) no capital market is formed: owners from the *nomenklatura* rarely invest their own money; more often, in a special way, they "capitalize" their power over people and things and their political connections. The profitability of dual status (a position in the state sector or a social organization) and joint ownership of a company that is an annex to a state enterprise immobilize capital. This organizational tying up of capital likens this form to ownership by organs of workers' self-management or the "crew";

• that the small inputs of the new owners destroy the anti-inflationary effect of the privatization maneuver in the state sector;

• only slight improvement of the supply of consumer goods (since the main customers are state-owned industry, the empire, and the state). However, it increases the flow of money to the market (through seizure by private persons of some of the revenues that in the past went to the state budget; buying off crews and workers' councils with wage increases);

• a compromise of the idea of privatization of the state sector in the eyes of the society (opinions on this are presented below);

• the possibility of shifting costs to state enterprises and the state budget.

The phenomenon of shifting costs appears in all forms of making owners of the *nomenklatura*, whether in the form of saddling the state budget directly (e.g., making profits from the export of food that is subsidized by the state or using subsidies to political and social organizations to purchase fixed assets that actually become the group property of the functionaries of the organization) or by throwing some of the costs of operating private companies onto state enterprises (exploiting the dual status of owners of a private company and managers of a state enterprise and the dual status of fixed assets in certain forms of "making owners of the *nomenklatura*"). We can put forth the hypothesis that the sudden worsening of the economic performance of the state sector and the swelling budget deficit may be due in part to the profits attained by the rapidly emerging new forms of ownership described here that link power and capital.[29]

The main advantages of this form are

- release of reserves known only to the managerial cadre of enterprises and more efficient use of productive factors (including the recruitment of labor that is in increasingly short supply);

- lowered costs of monitoring and creation of lukewarm (because there are no guarantees of the permanence of ownership rights) but clear interests in the reproduction of fixed assets and capital.

In regard to the transformation of the system, another advantage is the speed with which this form of privatization is taking place (owing to the tangle of material interests of the *nomenklatura* and the rationale of control by which the power elite is guided). This process not only reduces the frustration of executives in the apparatus, but it also gives the elite the feeling that they are in control of the entire operation and can bring about a symbiosis of this form of privatization with the centralized command system (if the expected penetration by Western capital does not take place). This form also does not require giving up the philosophy of rule that puts the interest of the state/empire over the interest of social consumption.

An advantage of privatization through political capitalism for the authorities is that they are not forced to adopt a troublesome, restrictive monetary policy (which would make political stability more difficult). Inflation destroys the small private sector operating in the consumer market, but owners operating in the privatized state sector are much less affected by it. They can always pass along costs in prices, especially if their major customers are state enterprises. Besides this, their own financial input and risk are small.

Evaluating Political Capitalism

Not all the forms of making owners of the *nomenklatura* described here should be evaluated in an equally negative way. The most pathological forms are ownership by social and political

organizations subsidized by the state and activity replacing make-
believe bureaucratic actions (e.g., fictional accountancy), or using
absurd laws (brokerage between various markets and kinds of
capital) in order to limit—often for doctrinal or "strategic"[30]
reasons—the expansion of the traditional private sector operated
by "people from the street." One may expect that other forms will
become economically more feasible after the simple reserves to be
had by exploiting the monopoly position of the parent state enterprise are exhausted and all possibilities of shifting to the state enterprise some of the costs of doing private business have been exploited. This rationality will be prodded by the development of
other forms of ownership in the state sector, about which I will say
more. Making owners of the *nomenklatura* may also help to eliminate the *nomenklatura* as a political mechanism.[31] After a short
time the new owners themselves probably will support more open
access to the private sector in order to become independent of the
state administration, which today controls the setting up of companies included in political capitalism and decides their duration.

Two analogies—one historical, the other contemporary, but
from a different geographical area—conclude this discussion of
political capitalism.

The first analogy concerns the process of Westernization of the
Ottoman Empire in the nineteenth century.[32] There, as in Eastern
Europe today (in those countries where transformation is taking
place), the penetration of the economy by Western capital was
subjected to dual control. Certain segments of the economy were
excluded from this penetration, and a buffer zone was created in
the form of arrangements that recall some of the forms of political
capitalism described above. Brokerage was the main area of such
activity,[33] with political functionaries given permission to engage
in economic activity on their own account. The local traditional
private sector was not included in the maneuver of "opening."
As a result the first phase of Westernization (like the first phase
of transformation described above connected with "ontological
opening") led not to the development of a universal market, but
rather to even deeper segmentation because each segment operated
in accordance with a different logic. The transformation was largely guided by the state (in keeping with its reformed rationality of
control and not its immediate economic interest), while the role of

the traditional private sector was marginal. The pace of transformation depended much more on economic units created through political favoritism (as in the companies in Eastern Europe described above, or commercial brokerage capital in the Ottoman Empire) than on the expansion of small, traditional owners, who were restricted to operating exclusively in the local market (which does not mean without profit). However, access to the most profitable markets—trade and cooperation with the empire, the state (government orders), and state industry—was reserved for persons from the area of political capitalism. In both cases expansion of the latter was accompanied by increasing tensions and divisions in the state administration itself. For in spite of its continued control of access to various forms of political capitalism, the central administration felt more and more threatened by the new power of owners from the *nomenklatura* (who, as one can see in Poland and Hungary, quickly attempt to become independent, attacking the *nomenklatura* as a mechanism of recruitment to positions of power). In both cases tensions increase between the central authority and the "provinces": as in China and the U.S.S.R., fears that penetration, Westernization, is a synonym of colonialization can lead to intervention by the army and the suspension of "ontological opening."

In both cases (the Ottoman Empire and Eastern Europe) the first phase of transformation, described here as connected with "ontological opening," does not result in an immediate improvement of traditional indicators of "openness to the world," such as the share of export and import in the GNP, foreign investments per capita, or export per capita. In spite of this (in countries with forms of ownership that do not permit penetration, which was the case in the Ottoman Empire and is the case in Eastern Europe) the first phase is a crucial one on which the success of all the rest depends. In the Ottoman Empire Westernization was disturbed by national conflicts and the breakup of the empire—a fate that perhaps lies in store for the U.S.S.R. The alternative might be militarization and recentralization (which also would halt the process of "ontological opening").

Finally, in both cases the opening/Westernization maneuver was introduced by the political elite and not by groups pursuing their own economic interest. The latter appeared later, together with the operators of political capitalism created from above. In Eastern Europe this political elite is the faction of "globalists" described elsewhere; in the Ottoman Empire that elite was the Young Turks.

The second analogy concerns institutional arrangements of the buffer zone in conditions of dependency. New studies of the dynamics of dependency in Latin America[34] show that recently the role of the state in the economy has increased there, and the state is pressuring multinational corporations to share markets (and profits) with local capital. This is supposed to facilitate the passage from purely negative dependency to dependent development. A similar problem faces the countries of Eastern Europe in their relations with the U.S.S.R. The introduction of various forms of political capitalism to the buffer zone in trade with the U.S.S.R. promoted by the state also seems to have the aim of rationalizing this exchange. It is expected that private companies working for a profit will be able to negotiate better terms than the state administration[35] and also make more efficient use of local advantages. This would reduce the immediate benefits for the Soviet side, but in the long run it might make trade more attractive and increase its volume. Of course, pathological forms are possible; e.g., dynamic companies turn a profit from the export of food subsidized by the Polish state and are in direct competition with the needs of the domestic market and fueling inflation.

Other Suggested Forms of Privatization in the State Sector

In addition to the program of state capitalism (implemented very intensively but rarely discussed in all of its complexity; rather, it is attacked as a political symbol), four other visions of privatization of the state sector in Eastern Europe are put forward.

1) The *transformation of state enterprises into joint stock companies with mixed capital*, with the participation of the Treasury and foreign capital. The legal basis of this form (and of the other ownership transformations) is the law concerning the Treasury that separates the enterprise from the indivisible inventory of state ownership and permits further ownership transformations.[36] Only in this last context can this law be evaluated positively, for

without further ownership changes there would be regression in relation to the status of the self-managed state enterprise.[37] Companies with mixed capital are being set up based on the law on economic associations (Hungary)[38] or the law on foreign capital (Poland).[39] The scale of the maneuver proposed by the authorities of both countries is considerable: in the case of Hungary it embraces 25 percent of all industrial output.[40] The foreign capital flowing into companies is supposed to make possible the modernization of enterprises and to increase their efficiency and chances of export of the West (joint ownership is a *carte d'entrée* to the European Common Market). The fact that most of the enterprises suggested by the Hungarian authorities for this form of privatization are working for the benefit of the Council for Mutual Economic Assistance (COMECON) as a whole[41] makes it attractive to the entire bloc. So far, however, both in Poland and in Hungary these companies have been forming at a rather slow pace. For example, whereas in Hungary $320 million have been invested in such shares, in Turkey shares for a value of $800 million have been purchased in only nine months.[42] In the opinion of specialists,[43] this process could be speeded up by the liberalization of wage policy (lifting the limitations imposed by the state). Yet this is difficult on account of the threat of inflation (especially in the case of enterprises producing for export and not the domestic market). Such wage differences also would give rise to social tensions and populistic egalitarian pressures. Shareholders also would have to be given a say in the selection of the managerial cadre of enterprises—but in this situation what would happen with the *nomenklatura* (not necessarily from the party, but the one introduced for security reasons), since many enterprises from the list are important for the "defense potential" (the machine industry, means of communication, and transport) and require contacts with enterprises in the COMECON that the authorities do not want to open up for the West?

2) The *transformation of state enterprises into joint stock companies whose shareholders would be private native individuals.* Two versions are possible.

First, *gratuitous ownership rights* may be granted to the employees of a given enterprise. The disadvantage of this version is the tying up of capital in a particular type of production, for the employee-owners will defend this production, fearing the costs of changes that would lower the value of their qualifications. In this form there also would be little re-creation of economic interests in reproducing fixed assets and capital, which is one of the basic goals of the privatization maneuver. Finally, with dispersed and nontransferable ownership, the employee-owners may be tempted to favor immediate consumption, which results in rapid decapitalization. Owing to its gratuitousness, this form also has no anti-inflationary effect. Furthermore, as M. Dąbrowski wrote: "Economically and socially unjustified property differences resulting exclusively from the place of employment at the moment of entitlement"[44] may appear.

Second, *shares may be sold to the employees of the enterprise*[45] and to outside persons (while retaining certain priorities for the employees). This version is suggested as a way to follow the experiences of Western countries.[46] The main advantages are the anti-inflationary effect that will help to balance the state budget and probably a better (than in the gratuitous form) re-creation of economic interests in the reproduction of all productive factors (and not only of labor). Finally, with ownership by people from outside the enterprise, the elements of a capital market appear. A number of difficulties arise here, however. First, assessment of the property is impossible without a market (which in turn cannot come into being without ownership changes). M. Dąbrowski[47] suggests auctions to break out of this vicious circle. While this does not guarantee an objective assessment of productive factors (but rather is a measure of the affluence of the interested purchasers), the main objective is to create owners and, as a consequence, to start up a market. The second problem is the small financial resources of the population.[48] Yet even here a solution can be found by considering various forms of guarantees (e.g., a mortgage on real estate). The increase of efficiency and accumulation after entitlement will become self-generating.[49]

A third way to create joint stock companies is the egalitarian vision of *distribution* among the adult citizens of *debentures* for the value of their share of the national property. (Such vision is seriously debated now—summer of 1990—in Czechoslovakia and in the Polish Seym.) These debentures would give the right to obtain shares for this value in a state enterprise of the debenture holder's choice that goes private through auction.[50] These debentures (rights of ownership to a part of property) also could be purchased by private persons and brokerage firms, for not everyone would be interested in being an owner and would prefer cash at once. The element of risk, choice, and economic dealing would favor the enterprising, for the choice of the specific enterprise would be up to the holder of the debenture. In Poland, certain preferred debentures are suggested for the employees of a given enterprise, who when it went up for sale would have first choice in turning their debentures into shares. Limits would be imposed on institutions (commercial banks, foundations, companies) buying shares from individuals. The auctioning of state enterprises would begin with areas where competition is possible already. The entire entitlement operation would have to be accompanied by energetic antimonopoly measures enforced by the state.

3) The *transformation of state enterprises into group ownership*.[51] Here also several forms are possible:

• ownership by *organs of workers' self-management*, without separate shares. These bodies would have the right to make decisions now reserved for the so-called founding organ (e.g., a further change of ownership forms, investment of part of the profit, change of the profile of production, sale of part of the fixed assets, division of the profit). Such ownership rights create a much more solid foundation for workers' self-management than solutions of the Yugoslavian type;

• ownership by *cooperatives* with membership limited to employees;

• ownership by *municipal bodies*;

• ownership by *foundations, trade unions, social and political organizations, associations*;

• ownership by various types of *public funds* (e.g., old-age pension funds).

The disadvantage of ownership without separate shares is the weakness of economic motivations. Its proposers regard this form as temporary, enabling the accumulation of capital and experience before passing to more consistent privatization with separate shares. This form could become stabilized and begin to live a life of its own, however, because of the interests of the functionaries of the organization, of regional administration, and so on; many of these people regard group property as a source of their additional, uncontrolled profits.

Also possible are various forms of more separate and full, but not yet absolute, ownership rights; these, too, are regarded as temporary solutions (e.g., enabling the accumulation of funds for the purchase of shares). These can be various forms of *leasing* the state enterprise or parts of it to groups of employees (sometimes with the retention of the dual ownership status of fixed assets, which so-called task groups among employees can use for their own account when these assets are not in use by the enterprise).[52] Another possibility is the *employee-state company*, with preferred shares given to employees at the outset in order to retain the self-managed nature of the enterprise, and a gradual increase in the percentage of shares held by employees.

4) *Organizational ownership in the form of so-called holdings,* whether "natural" (banks, foundations) or created especially by the state in the form of enterprises to which other enterprises are entrusted and are evaluated not on the basis of the volume of a certain output, but on the basis of the profit from the capital and fixed assets entrusted to them. This form is especially valuable during the *restructuralization* maneuver in the economy.[53]

The authors of all of the proposals presented above are aware that faulty macroeconomic decisions (often caused by political motivations)[54] and their effects—e.g., inflation—can wipe out the benefits and destroy the economic motivations resulting from privatization. Different forms of ownership have different degrees of resistance to the devaluation of money, which is least painful to various forms of state capitalism and organizational ownership and most hurtful to separate, individual ownership.

Forms of Privatization in the Socioeconomic Context

The dynamics of the crisis on one hand and the solutions of economic policy on the other can have an important influence on the success of individual variants of privatization of the state sector. Also significant are public attitudes, especially in a situation of democratization from the top, when the new elite entering the public scene is uncertain of its base of support and gauges it (by trying catchy slogans) in the course of the political process.

Dynamics of the Crisis

Starting in 1988, the lingering crisis of the Polish and Soviet economies (and to a lesser degree, the Hungarian economy) has been moving toward recession combined with a rapidly accelerating inflationary spiral and deepening disequilibrium (material imbalances) of the economy. This peculiar "crisis within a crisis" is connected with a physical decline of production in the state sector. The reasons for this decline are complex: the limitation of cooperative import,[55] increasing fuel and energy difficulties,[56] a decline in the efficiency of state enterprises,[57] and a reduction of employment in the state sector.[58] The last two factors do not necessarily mean a decline of economic efficiency in the entire system, which is made up of various forms of ownership. For it is possible that they are due to both the illegal flow of productive factors to the so-called second economy (where they are used much more efficiently) and with the shifting to state enterprises of part of the costs of the form here called political capitalism. In this form new goods and services are produced, however, and productive factors seem to be used more efficiently. Yet the redistributive effect of this form of privatization (even with an eventual increase of efficiency in the system as a whole) strikes directly at the state sector and the state budget (decline of efficiency, insolvency, and subsidies). The influence of political capitalism on recessionary tendencies in the state sector is linked not only with a shifting of costs, but also with jacking up the prices of foreign currencies in auctions and the free market (which for companies entering this form of ownership is not a great burden, for their customer as a rule is the state sector or the empire, which do not consider the costs). Another source of recession is the progressing anarchy of economic life. There are many reasons for this, one of which is the scenario of the economic reform, consisting in a further fragmentation of the economy and segmentation of the market. With dissimilar rules in the individual segments of the economy and with the administrative rationing of some productive factors (labor, energy, etc., depending on local conditions), the actual hierarchy of forms of ownership takes shape on a low level of the administration, irrespective of the policy of the decision-making center. Material links with the private sector and the sector of political capitalism gradually seem to dislodge party-economic cliques, for in contrast to the new cliques that are forming the latter are unable to provide the local apparatus with viable survival strategies. Inflation also has an anarchic influence on the economy. One of the effects of inflation in the state sector that causes economic anarchy is slowdowns in payments: it is not worthwhile for enterprises to pay their bills on time when the value of money is rapidly declining. For some enterprises, however, this means operating on the edge of bankruptcy and with insufficient funds to continue production.[59]

The recession is accompanied by an increase of subsidies to the state sector, a budget deficit, and higher taxes, which in turn intensify recessionary tendencies. As regards the budget deficit, both Poland and the U.S.S.R. are for the first time experiencing the economic cycle of public choice, which has been described many times in Western literature.[60] The political process set in motion in Poland after the "round table" had its measurable cost. The attempt by the Rakowski government to put together an electoral coalition with the United Peasants' Party resulted in an increase in the purchase prices of agricultural products to the so-called parity of income levels.[61] With an overpopulated agricultural sector[62] this often meant raising purchase prices above market equilibrium prices ("bazaar" prices). With no rise of retail prices (because of fear of destabilization before the elections), this cost the state budget about 800 billion złotys.[63] More difficult to calculate is the cost of low-interest credits for persons operating in the political capitalism sector, who in this way were encouraged to support the Rakowski team. In the pre-election period the budget deficit (worsened even more by wage increases, which often were politically motivated)[64] swelled twofold. In the U.S.S.R., in turn, the electoral cycle was coupled with cooperation of populist leaders (with their antibureaucratic slogans) in order to neutralize (unsuccessfully, as it turned out) aspirations of national minorities, which united local power apparatuses and communities. This cooptation was also reflected in tax policy (as in the egalitarian slogans of the populists) and in spending foreign currency reserves to purchase consumer goods (the E. Gierek method, which was used in the early seventies and was imitated in the economic blueprint agreed upon by Gorbachev and Yeltsin in August 1990) in order to pacify the public feeling before the elections, or decrease inflationary pressures rooted in shortages.

The inflation that accompanies the recession is especially ruinous for the small private sector. Political capitalism is more resistant to its negative effects, and at the same time adds fuel to the inflationary fire (by jacking up the prices of foreign currencies at auctions and by bribing workers' councils and crews with wage increases so that they would consent to privatization and the setting up of companies, with simultaneous easy access—on account of political connections—to credits and subsidies).[65] It is worth remembering that inflation in Eastern Europe has two characteristics that do not appear in inflation in the capitalist world. First, it can be called "shortageflation" (in which all real increases are gobbled up by the deeply unbalanced economy and do not slow down the inflationary spiral).[66] Second, it is so-called sterile inflation,[67] for it does not prod adaptation measures in state industry (e.g., a regrouping of productive forces). This lack of reaction results from forms of ownership (no economic interests and soft financing because the state enterprise is not economically responsible) and from materials barriers that make it impossible to increase supply, in spite of deep disequilibrium, high demand, and high prices. Though forms of political capitalism do not reduce inflation (they may even increase it), they may contribute to changing its "sterile" nature. For this form of ownership puts in motion physical reserves that make it possible to overcome certain materials barriers. At the same time, however, in political capitalism the pace of founding new companies is slow, for this form is fused with (built into) concrete state enterprises. Thus it is a form that does not promise rapid restructuralization of the economy, whose present structure is one of the main causes of inflation because branches producing means of production are dominant over branches producing consumer goods. Other forms of privatization (e.g., the purchase of shares) also are a potential means of combating inflation and the budget deficit,[68] but political capitalism is not such a means.

Meeting obligations to the COMECON and acquiring foreign

currency in Western markets at all costs lead to a phenomenon unknown in the capitalist world (at least in the developed countries): export in competition with the domestic market. Political capitalism is an important countributor to this process.[69] The accumulating effects of disequilibrium that result from such competition (and also of the investment policy[70] in order to meet the obligations of specialization in the COMECON) only increase the market value of command over scarce resources, which is the main motivation behind setting up companies of the political capitalism type. Other forms of ownership (including the traditional private sector) are only grappling with the negative effects of this situation.

Economic Policy

In Poland, where the economic crisis is the most dramatic (though the situation in the U.S.S.R. is extremely difficult), three variants of an emergency stabilization policy have been put forward. The variants differ fundamentally, though in the longer-term perspective all use similar (though apparently understood differently) clichés: "introducing market mechanisms," "changes of forms of ownership," and "opening."

The first variant (supported at the "round table" by the opposition side)[71]

• seems to overestimate the role in the economy of political factors (such as various social councils—e.g., of planning, or wage-price agreements and contracts between the government and the trade unions) and underestimate economic solutions (in particular, privatization measures in the state sector);

• searches for a reduction of recessionary tensions chiefly through lightening the country's foreign debt obligations and increasing cooperative import;

• threatens to cause hyperinflation with the proposal to implement the indexation of wages. This idea was put forward by Solidarity before the elections in 1989 for political reasons and already during the "round table" discussions was thrown onto the enterprises (in a way that seems to be a compromise with the government position, but which in fact only increases inflationary pressures). The latter would have to come up with the funds for wage increases on their own (by raising prices). The nonobligatory nature of the "round table" (at least on this question) and the handing over of the decision on the form of indexation to the new Parliament (with 35 percent Solidarity deputies in the Seym and 99 percent in the Senate) led to a further modification. The uncontrolled pre-election payments of wages in the state sector and the huge budget deficit, together with the newly acquired feeling of responsibility, prescribed a quiet backing away from radical indexation.[72]

As regards the position on various forms of ownership, making owners of the *nomenklatura* is attacked for political reasons (to build identity, to latch onto the slogans of the excluded populist wing of Solidarity,[73] to exploit emotions), while in fact no other program of privatization of the state sector is put forward. Advocates of this variant limit their actions to supporting slogans of the development of the traditional private sector, the "equal rights of sectors," and workers' self-management.

The second variant of stabilization policy is radically populist (it is accepted today by part of the All-Polish Agreement of Trade Unions and the party apparatus, but also by some of the worker "masses" of Solidarity). As the crisis worsens, the main idea of this program, which is to shift the costs of the stabilization policy to the more affluent part of the society, may become more popular. Certain elements of this program, somewhat toned down, are already beginning to appear in the proposals of groups that heretofore had held a different position (even among the monetarists). The most noticed proposal of the populist stabilization and anti-inflationary policy was formulated in autumn 1989. Its author[74] proposes:

• a temporary tax on above-average personal incomes (per person in the family) after the deduction of productive investments from personal funds and the payment of credits taken out for productive purposes. A tax of 10 percent is suggested for two to three years;

• a compulsory loan deducted every month for one to two years from the entire nonagricultural population with incomes per family member considerably higher than the average (e.g., 1.5 times higher) of half of this excess. The loan would be successively returned together with interest equal to the rate of inflation after the most severe phase of the crisis has been overcome;

- a partial and temporary freeze of savings (while raising the interest to the rate of inflation);
- elimination of the two-currency system, the free traffic in foreign currencies, and the sale of goods for foreign currencies in the Pewex shops. In the opinion of the author of this proposal, the purchase of foreign currencies from the population fuels inflation in two ways: by running up prices at foreign currency auctions for enterprises and by increasing the number of złotys in the hands of holders of foreign currency. Egalitarian demands also increase. At the same time, high import duties are suggested for private imports, which would be remitted if the goods were sold to the state at the official exchange rate of the dollar. In the opinion of the author of populist program, even under these conditions such import would be quite profitable, while the state could reduce the budget deficit by selling goods at market equilibrium prices;
- a tax on above-standard dwelling space.

At the same time, a number of measures are suggested to restore market equilibrium and bring supplies into balance.

- First, a tax on investments made by enterprises of half of the sums paid to contractors. This would encourage a rapid completion of projects and discourage unjustified investments.
- Second, increasing the production of meat by changing the structure and prices of fodder available in the market and putting to work reserves of labor (and buildings) on average-sized farms. This maneuver would also require a change in the function of state and collective farms (which would become granaries for small farms) and a change in the structure of import. This populist variant would not require as big an increase in the price of food as discussed at the "round table." The present Solidarity government policy of "introducing market mechanisms in agriculture" is formulated from the perspective of large farms. It calculates the costs of machines and hired labor, but does not consider the reserves of personal labor of the overpopulated Polish countryside (30 percent of the population resides in the villages). Raising purchase prices will not put these reserves to work or increase the output of meat on average-sized farms, where the main barrier is the shortage of fodder.
- Third, restructuralization of industry, which requires renegotiation of production specialities in the COMECON. Here it should be emphasized that the populist proposal (both in Poland

and in Hungary) clearly accents the national interest. This populist variant has two serious dangers: it is highly anti-efficient (especially as regards the private sector and the starting up of new ventures), and it has great potential for repression, since most of the measures suggested require greater administrative controls and sanctions.

This variant (closest to the so-called stabilization proposals of Wladystav Baka, which were announced in the autumn of 1987 when he was still president of the Polish National Bank) is one of "hard money" with the simultaneous liberalization of price policy (the so-called monetary-market variant).[75] This would be a restrictive monetary policy reinforced by a strong central policy of restructuralization in industry. It would also reduce the growth rate of demand, both for households and enterprises, and probably would reduce the easy profits of the private sector. This variant would require a reversal of the ruinous effects of shortageflation and creation of effective mechanisms to spur economically rational adaptation reactions on the part of enterprises. One of the ways to accomplish this might be to create a securities market and make ownership changes in the state sector, though the supporters of this variant do not expect a rapid rationalization of behaviors from ownership changes, which were undertaken in conditions of great disequilibrium and monopolization.[76]

This variant sharply criticizes the Rakowski government policy that is based on the tacit assumption that the inflationary spiral combined with privatization in the variant of political capitalism (with the material reserves thereby released) will stimulate adaptation measures in the sense of raising output and changing its structure, especially if laws are passed to make it easier to set up companies. The supporters of the monetary-market variant emphasize the anarchic effect of the policy of the government based on the above assumptions, especially when it is combined with an outflow of money dictated by political considerations.

• The fourth variant is the stabilization policy proposed in the Leszek Balcerowicz plan, introduced in December 1989. This plan is based on tight fiscal and monetary control and "correctional inflation" as a cure for inflation (with increase of prices at once, through government decision, to the level of the "consumer demand barrier." The intent is to push producers to reduce costs and lower prices in order to survive in the market.

Social Attitudes toward Ownership Changes

Social attitudes favor the privatization process in the state sector. Polls by the government Center for the Study of Public Opinion in April 1989[77] showed a clear increase in the acceptance of privatization in comparison with polls taken in 1987. While in 1987 a majority supported privatization only in the handicrafts and retail trade, in 1989 a majority supported the privatization of all forms of economic activity (excluding banks). In 1989, 58.6 percent of workers and 64 percent of managers accepted the privatization of state industry in the form of companies with the participation of foreign capital and 64 percent of workers and 77 percent of managers accepted privatization in companies with the participation of the crew. When respondents were asked about transformation of the crew-participation type for the enterprise in which they themselves were employed, the number of supporters among workers rose to 71 percent, but among managers declined to 68 percent. There were fewer supporters of selling shares to persons who are not employees of the enterprise. In a study made by Bogdan Cichomski and Witold Morawski,[78] this form of privatization was supported by 35 percent of managers and 17 percent of workers.

The strongest supporters of all forms of privatization were engineers and technicians. Polls showed that the setting up of companies by private persons had social acceptance: only one-fourth of the respondents suggested limiting this to small firms. The attitude toward forms that I called "political capitalism" is interesting. In answer to the question "Who should run the enterprise so that it would operate better than before?" 35 percent of managers and 20.2 percent of workers chose the reply "A high-class specialist-manager, who leases the enterprise from the state on the basis of a contract with the ministry concerned. The crew does not participate in management."[79]

The above views are coupled with the opinion that it is necessary to take politics out of the economy at the enterprise level: two-thirds of workers and four-fifths of managers were against any kind of interference by political parties in the enterprise's operations. Acceptance of wage differences in the enterprise also rose. In 1989 57 percent of workers (10 percent more than in 1987) accepted wage spreads in which managers would earn three times more and engineers two times more than workers. This was accepted by 89 percent of managers.[80] Workers were somewhat more conservative as regards the system than were managers: 30 percent of them agreed with the statement "one doesn't have to change the principles, only find the right people," with which only 20 percent of managers agreed.

There is clearer resistance to privatization in the state sector among activists of institutions that would lose influence after privatization. Thus the Forum of Workers' Councils (a national association of workers' councils) rejects any formula other than "workers' self-management ownership" (group ownership of the crew without separate shares),[81] which is supported by 30 percent of workers.[82] Also the discussion at the second National Ideological Conference of the PUWP (Communist party) showed that "strategic reasons" (holding on to state property as the foundation of political domination) were regarded as just as important as efficiency arguments.[83] It is interesting that the new generation of full-time employees of the Communist party (with economic education and some practice in "political capitalism") was much more willing in 1987 to accept ownership changes in the state sector.[84]

The problem of privatization (especially the form of political capitalism) also became one of the pivots of articulating differences in the factional struggles within the power elite. W. Baka's attack on making owners of the *nomenklatura*[85] seems to be linked with his competition with the 1987 prime minister, Mieczyslaw Rakowski, and not motivated solely by fears that this form of privatization will bring only redistributive and not productive effects. Baka, who spoke as a secretary of the Central Committee of the Communist party, is also a participant in the process of redefining the identity of the party in relation to the government, and so there is a tendency to exaggerate differences of ideas. The opposition, in turn, which at the "round table" presented the Social Democratic/workers' self-management variant, was primarily guided by the belief that any other kind of change in the system would split its potential base of support. After the victory in the parliamentary elections, the opposition began to pose the problem of privatization in the state sector more clearly (though more cautiously than in power circles, owing to the ideological genealogy of many Solidarity activists and experts).[86] It should be added that many participants of the form called political capitalism entered the Seym (party seats).[87] They also organized themselves into a new pressure group called Economic Action (established under the auspices of the Rakowski government), and in a meeting with General Jaruzelski (before he became president) they argued for the need for greater access to ownership in the state sector.

Yet in an interview in the Communist party's weekly journal, *Polityka*,[88] Prime Minister Rakowski emphasized the necessity for abandoning the personnel policy called the "*nomenklatura.*" It seems that making owners of the *nomenklatura* and the peculiar capitalization of power (which becomes a *carte d'entrée* to a company) logically lead to the next step: The same people to whom the authorities allowed access to ownership now wish to free themselves from dependence on political and administrative factors, for in every concrete case the latter can still destroy the flimsy construction based on a coupling of positions in a state enterprise and in a private company. Though apportionment of ownership and legal guarantees as well as less arbitrariness in making owners of the *nomenklatura* may reduce some of the sources of profit (e.g., the uncontrolled manipulation of costs), these profits will be made more secure and political capitalism may become more economically rational.

Thus in the economy the transformation phase of the system boils down to the first in a sequence of three steps. This is the maneuver of "ontological opening" (different versions of privatization in the state sector), which in turn is supposed to make it possible to enter into new relations with the world capitalist system. The third step—the penetration by Western capital—is expected to initiate dependent development, though the peripheral status of the system (but on other principles) will continue.[89] Here we can observe a strange paradox: without this crisis the elite would not have taken the risk of "ontological opening," but this opening is extremely difficult in conditions of the crisis. A number of short-term moves of the stabilization (anti-inflation) policy may prod the process of privatization and determine the chances for success of particular forms of privatization. It seems, though, that both the historical inevitability of creating a market (since the inefficiency of centrally controlled allocative processes is already bringing about the absolute—and not only the relative—pauperization of the societies of the countries of real socialism) and the dynamics of social consciousness make the privatization maneuvar (without prejudging its forms) inescapable. A slowdown and even temporary reversal of this process are possible, however.

In Poland the first steps have been taken toward privatization of the state sector. In February 1990 a bill to modify the law concerning state enterprise was sent to the Seym and accepted. This bill clearly states that the organ of state ownership is the Treasury and not, as could be read from the law of September 1981, the enterprise (or rather, its workers' council). This is supposed to prevent the uncontrolled (via *nomenklatura* companies) selling of property, often below its real value, and to curtail speculation in land and buildings.

Two other bills are in preparation in Poland: on privatization of the state enterprise and on the Council for National Property and the Agency for Ownership Transformations (bills in *Życie Gospodarcze* No. 7, February 1990). They lay out a commercial path to privatization via the agency subordinated to the prime minister and under the supervision of the Council for National Property appointed by the Seym. Certain preferences are foreseen for employees: 20 percent of the shares of the enterprise (but not more) can be sold to employees on more favorable conditions.

The major opponents of these bills are: workers' councils of enterprises, which are interested in wide-scale employee stock ownership and unhappy about increasing the role of the state in appointing and dismissing managing directors, among other things, and also the populist Economic Council of the Council of Ministers. The latter body is in competition with the Economic Committee of the Council of Ministers headed by Leszek Balcerowicz and having decision-making powers. The negative position of the Council (see *Rzeczpospolita*, 16 February 1990) is expressed in proposals of various forms of "socialization" instead of privatization and in the demand for more political control over the entire process.

Fears are also voiced that explicitly naming the Treasury as the owner might create an automatic mechanism for the transformation of the foreign debt of the Treasury (where, in the world markets today, one dollar of the Polish debt can be purchased for about twenty cents) into ownership rights in state enterprises.

According to recent data,[90] nearly 42,000 cooperatives in the state sector in Poland are mostly the realization of political capital-ism (*nomenklatura* companies), as described in this chapter. The NIK (the Main Chamber of Control) estimates that nearly one-third of these firms should be taken under legal scrutiny due to strong suspicion of illegal activities. "*Nomenklatura* companies" control between 10 and 20 percent (depending on calculation) of fixed capital in the state sector (or, state sector turning into individual/group ownership).

The new law on enterprise recentralizes property rights and cre-ates a barrier for such shift of property rights decided on factory level. It is unclear, however, if it would be retroactive, delegalizing *nomenklatura* firms, mentioned above. It is unclear as well what would be the impact on capital formation of the Seym's legislation (June 1990) on "unjust profits," introduced to meet populist pressures.

There is a strange paradox here. For what is particularly pain-ful and irritating in "political capitalism" (*nomenklatura* com-panies)—namely, the possibility of shifting part of the costs to state enterprises and the state budget—can be regarded (from another perspective) as the main advantage of this form of ownership. The reason is that we have to do here with a more rapid formation of capital. After forty years we have found ourselves once again in the phase of primary accumulation.

The capital formed in the forties and early fifties at the cost of agriculture and invested in the state sector was largely wasted. The state sector is a dysfunctional bankrupt. And now the formation of new capital is taking place at its cost. Whether this will be a ration-al operation will be decided only in the next phase, however—namely, the future of this capital. Will it become the foundation of real privatization competing in a purely economic game without support in the mechanism of power (as in the phase of political capitalism)? Success will be determined by the openness of the econ-omy, diversification of the accumulated capital, and continuity of the process (compare with Japan of the 1880s, and a negative ex-ample: the Philippines of the 1970s).

There is no rational privatization without capital, however. Other alternatives are small savings (eaten up by inflation) or transformation of the debt into ownership rights (e.g., one dollar purchased from a bank by an investor for thirty cents and giving him the right to purchase a dollar's worth of assets in the state sector). Against this background, political capitalism shows certain advantages, especially when its more blatant forms of using power in speculation are limited (by the minister of finances). Examples of such speculations include the practice of extending monopoly status to a private company by exploiting the monopoly position of an enterprise in which the owner of the private company continues to be the managing director of the state enterprise; making fortunes on the export of production subsidized by the state—such as, until recently, food—or using subsidies to political parties for economic activity, which gives profits to the apparatus.

One might also expect that attacks en bloc on this form of accumulation will distort it even more: Political capitalism will change into finance capital, and the funds accumulated at the cost of the state sector will not serve further privatization but will end up in the branches of foreign banks in Poland and flow out of the country.

Appendix. Global Capitalism—Local Socialism: Toward the Dissolution of COMECON

In my opinion, the reforms taking place in Eastern Europe today (economic as well as political ones) are first and foremost an attempt to redefine relations between local socialism[91] and global capitalism (global in the sense that it dictates to socialism the latter's place in the world division of labor). Though socialism tries to imitate the capitalist way of organizing production and exchange, it lacks the ontological foundations of capitalism in the form of private property and the economic interests linked with it. The reformulation of relations with capitalism, as I have shown, is motivated by the desire to weaken the effect of the subarticulation of socialism to capitalism and to try to move from negative dependency to dependent development. This requires fundamental changes in property rights and political institutions: guaranteeing new property rights and social stability during the period of their introduction.

Such "ontological opening"—as I called it—is also followed by transformations inside the COMECON. Thus a reinterpretation is being made of the models of Eastern Europe's dependency on the capitalist West and on Moscow. For if my hypothesis[92] is valid that in the past the COMECON was a way in which the bloc adapted itself to its subarticulation in relation to capitalism, then the limitation of this subarticulation (as a result of privatization and the penetration of Western capital) will do away with the need for this institution. In the past one of the aims of the COMECON was to impose on the countries of the bloc production specialties—often unfavorable from the countries' point of view, but reducing uncertainty and tension in the empire as a whole owing to the "import substitution" effect. The COMECON also was a mechanism forcing transfers of products and foreign currency on the countries of the bloc, as well as an instrument for redistribution of the costs of subarticulation (which are greater in the economically less developed countries of the bloc). The second goal of the COMECON was to soften the shocks occurring in individual countries of the bloc after the sudden worsening of relations with the West (for example, the U.S. sanctions against Poland in 1982). The rapid worsening of the economic crisis in the U.S.S.R., however, makes Moscow less willing to act as a shock absorber by subsidizing some countries when their economic situation worsens on account of the imposed type of production specialty that is an "import substitution" for the entire bloc. What is more, the worsening quality of East European products considerably reduces the value of "import substitution," for it widens the technological gap between the empire and the West. The new approach—the possibility of the Finlandization of Poland and Hungary (intended to stimulate the inflow of new technologies and capital to the bloc)[93]—will relieve Moscow of responsibility for "evening out levels" between countries of the bloc, without threatening the Soviet Union with the loss of products previously exported there from Eastern Europe (and most often unsellable in the West).

Both reasons—reducing subarticulation and the economic crisis in the U.S.S.R.—make the COMECON not only less necessary, but also too costly for Moscow. Hence researches are wrong who claim that it was the flaws of the COMECON as a mechanism of economic integration that led to the efforts to reform it,[94] for the COMECON was never conceived as such an instrument.

Even if COMECON ceased to exist, the specialization agreements signed in the middle of the 1980s[95] would not necessarily be canceled. Today these agreements are enforced by instruments other than COMECON structures: e.g., agreements between enterprises (exploiting the interest of enterprises in survival) and also through private companies (chiefly associated with new owners from the *nomenklatura*). At the same time, there is ever more frequent talk about the possibility of abolishing the transfer ruble trade zone and moving to settlement of accounts in dollars.[96] This will have major repercussions for all the COMECON countries. If this is not attended by a devaluation of the ruble (currently overvalued in relation to the dollar), then the same transactions that were in balance in rubles could mean an annual deficit of $1 billion for the Polish side.[97] Another consequence might be a reduction in the physical volume of trade. Forced to pay each other in dollars for their products, the East European countries would prefer to buy higher quality Western goods for these dollars. This could make it hard for some enterprises to sell their products, resulting in a decline in output, and even in unemployment.[98]

The present attempts to reinterpret the relations of Eastern Europe with the capitalist world and, as a consequence, with Moscow are not the first such attempt. In fact all the previous crises revealed the cumulating effects of subarticulation in relation to capitalism on one hand and the cumulating effects of the dysfunctionality of the COMECON as an instrument for the adaptation of the bloc to this subarticulation on the other. In each crisis an attempt was made to redefine these relations or even to gain a place in the Western division of labor. The attempts of the 1970s (modernization for Western credits granted in exchange for "window-dressing" liberalization) turned out to be not only naive but also dramatic in their effects (the huge foreign debt). It was only the crisis of the 1980s that forced the articulation of the notion of "ontological opening" and attempts to remove the systemic causes of subarticulation through ownership reforms. As I pointed out in chapter 2, Eastern Europe is only at the beginning of this road, but only this direction of changes can alter the relations between local socialism and global capitalism and, as a result, also alter relations inside the bloc of countries of real socialism.

However, even the success of ownership reforms (privatization) in Eastern Europe and the gradual penetration by Western capital (and, more importantly, by its logic) will not change the peripheral status of Eastern Europe in the world economic system. This will be a peripheral status caused by other mechanisms—rules of the market—and not, as presently, the impossibility of following these rules in Eastern Europe on account of its ontological peculiarity. What is more, this will be peripheral status with hopes for dependent development on a higher qualitative level than the present one. To sum up: the reinterpretation of the model of dependency (in relation to the West and to Moscow) is the crucial—and perhaps causally antecedant—moment of the transformation presently taking place in Eastern Europe.

Part Two

The Public Scene during the Decline of the Socialist System

Introduction:

New Configurations and Their Dynamics

August 1989

The breakthrough in the socialist system is accompanied by sudden changes on the public scene. First and foremost, the possibility opens up of "political wheeling and dealing," which is a departure from the situation of "power without politics" that is characteristic of the monoparty system,[1] in which the Communist party with its "myth of the avant-garde" laid claim to the role of the historical substitute for social forces (whether for those recognized as not "progressive" enough or for those eliminated through nationalization of the means of production). Today some of the opposition circles have been recognized as the "constructive opposition in exchange for assistance in stabilizing the social situation at home. Yet this is an evolution in the direction of what can be called "politics without power" (this applies to the U.S.S.R. as well as Poland). For the struggle for influence on the public scene and the feverish efforts of all of the actors to reshape their political identity are not attended by real control over economic processes or over the executive apparatus of the state.

The reasons for this strange anarchy of the period of transformation are complex, and I will deal with them in detail below. The opposition, which until now has operated in the poesy of moral objection or has fought for recognition of the universal rights of the individual, is becoming a participant of the official political process with its rules of the game and rhetoric. As we have seen in

Poland since the parliamentary elections, this leads to a dramatic crisis of identity and divisions within the opposition. The effort to alleviate this crisis—an example is the behavior of the opposition in the Seym—is a peculiar avoidance of responsibility, as in the government crisis of July 1988, while the authorities, in turn, attempt to share this responsibility at any price. This game explains a number of political behaviors in the first weeks after the elections in Poland (until the formation of the new government) and also explains shifts in accenting the importance of particular institutions and in directing the flow of decisions, which resulted in a shift of the hard decisions to the Seym, where the opposition cannot avoid responsibility for often dramatic choices.[2]

The first stage of transformations on the public scene (before the "round table") was the formation of a new center made up of the faction of the ruling group in favor of "reforms" (a term that is still hazy in this stage) and the faction of the opposition disposed toward cooperation. Concomitant with this was a change in the language of both sides, often to a call for peace for the sake of the reforms.[3] At the same time, in public situations the black-white language returned (e.g., the "*your* president—*our* prime minister" position formulated by Adam Michnik during the July 1989 crisis). In my opinion, this is linked with the logic of democratization from above. The opposition elite sprang up from society's overall rejection of the persons and symbols associated with the communist system (but not necessarily rejection of institutional arrangements, e.g., in ownership) and does not yet know the specific expectations of its electorate. Thus, the opposition elite feels safer in the domain of symbolic politicizing, the more so in that the elections (when all the reformers from the old regime ruling circles were defeated) repeated this all-inclusive rejection. This being so, the opposition elite regards its behavior in the Seym as, among other things, an opportunity to build up (or get to know) a more specific base of support gathered around concrete interests. Yet this carries the danger of splitting the heretofore uniform electorate. This accounts for the reversions to the rhetoric that ensured unity in the past (e.g., sharp attacks by Solidarity's Citizens' Committee deputies during parliamentary interpellations concerning the presence of Soviet forces in Poland, as in the 2 August 1989 transmission of Seym proceedings on Polish Radio "Program I").

This "double-speak" of the opposition, with pulsating waves of radicalism for the popular use and the pragmatism of "control for the sake of the reforms," is also an attempt to react to the dangers, and—at the same time—unavoidability, of sharing responsibility for socially unpopular decisions. All of this, however, deepens the crisis of identity of the opposition.[4] The Communist party also is beginning to look for its specific base of support.

The formation of the new center is discussed in chapter 3, most of which was written in January 1989 (before the "round table" talks, though in the course of preparations for them). The appendix to chapter 3 on the new political geography (i.e., the social makeup of the voters who supported Solidarity candidates and thereby sided with the opposition part of the new center) was completed in August 1989 and confirms the intuition contained in the earlier analysis.

The next stage of transformations on the public scene (which is the subject of chapter 4) deals with internal differences in the new center and even signs of its breakup. Two political events were the catalysts in Poland. The first was the "round table" with its four "deals":

• the legalization of Solidarity in exchange for the stabilizing influence of the opposition;

• freer (though "nonconfrontational") elections to the Seym and free elections to the Senate in exchange for the opposition's sharing responsibility for difficult economic decisions;

• the creation of the new, powerful institution of the president (also limiting the Seym)[5] in exchange for a further reduction of the so-called "leading role of the party." Today it is the president—not the Communist party—who is supposed to be the guarantor of stability and continuity of governments both in relation to Moscow and the West. This function in the past was one of the two arguments (in addition to the personnel policy of the *nomenklatura*) used to justify this "leading role";

• the agreement of part of the opposition to participate in the work of a body that is a sort of extended center of the prerogative state.[6] This body treats law as an instrument of politics and conducts negotiations in a triangle: Committee for National Defense (or its counterpart, depending on factional lineups),[7] the Church, and members of Lech Wałęsa's Citizens' Committee as a necessary supplement to the constitutional process. The opposition agreed to participate in this Committee on Understanding[8] in exchange for the promise to move gradually toward governments of law. Yet, as I show below, the logic of the political process of the period of transformations is pushing both sides (the opposition as well) to prolong arrangements of this type.

Other points of the above "trade-off" are being reformulated, such as the relations between the office of the president and the Communist party.

The second event in Poland that speeded up transformations within the new center—and even its fragmentation—was the parliamentary election in June 1989. This election had three important results.

The first was the spectacular victory of the opposition (but, as we see from the new political geography,[9] a victory of the Solidarity-affiliated Citizens' Committees rather than of Solidarity as a workers' movement). This victory, as I show below, brought about a crisis of identity of the Citizens' Parliamentary Club, whose symbolic base of support is still the workers' trade union Solidarity and the traditions of 1980–1981, but whose real electorate (whose voice must be considered) is other social groups that often enter into a conflict of interests with this symbolic reference group.[10] The twists and turns of the Citizens' Parliamentary Club (CPC) during voting in the Seym on issues that divide the society are expressions of this crisis. For example, farmers (a considerable part of the electorate) were included under indexation, yet simultaneously "market mechanisms in agriculture" were introduced and the lid was taken off purchase prices of farm products, which only fuels inflation. As one of the deputies of the CPC said during a discussion in the Club, this is a "sacrifice of the economy on the altar of politics"—hence, exactly the error that was committed by the previous political teams.[11] The election victory was achieved thanks to the tactic of encouraging people to vote en bloc—for the entire "Wałęsa team"—without discussing the different programs of individual candidates and with the centralized (in the Citizens' Committee) selection of most of them. This became one of the reasons for divisions in the segment of the opposition which previously had agreed to enter the new center.[12] Other important factors were the power of the Church and the allusions during the election campaign to the rejection of the old regime lock, stock, and barrel (such as, by crossing off all the names on the Communist party list, regardless of the individual views and behaviors of the candidates). Paradoxically, recourse was made to (and a smashing victory achieved thanks to) the same fundamentalist attitude that the opposition bloc criticized at the "round table" when it entered the new center.

The second outcome of the elections which had an important effect on the political process was the defeat of the so-called national list of reformers from the ruling team. The defeat was caused by the requirement that more than 50 percent of the votes was necessary for election, a requirement that resulted from excessive optimism based on faulty calculations.[13] Another mistake was the failure to take into account the polarizing election strategy of the provincial Citizens' Committees and the Church.[14]

The third outcome of the defeat of the Communist party (PUWP) was the laying bare once again of the strength of the full-time party machines' resistance to the reforms implemented from above. Communist party reformers were crossed off the ballot not only by Solidarity voters but by conservative groups (mostly low-level party members). A poll taken among newly elected party deputies showed that only 41 of them out of 124 candidates had received any help from the apparatus during their election campaigns.[15] Today this situation is the source of complicated attitudes in the Club of Deputies of the PUWP: rebellion against the apparatus and the need to establish their own identity and autonomy ("we are just as important as the Central Committee"),[16] insecurities due to having been elected in the second round (with lowered requirements concerning the percentage of votes needed for election), and at the same time, pride that each of them won on individual merits in spite of belonging to a bloc that did not receive support and was evaluated negatively by the voters (in contrast to the situation with the members of "Wałęsa's team").[17]

The results of the elections breached the arrangement negotiated at the "round table" that was based on the four "deals" described above. The political aspirations of the opposition greatly expanded—even to thinking about forming its own government (as in the phrase, "your president—our prime minister," formulated by A. Michnik in *Gazeta Wyborcza*[18] and repeated by Wałęsa during a meeting with President Jaruzelski).[19] The shock in the Communist party added to the frustrations of the party machine, where the passive boycott of the changes taking place intensified the crisis in the ruling coalition (as evidenced by numerous statements by members of the Democratic party[20] and United Peasants' party and also the pattern of voting for the president).[21] All of the above elements plus the unforeseen turn of events in China[22] considerably weakened the office of the president (elected by a majority of one vote and in a climate of weak support from Moscow) and also undermined the entire political framework negotiated at the "round table" and based not on a numerical majority of Communist party deputies but on a uniform and disciplined coalition.

An interesting mechanism came to light here. The reformers in the Communist party undertook political reforms not with the intention of giving up power, but in order to create a more effective stabilizing mechanism in conditions of a severe crisis. It was expected that the "national list" would be elected and would still constitute the center of power (and one endowed with a new legitimacy), while the institutions to which the opposition would be admitted would be more or less phony (like the previous ones), with real power behind the scenes: not necessarily in the Political Bureau of The Central Committee of the Communist party but, for instance, in the committee for implementation of the "round table" agreement, created in April 1989 and dominated by inner security officials connected to General Kiszczak; by Catholic Church officials headed by Bishop Bronislow Dojbrowski; and by leading people from the KOR (Committee for Defense of Workers) branch of the ex-opposition. The possibility of a "paper revolution" was strongly accented by the opponents of "transition through transaction" in more radical opposition groups. The Communist party reformers wanted to keep—through the presidential office reserved for Jaruzelski—control over regional self-government (which would oppose the opposition's creation of its own executive apparatus).[23] But party reformers did not foresee the breakup of the coalition with the facade—not the oppositional—parties. The public rejection of the so-called leading role of the Communist party by some members of this coalition in fact reduced this role.

Finally, the enigmatic stance of Moscow was unexpected, a stance that is associated with the intensifying conflict there in the triangle of party, army, and KGB. It is characteristic that signs of a power vacuum in the center appeared in a situation when the newly legalized opposition was not a socially recognized "new power." A somewhat surrealistic comparison comes to mind. In August 1980 the Interenterprise Strike Committee in Gdańsk Shipyard (surrounded by cordons of police ready to move in) was regarded as the new center of local authority.[24] This process intensified, but it ended when the strike committee began negotiations with the government—which was simultaneously an act of mutual recognition and of self-limitation of the sides. The Committee remained the representative of the workers; the government, of the powers that be, but without the claim to be the Leninist avant-garde.

The summer of 1989 was a peculiar inter-regnum stage, when the opposition was already speaking about its own government and the existing center was in a deep crisis. People saw this arrangement as sort of a holiday decoration and tried to take care of their business as before, outside the institutional channels, of which the opposition was now a part. Wildcat strikes were spreading, and members of the Citizens' Parliamentary Club were complaining about apathy and the "absence of a civil society."[25] Moreover, this breakup of the previous center of power had only increased the license of the apparatus at the bottom; owing to the enduring atomization of the society, no alternative, oppositional power elite had appeared at the top.

The above factors, together with the crisis of identity of the opposition following legalization, led to the disintegration of the new center. This is especially true because the opposition is inevitably threatened by the trap of joint responsibility, even though its real influence is miniscule, which is due not so much to the decision-making procedure[26] as to factors completely outside its control (e.g., long-term obligations in the COMECON and economic relations with the U.S.S.R.).[27] Paradoxically, the severity of the crisis combined with legalization of the opposition led to a shrinking of social confidence in the opposition. In reaction, the opposition retreated to the "safe" ground of symbolic politicizing and empty, formal protests (e.g., the declaration of the Senate after the unilateral introduction of market mechanisms by the Rakow-ski government on the last day of its rule, July 31, 1989, published in *Trybuna Ludu* of 2 August 1989).

All the above processes are deepening divisions within the new center—both in its "coalition" and opposition wings.

In the Citizens' Parliamentary Club, in turn, the first weeks of its activities laid bare a clear division into supporters of building democracy "from the top" and "from the bottom," into economic pragmatists and supporters of yielding to populistic pressures.[28] Also becoming ever more clear are divisions between the trade-union segment of the opposition and the segment leaning toward the role of a political party.[29] Divisions are also appearing in the structure of the Citizens' Committees. The main Citizen Commit-tee (attached to Lech Wałęsa) was built on the principle of a pe-culiar selection that excluded not only populistic circles, but also liberal and so-called national elements. The local committees, on the other hand, either were formed by those forces excluded at the top or are now entering into cooperation with some of them. Simultaneously, horizontal links between local committees are being formed (in order to prepare for elections to regional councils and to coordinate political actions in their own regions, including actions of the "nonparliamentary opposition").[30] This is competi-tion both for the regional authorities of the trade union Solidarity and for Wałęsa's Citizens' Committee. This also makes even more paradoxical the situation of the Citizens' Parliamentary Club. This body does not have its own structure linking it with the voters, and its potential party ranks are divided and beginning to lean toward groups that were excluded from the "round table" talks. For the latter give them more room for maneuver, and not the role of a compliant mass, as in the case of being subordinated to the Citizens' Parliamentary Club.

Similar deep rifts are becoming visible in the Communist party and the coalition. We now have not only two factions of reformers that remain in conflict (about which more is said below), but also a conflict between the central authorities of the party and part of the apparatus and the newly elected Club of Deputies of the Commun-ist party in the Seym. There are also clear divisions between the functional segments of the central party machine, for example, on the question of introducing market mechanisms in agriculture between the Economic Committee of the Central Committee and the Agricultural Committee.[31]

The breakup of the new center described here (to which chapter 4 will be devoted) is also associated with the logic of democratization from the top. The recurring waves of radicalism and the politics of symbols as well as the increasing unpredictability of the behavior of the opposition in the parliament are signs of the opposition's lack of confidence in its base of support and its attempt to use the rhetoric that worked in the past.

The second threat that explains the logic of the political behaviors of the so-called legal opposition at this stage (before forming a government, June–July 1989) is the avoidance of responsibility for difficult but unavoidable economic decisions. One of the manifestations of this "passing the buck" is the refusal to enter a government of national understanding (or, as Prime Minister Kiszczak calls it, a government of a grand coalition).[32]

In June and July of 1989, in the face of such a refusal (combined with the breakup of its own coalition and the crisis of the new center), the side linked to the communists and conventionally called the "party-government" side (but in fact the center of the prerogative state that changes its makeup with changes in factional lineups and in the hierarchy of institutions) could choose two possibilities of organizing the political scene.

The first alternative was to continue the present situation of dyarchy. Such a proposal was made in a talk between Jaruzelski and Wałęsa and met with the former's approval.[33] Hence behind the scene of constitutional institutions (in June and July 1989 making up an internally contradictory system in which the constitution sanctions the "leading role of the Communist party" yet in which this party no longer has a majority in parliament or even a working coalition) would function a so-called Committee for Understanding (or similar body) that would be the real center of the prerogative state. Through the understanding of a narrow staff close to the communist Committee for National Defense, the Church, and Wałęsa's Citizens' Committee (and of Wałęsa himself) this body would determine the shape of decisions before they were sent to the parliament for approval. In the past a similar function was performed by the Political Bureau of the PUWP, and later by the Committee for National Defense. This formula would be advantageous both for Jaruzelski's reformers and the Citizens' Committee. It would give them more influence than they get from the formal balance of forces in the Seym (where the reformers lost, and the opposition was limited by the principle of "nonconfrontative" elections). Such a solution, however, is coming under attack both by the other members of the government coalition (United Peasants' party, Democratic party) excluded from the Committee and by the party machine, which is generally dissatisfied with the shift in the center of the prerogative state.[34] A somewhat surrealistic election slogan of the candidates supported by the party machine and directed against dyarchy was "law and not deals."[35] They had in mind here enforcing the formal constitutional principle of the "leading role of the party" as well as its broader informal aspects (which are illegal according to Western concepts of legality).

The second element of the first form of rule in the event of the refusal of the opposition to enter the government is to channel all tough decisions through the Seym. This, together with "live" broadcasts, would create the impression of full joint responsibility of the opposition for the line of policy.

The third element of this idea is a further limitation of the role of the Communist party ("giving up the captain's bridge in exchange for holding the same course")[36] and speeding up the law on parties (among other reasons, in order to institutionalize divisions in the opposition). It seems that this element (and perhaps the other parts of this idea) collapsed with the departure of Orzechowski and the victory of Rakowski's line at the Thirteenth Plenum of the Central Committee of the PUWP. Representatives of the party and of a new generation of activists interested in reanimating the party (elsewhere I called the latter populists, in distinction from Orzechowski, a globalist)[37] entered the Central Committee.

The second alternative (which seems to be represented by Rakowski as the First Secretary of the PUWP) is to move away from dyarchy and enforce again the "leading role of the Communist party." And not only symbolically, as when the Club of Deputies of the Communist party (and not the president) put forward the candidate for prime minister before the Seym (a candidacy that Rakowski "recommended" to the Club),[38] but in fact.[39] Rakowski probably speculated at this time (summer 1989) on conflict between the branch of the KGB supporting the Polish "round table" and Kiszczak's "openings" and hard-liners in the Soviet Communist party (with Yegor Ligachev) and on the visible weakening at this time of the KGB side with the dismissal of Chelnikov. Nomination of Kruiczkov and strengthening of the KGB (globalist) faction ended the above speculations. Another element of this idea is to close up the ranks of the Club of Deputies of the Communist party and simultaneously to subordinate it to the Political Bureau. This was Rakowski's aim when he spoke about the necessity for "unity of leadership" at his first meeting in the Club. Another element of this conception is to restore the unity of the coalition. One of the first moves in this direction was Rakowski's alliance, when he was still prime minister, with the United Peasants' party for the right to set purchase prices of agricultural products at a level guaranteeing "parity,"[40] which outrageously increased the costs to consumers. Finally, as in the previous solution, an attempt will be made to enforce joint responsibility of the opposition by channeling all tough decisions through the Seym.

The third alternative (which was formulated during the "round table" talks by—surprisingly—one of the notorious hard-liners, Z. Cypryniak) was that Solidarity form a government on its own responsibility (with its own prime minister) but in coalition with the Communist party. This proposal was not taken seriously by the opposition, which did not know at this time that Cypryniak was (together with Andrzej Gdula, one of the main directors of the "round table") a member of the so-called A. Lukjanov Committee in Moscow. This committee—not fully formalized—was responsible for monitoring and interpreting for Soviet authorities the crisis and transition in Eastern Europe. It is worth underlining here that the main figures of the "round table" from the communist elite side in other countries were members of this committee (e.g., Hom in Hungary and Ademiec in Czechoslovakia).

The last alternative was consequently put in practice but modified, and a new government coalition was built in parliament from the Peasant party (ZSL) and the Democratic party (SD). Communists kept the presidential office; the new coalition, dominated by Solidarity, kept the government.

Each of these conceptions creates its own dynamics and field of conflicts. The second one would introduce a contradiction between the role of the Communist party and the results of the elections. The first one—based on dyarchy—would shatter the legal system and lower even more the authority of the state (and we have to remember that the fear of anarchy was one of the reasons of undertaking political reform with the consent of the old center of power that felt itself to be without real control). In such a situation the third alternative—the most radical one—looked, paradoxically, the most realistic.

These three eventual lines of development of the political setup in Poland can be presented in a diagram as follows:

As we can see, whichever way political development takes, one general idea is behind it—to stabilize the balance of political forces and to guarantee the smooth carrying out of often painful and unpopular decisions in conditions of a severe economic crisis. The successive solutions are an attempt (often only a change of accents) to reduce the often unforeseen tensions that appear in this process: e.g., dyarchy, or "overloading" the Seym with difficult decisions, is an alternative response to the refusal of the opposition to take part in the government and a way to divide responsibility. The situation is similar in other socialist countries. For example, in the U.S.S.R. the recently formed Interregional Understanding of Deputies can be interpreted as a reaction to the increasing pressure of nationality interests. The "Understanding" (with its strong populistic, antibureaucratic accents) is searching for common ground that unites people in support of reforms and cuts across national movements.

Returning to the situation in Poland, against the background of the processes outlined here, three characteristic phenomena were taking place immediately after the 1989 parliamentary elections:

• the activity of a nonparliamentary opposition of various shades (including the official trade unions, the All-Polish Agreement of Trade Unions, which were established during martial law as an alternative to Solidarity). These official trade unions are having a radicalizing influence on the now legal Solidarity,[41] which makes it even more difficult for the Citizens' Parliamentary Club to operate and increases populistic pressures on it;

• a rapid differentiation of the society as a result of the economic crisis and of the reforms. This introduces a more complicated

Stage I: Formation of the new center

Populists in power	New center	Populists in opposition

↓
"Round table" with
its four trade-offs ⟶ Elections ⟶ **Stage II:**

Breakup of the new
center; revision of
the four trade-offs

→

Government without the opposition

Alternative I:
Dyarchy, hard decisions through
the Seym, law on parties that
would limit the Communist
party and fragment the opposition

Alternative II:
Enforce the "leading role of the
Communist party," unify the old
coalition, divide the responsibility
by channeling tough decisions
through the Seym

Alternative III:
Solidarity forms government, dissolution of the Communist party
(change of name), keeping behind
the stage the informal decision
center: Komisja Porozumiewawc-
za do realizacji "porozumienia"

Key: ⇢ rejected alternatives
→ selected alternative

map of economic interests into the process described above, and not, as before, simple wage equalizations;

• increasing anarchy in the executive apparatus of the state and the economy, leading to what in the introduction was called "politics without power." This anarchy cannot be explained only by the Communist party resistance to the line of reforms or by the struggle between factions seeking different programs of change. It seems that we have to do here with a wholesale loss of control in the hierarchical order. After central-level authorities lost in the elections, the executive authorities of the local level became aware that the same fate lies in store for them. In this situation they are planning a strategy of survival[42]—they are ceasing to look to this level and know that even open disobedience is no longer risky. The local economic administration reasons the same way in relation to the state economic administration. Such a general feeling of uncertainty (and efforts to reorient the strategy of survival, overturning old loyalties of the client type) is also appearing after the elections in the U.S.S.R.[43]

In the following reasoning I will not attempt to explore the entire tangle of the phenomena outlined above. I will deal only with selected factors, including:

• the conflict over visions of the future between the party factions of populists and globalists;

• the crisis of identity in opposition circles connected with legalization;

• the "round table," but only in one of its aspects: namely, as a characteristic communication ritual;

• the anarchy of the transition period.

I will also take up some theoretical implications of the process described here, such as:

• the dilemmas of democratization from the top, when the reformatory elite operate in an atomized, post-totalitarian society and in some measure represent theoretical interests (e.g., the necessity for ownership changes and the establishment of a market) and are just beginning to search for the historical—real—carriers of those rights (e.g., property rights to ex-state property). And sometimes, as in the model of political capitalism, from the ground up the reformers are even creating such carriers (the *nomenklatura* made owners) who would seem to conduct their interests in the direction of changes planned from the top. What is striking here is the danger of repeating the Leninist model of the avant-garde, both by the reformers from power circles and by the opposition, or rather, the opposition entering into the power system;

• the hypothetical direction of transformations of the system of political institutions in comparison with the models of "Rechsstaat" (a state based on governments of law) and "Standesstaat" (a state that is a peculiar form of absolutism, characterized by a segmented state and few domains of power regulated by different rules and legitimating arguments.

Chapter Three

Stage One:

Forming the New Center

March 1989

One of the most typical elements of the breakthrough in the socialist system is the regrouping of the previous configuration of forces
on the public scene. What is interesting is that similar trends
(though in a somewhat different from and with varying degrees of
intensity) are appearing in all the countries of Eastern Europe
which are reforming their systems, from the U.S.S.R. through
Poland and Hungary. In all these countries a *new center* is clearly
emerging, which is made up of a pro-reform faction of the ruling
group and part of the opposition. At the same time, economic interests with in the society itself are beginning to be marked off by
differences, and some of these interests are already playing a role
on the public scene, whether in the quasi-political representation
of the nascent class of new owners or in the populist expression of
groups bearing the main costs of the crisis (and of the reforms
imposed from above). The latter orientation appears in the factions that are outside the new center, factions of both the ruling
group and in the opposition. Thus on one hand we have a new
"political class" (*avant-garde of the establishment*)[1] that has
emerged from parts of the two previous political classes (which in
Poland crystallized during the open phase of the conflict in 1980
and 1981 and to this day remain in opposition to each other; in
other countries they are more latent). On the other hand, "wings"
are forming that are connected with groups and interests different

from those on which the new center is based. These wings, which consist respectively of splinters of the formerly homogeneous opposition and ruling groups, differ from each other in symbolic allusions, the past, and immediate political interests. At the same time, however, they appeal to similar groups of the society and in their attacks on the center manifest a similar anti-elitist orientation.

The distintegration of the former configuration of political forces is accompanied by a dramatic *change of language*. The splinter group of the opposition declares its readiness to enter the new center by abandoning public use of language colored by ethical values or the "politics of rights" (the appeal to the inalienable rights of the individual). It was this language in the past that cemented this opposition and transformed an atomized society into a collective subject, which on the basis of "moral right" came out in favor of denying the *nomenklatura* access to power. Some members of the power apparatus are entering the new center by resigning from the ideologically motivated and preempted "historical right" in favor of a new language of politics: the language of control (*joint control of the new elite*) over the reforms and the rest of society in order to "minimize the risk"[2] of the period of transformation. As I show below, this is accompanied by other, equally dramatic concessions by both sides, which are a condition for the formation of the new center. On the "wings" there are attempts to fit specific interests of selected participants of the production process into a systematic whole. This second phenomenon is perhaps even more important than the formation of a new political class. Alliances of part of the ruling group and part of the opposition have appeared in Eastern Europe in the past,[3] but never before have economic interests functioned as a factor of politics. The public scene was dominated by material claims (everyone wanted to get a bigger piece of the pie from the state redistribution of funds) or by symbols mechanically taken over from tradition or finally by "theoretical interests"[4] (e.g., the call for ownership reforms, in spite of the lack of personal material interest, for according to theory such reforms promote more rational economic management). Previous protests chiefly concerned the spheres of distribution and consumer claims (real wages). Today, however, the public appearance of economic interests is combined with a collision of roles in the production process. This conflict intensifies with the progress of the reform that is creating "owners" in the state sector.

The above situation is somewhat complicated by the return on both "wings" of the language of ideology rejected by the "new center": a "class" language in the splinter group of the former power bloc and a fundamentalist language in the wing of the opposition that evokes the mythologized image of Solidarity (in order to emphasize more strongly the "betrayal" of the splinter group entering the avant-garde of the establishment). This return of ideological language is coupled with difficulty in expressing the economic interests of their respective social bases. Sometimes, however, this language is an instrument for realizing these interests.

A second factor complicating the public scene is the still considerable role of organizational subjects and interests. Sometimes they break off and divide the emerging new configuration, and sometimes they intertwine with the interests of particular factions of the former "political classes." Thus on one of the wings an alliance is forming of populist orientation along with the interests of the trade-union structures set up after the delegalization of Solidarity (All-Polish Association of Trade Unions—OPZZ), while in the center a similar alliance is emerging of part of the opposition entering the new center along with the workers' self-management movement. Promotion of the idea of a workers' self-managed economy allows this part of the opposition to postpone taking a position on ownership changes in the state sector which might divide its present base of social support.

Generally speaking, in the first phase of the breakthrough in the socialist system polarization (evident in the phrase of open conflict) yields to a more complicated map of conflicts, while the two formerly monolithic sides (or the sides that presented themselves as such) become openly split. The course and scale of the above process varies in the individual countries of Eastern Europe and depends on the way and scope of the previous organization of society into a political class and also on the seriousness of the collision of interests, which is linked with the intensity of the crisis and the type of reforms implemented from above. *The trend, however, is the same everywhere: from polarization to a more complicated map of conflicts—from the orientation toward universal values and the fight of the society with the state over more room for independent action—to differentiation of interests within the society itself: the formation of a new center on the one hand and the political representation of selected economic interests on the other.*

The above process is consistent with the logic of historical transformations. The French Revolution, as one of the phases of transition from feudalism to capitalism, was coupled with the formation of a political class[5] (as in Poland in 1980 and 1981), while at the same time the crystallization of social classes dividing society ran for the most part independently, on a parallel track. Only the fusion of these processes (which is taking place in East Europe today) combined with the breakup of the political class from the earlier phase of the crisis and the reorientation of its individual segments to different social classes, accelerated the breakthrough in the system. The political scene became linked with the economic rhythm of the society.

Additional elements characteristic of this phase of the breakthrough in Eastern Europe are

• a severance of generational continuity both in the power circles and in the opposition. As regards circles of the intelligentsia, this is true for all of Eastern Europe. Additionally, in Poland one can observe the appearance of a new, post-fundamentalist mentality among protesting workers, which is also a sign of a break in generational continuity. In other countries this phenomenon does not appear because there is a lower degree of political organization of the working class and a lack of earlier phases of open protest;

• the creation by the authorities of new actors on the social scene, which is coupled with a market reform imposed from above that has the aim of spawning owners in the state sector. A striking feature of this process (which in all countries, interestingly enough, is taking place *before* the respective legal regulations have been changed) is its similarity to the earlier building of real socialism, which was also from above. Now, as then, the authorities are realizing a certain vision, namely, their idea of the capitalist mode of production, which is closer to the ideological connotation of Marxism than to the historical reality of capitalism. An "owner" in nineteenth-century style is being created, personified, and equipped with a stricter labor code as an instrument of accumulation. It is not understood that capitalism today is first and foremost financial institutions (holding companies), movement of capital and information, and the "exploitation" of fixed assets (innovations) rather than the exploitation of people. So perhaps the "classical" system that was described by Marx and existed nowhere else but in *Das Kapital* will arise in Eastern Europe.

The aim of this chapter is to make a more thorough analysis of the above phenomena. Three of them are emphasized:

• the emergence of the new center and the political representation of some economic interests;

• the severance of generational continuity in the power elite and the opposition;

• the postfundamentalist mentality of young workers that was manifested during the waves of strikes in 1988.

The New Configuration of Political Forces: Poland, 1988–1989

The appearance of the new center in Poland in 1988 and 1989 is coupled with divisions both in the power circles and in the opposition. The new political class, which is made up of parts of formerly opposite camps, is a specific avant-garde of the establishment. In other words, it is a group of people with a rather similar status (education, prestige, affluence) who are united by a feeling of responsibility for social peace and who support the economic reform being imposed from above. The power segment of the party machine entering the new center does this for the reasons explained in chapter 1 (a reformulated rationality of control, the imperial interest). It needs the "constructive" opposition as a shock absorber of social tensions and as a source of impulses (challenges) for the routinized, inert, and nonsteerable executive power apparatus. The opposition, in turn, as one can see from the Solidarity reactions[6] to the Tenth Plenum of the Central Committee of the PUWP,[7] is willing to play this role in exchange for the legalization of trade-union pluralism and even limited political pluralism.[8]

This willingness did not appear in the power elite all at once. Its first spontaneous movement was the search for other guarantees of the reforms besides recognition of the "constructive opposition."[9] The leadership staked more on strengthening the pro-reformatory executive apparatus (as Gorbachev is doing), on making it materially worthwhile for part of the powerful in the party machine to be interested in a continuation of ownership reform in the state sector (by consenting to the fusion of power and capital, as explained in chapter 2), and finally on removing politics from management of the economy and excluding the party (as well as the opposition) from places of work. However, the clear resistance of the party machine to the last point and its formation of a populist faction attacking both the fusion of power and capital[10] and depoliticization of places of work (but at the same time indicating readiness eventually to support the opposition postulate to legalize Solidarity)[11] forced the Jaruzelski-Rakowski circle to change its strategy and to look for contacts with the "constructive opposition."

In this way a new center began to emerge. The common philosophy of rule of both the ruling and the opposition splinter groups in this new center is an order based on the *liberalization of group interests.* To put it another way, it is an order based on working out a system of laws that would be neutral to various ideas competing with each other and would allow individuals and groups to realize their interests (e.g., individual adaptation to the economic crisis) as long as they do not encroach upon the freedoms of other people and do not threaten the stability of the state. The public good here is understood as the interest of individuals plus the stability of the state, rejecting paternalism toward selected groups and refusing to carry out a priori ideological assumptions and goals. In order to work out such a system of rights, the ruling group seems willing to give up the clause in the constitution on the "leading role of the Communist party" and wording emphasizing the special role in socialism of the working class.[12] The "constructive" opposition, in turn, is willing to desist from forcing state paternalism and to curb its more radical groups to reduce the threat of destabilization (by supporting with its authority the "consolidation plan" that assumes inevitable social costs of the reforms).[13]

The populist wing, however, expresses the interests of social classes or parts of classes that have the least chance in the market game, demanding for them preferences and state paternalism and the right to express dissatisfaction even at the cost of stability.[14] This is true of both the part that is closer to the ruling group populists[15] and the part that is a faction of the opposition.[16] The social base of these wings consists of young workers and young people in general, pensioners, groups that cannot benefit from profits in the new relations of production, and poor people who most fear inflation, which is difficult to control with the planned withdrawl of the state from the economy. A similar configuration of forces is emerging in Hungary and, with modifications, in the U.S.S.R. (where in the wings, in addition to social problems, there are nationality problems; in the new center, where Gorbachev is supported, in the name of stability the reforms are coupled with a defense of the political order, which impedes the expression of nationality aspirations).[17]

In this context it is worth considering the problem of *radicalism*, for the situation is highly interesting. On one hand (on the wings) we have *extremism without radicalism* and on the other, *two varieties of radicalism* in the new center. The part of the ruling group entering this center is more willing to introduce market mechanisms and accelerate the creation of new owners (owners from its own ranks), while the "constructive" opposition in the new center puts more emphasis on the liberal vision of law and legality[18] and less on the necessity for abandoning state paternalism in the economy. Moreover, this part of the opposition tends to favor the expansion of workers' self-management and the development of the traditional private sector rather than ownership reforms in the state sector.[19] Yet the Working Group of the former National Committee of Solidarity[20] on the wing defends the right to extra-institutional political protest (politics of the street, "fighting squads") for those groups that have no chance in the market game proposed by the center. The Working Group also opposes the creation of owners from the former *nomenklatura* and represents worker experiences in this question.[21] What is interesting, however, is that this group (former trade-union organizers at the plant level, chiefly lower-level technical supervisors) also questions the expansion of workers' self-management, which seems to be supported by the opposition faction in the new center. The Working Group (especially its Gdańsk faction) is interested in a so far enigmatic "third way." Because of the ambivalence of this project and firm opposition to the social effects of the market reform, this group can be described as *extremism without radi-*

calism. The eventual transformation effect of the activities of this group seems limited because, regardless of its intentions, it supports "classical" state–controlled socialism, with the state as owner. This group is ready to fight with the state, as Solidarity did (thus using a mixture of trade union and political instruments), but within the state-controlled system. It will fight over the distribution of funds but not for a change of the system. This faction evokes the myth of Solidarity (with the idealization of its politics) in order to emphasize more strongly the "betrayal" of Wałęsa's group, which is now entering the avant-garde of the establishment. The Working Group finds itself in a typical historical situation conducive to the rise of extremist movements.[22] The elements of this new situation are: a *threat to its position* (neither of the activist groups of the Working Group is included in the new center by Wałęsa, and their social base (workers) is losing out in the market game) and *disorganization of its political reference group* by the breakup of the former identity of Solidarity (as a result of the about-face made by Wałęsa).

The second wing, which is made up of part of the former political class close to the ruling group, is less homogeneous. It embraces the populist apparatus of the new trade unions (the All-Polish Association), members of the party who see a betrayal of socialism in the ownership reforms and recognition of the opposition, and finally the executive power apparatus that regards the "policy of understanding" as a manifestation of disloyalty of the center. This last group has no vision of an alternative order and is not even concerned about the interest of the party as a whole. As studies have shown,[23] its objections are due to fear of uncertainty and loss of face, while its vision of the situation is based more on limited experience in some department of a party committee than on ideological premises. As in the case of the wing forming from the opposition, in this wing we observe a threat to its position, a crisis of identity, and disintegration of its political reference group. There is no myth to which one can appeal, the situation during the abolition of serfdom from above in Russia in 1862.[24] Before that, serfdom had been regarded as an obvious pillar of autocracy that needed no justification; until recently the dogma of the "leading role of the party" was regarded in the same way. In both cases the reaction to the abolition of dogma was similar. The change by the czar of his position on serfdom and by the communist power elite on the role of the party was met with silence by the Russian gentry and by the Polish party machine respectively—both dependent on the state, unaccustomed to expressing their own position (that in the past did not need justification), and caught in the trap of their own calls for "reforms." Another analogy with czarist Russia comes from the later period of Stolypin's reforms (1906). This was another attempt made from above to create conditions for economic growth and even for a breakthrough in the system. The control functions of rural communities (with their egalitarianism, self-control, and redistribution effect) were lessened in favor of the new middle class and its economic interests, as in Eastern Europe today. A law on associations was passed[25] and there was greater participation in rule through a new Duma. Finally, a populist opposition arose (and eventually won out through a tangle of revolutionary processes with the anarchy of war).

For its actors, the above situation is not a zero-sum game, for each of the sides wins something. This does not apply to the rest of society. There are groups that cannot win—in the society the distribution of benefits and costs is much more uneven than among political participants. For instance, young workers with the lowest qualifications[26] can benefit from the reforms only by getting out of their own social category (e.g., by raising their qualifications). As regards the benefits to political groups, the party elite gains (though its lower-level workers lose) because it acquires a new identity as the "initiator of reform"; the government acquires a buffer or stabilizer for the difficult economic reforms and enfranchisement of the *nomenkaltura*. Even if the legalized opposition did not play this role, the temporary lack of stability (caused by the competition of two trade unions in the enterprise) also could have advantages for the government: there is a hypothesis that COMECON partners plan to purchase the Polish debt, and social unrest pushes the price down. There is also talk about the purchase of part of this debt by Western financial circles, which are pressuring Poland for liberalization. Finally, Solidarity gains legalization, and the All-Polish Association becomes known as a radical defender of the working class.

Recent surveys conducted in industry[27] show that the newly emerging configuration of political forces does not have strong support in social attitudes. Paradoxically, there is greater support for the populist wings of the party and opposition factions than for the new center. Though everyone expresses verbal support for the reform, various groups understand it differently. The workers do not want a market, but they support the opposition (they are not in favor of the liberal model of democracy); managers support ownership-market reforms, but are against trade-union pluralism (on account of tensions in the enterprise), though as a rule they favor political reforms. Though these studies confirm the thesis, often cited to legitimize the new center, that party members differ little in their attitudes from nonparty members and believers, this only supports my conclusion that the new political class has no social base. Its program is much more attractive to itself than to the rest of the society, which in its various groups (and for various reasons) supports only some fragments of this program and rejects the rest.

What will be the outcome of the presently emerging configuration of forces? An important factor is that for the members of the new center, ownership changes in the state sector are more of a "theoretical" than a "real" interest. They will not become the new owners in the political capitalism structure. Such owners for the most part will be recruited from party machine executives. Supporting these new owners is not decisive on the political scene, and such support of the old communist regime may even become troublesome for the new center if populist attacks intensify. In such a situation one could expect the point of compromise to be shifted to an expansion of workers' self-management in the economy. Such a solution would blunt the conflicts connected with the creation of owners in the state sector and for this reason may seem politically advisable to the members of the new center, though it is an economic blind alley. Augmenting the probability of such a development is a well-organized workers' self-management movement, the only one that has members both in the Seym and the enterprise.[28] The economic interests of the wings also might restrict ownership changes in the state sector. Thus at the present the emerging new configuration of political forces does not have— at least in the economic field—much potential for change. For most participants political interest predominates: they want to preserve their identity and expand their spheres of influence. This combined with lack of clarity as to the preferences (and even the composition) of their social base may lead to the workers' self-management solution, which is economically disastrous but politically advantageous to most of the actors on the public scene. Only when ownership changes in the state sector create a national market and a strong political representation that guarantees the stability of the new economic order will one be able to speak about a transformational configuration of political forces. Such a situation does not yet exist, but perhaps it is only a question of time. The new configuration contains so many blockades and possibilities of compromise leading to a blind alley that it does not seem to be a panacea for the crisis. Thus in the long run it is unstable.

The Severance of Generational Continuity

Elsewhere[29] I wrote about imagination as an essential factor of politics, which is understood not only as moving within the area of what is possible but also expanding this area. The problem of imagination is especially important in critical periods. The clear severance of generational continuity both in opposition circles and in the executive party machine combined with an overrepresentation in Solidarity of people who were active in politics in the past (on the average one generation older than the core of the communist/inner security leadership initiating the present political agreement) may complicate the public scene even more. Ex–Polish Youth Union (1948–1956) members and older persons[30] are intermingled in Solidarity advisory circles with people who are more experienced in fighting with this generation. The latter, such as the Catholic Intelligentsia Club network, have been entangled in various ways with the political establishment for more than a dozen years.[31] Both of these groups know the power apparatus from the turning point of October 1956 and from the 1960s. These people more often use modified ideological language than do the younger post–Polish Youth Union (ZMP) generation that matured in the Gierek period of ritualized ideology and in the apolitical structures of the Polish Students' Association (ZSP) or the Ministry of Internal Affairs. As someone once aptly noted, it is easier to change one's views than one's way of thinking.

Under these conditions the recruitment to Wałęsa's Citizens'

Committee of many people with leftist views (perhaps as a conciliatory gesture to the authorities) may turn out to be embarrassing for the ruling group, which wants to build a post-socialist, quasi-capitalist order. Unlike previous generations of the party executives, this one is not saddled with a feeling of responsibility for the shape of real socialism—it was made without their participation. The gambling temperament so characteristic of the members of the new power apparatus perhaps has its sources in the initiating experience of this generation in the events of 1968 (obviously on a different side of the barricades than the March generation—student movement activists—in the opposition). They were then a largely manipulated instrument of the intergenerational contest in the power apparatus, a tug-of-war that was a confused mixture of anti-Semitism and de-Stalinization. Perhaps their reformatory activity today is an attempt to show that the motive of de-Stalinization was the chief motive? Perhaps they want to prove something to their opponents of the day-before-yesterday, with whom this initiating conflict bound them more strongly than with the people of their own camp, who were from another generation? The members of the present power apparatus are not afraid of competition and have no complexes. They want to compete and to win, without enjoying so much of an edge that it would spoil the taste of the contest.

A break in generational continuity also can be observed in the wider sense—not only in the circles revolving around the political game. In my opinion, this discontinuity between successive generations of the Polish intelligentsia is well illustrated by the complicated reaction to the political and intellectual career of Jan Strzelecki, who died tragically in 1988 at age 69. What is striking is the feeling that he is so remote, even though Strzelecki should be closer to my generation (40s and younger) than other members of his generation. He was never an active Stalinist (destroying people), and he was not an opportunist. So if strangeness is felt even in relation to him, then how much greater must be the gulf between my generation (and younger ones) and the so-called generation of revisionists and the still earlier generation of ZMP members and people of the party? An understanding of this is important for analyzing the present and future political process in Poland (and in Eastern Europe, for this discontinuity also appears there). For in the new center, Strzelecki's generation is overrepresented on the side of the opposition. Using the example of Jan Strzelecki, let us look at this discontinuity more closely.

After World War II Strzelecki led the young socialists, and after the merger of the Polish Socialist Party with the Polish Workers' Party he was a member of the Communist party until his expulsion in 1979. From August 1980 until his death he was an adviser of Solidarity, who in the last years of his life sought to find a bridge between personalistic Catholicism and his version of socialism. The generational discontinuity manifests itself not only in the striking features of Strzelecki's biography (and the biographies of many people of his generation), though this factor is important. He participated in the Warsaw Uprising, and for him faith in "progress" and in the possibility of organizing life after the war in accordance with communist values so alien to most people of my generation today was a psychological condition for surviving the occupation. This faith pushed him into the camp that promised such "progress." In comparison with the suffering caused by the war, the suffering caused by Stalin's "progress" (about which he knew) did not seem excessive. He was also the editor of the underground journal *Płomienie* (The Flame) and was aware of the nature of Nazi (and Soviet) totalitarianism.[32] Oddly enough, it was this knowledge that inclined him to take the first step on the road that made him share the responsibility (at least in his own conscience, which determined his later political activity) for the shape of real socialism in Poland. Strzelecki succumbed to the arguments of Julian Hochfeld that one should support—even falsify—the elections in 1947 in order to legitimize the communists in the eyes of the "West" (which was supposed to make it possible to retain ties with "Europe" and avoid the "Soviet way to socialism").[33]

Strzelecki was secretary of the Communist party in the Union of Polish Writers after October 1956 and then a silent witness (though he helped certain individuals) of the anti-Semitic generational revolt of 1968. (In 1968 one of the Communist party factions, the Moczar-Kępa group, spread anti-Semitic propaganda connected with the brutal dismissal of Poles of Jewish origin from the movement and from positions in science. One motive behind this policy, which led to massive emigration of the remaining Polish Jews, was generational pressure for upward mobility for younger people in the party machine.) In 1980 Strzelecki became an adviser of Solidarity, one of those who convinced the Strike Committee in the Gdansk Shipyard to accept in the text of the Agreement the canon of the "leading role of the party"—in the name of compromise, which for him seemed to be the highest value. It is no accident that at more or less that time he wrote in his notebook (as a note to Czesław Miłosz's *Dom rodzinny: Europe* (Europe the Homeland): "Miłosz wrote that the socialists were too intelligent to believe in their own words. This is true for words that concern the doctrine of complete liberation, but not true for everything connected with the minimum program, which for a long time has been the main area of their action. And here they have made the world more human, and this was the most important thing." The strangeness of this attitude to the younger generation is not so much because the younger generation is more radical but that they have a *different radicalism* and above all a different way of thinking. It was not opportunism (as some claim) that made Strzelecki stay for so long in the Communist party. His decision to join the PUWP resulted not only from the now trivial argument that "only from the center can one have influence" but from the much more complicated motive of *self-sacrifice*. For him participation in an organization that denied, as he knew, the values he cherished was a *"choice of brotherhood"* from the "primitive mysticism of plebian Marxism";[34] it was the sacrifice of himself (and more generally, the ideals of the intelligentsia) in the name of the "interest of the masses." In the background of this decision was the vision of the prewar, beggarly, already symbolic Annopol, a poor part of Warsaw which haunted him and other socialists.[35] In my opinion, this attitude is a complicated mixture of a *guilty conscience* (for being in a relatively privileged situation) and a sense of his own *superiority*. The latter is present in the assumption that the values sacrificed to the party are not important "for the people" (who are chiefly concerned about their daily bread). It was Solidarity that finally put an end to regarding workers as mindless laborers. Yet among some politicians who regard themselves as representatives of the society one can see a division of values into those belonging to "intellectuals" and those belonging to "workers."[36]

The belief in his own "differentness," (combined with rebellion against it, expressed in the refusal to derive benefits from it) returns in Strzelecki's notes from 1956, in which he stresses that "I don't want to save myself on my own," does not want to be better, more moral than others. In other words, better than those "from the people," who do not even have the chance of making a gesture of rejection, for no opportunity will "come up" if one is not a "personage," a participant of the elitist public scene. Then came 1968. In Strzelecki's opinion, handing in one's party card precisely then (as late as then) would have meant that everything before this (Stalinism) had been endurable and that only anti-Semitism guided from above was the reason for the break. And here is another paradox (as in the case of the falsified elections in 1947): he remained in the party because everything had been horrible from the very beginning. From then on he often used the phrase "I am a hostage." In other words, he has to be in the party so that others can be "safe": he holds the rulers in check with the threat of turning in his party card, which was supposed to make them more moderate. Here again there are elements of pride and an egocentrism that is so alien to young people, which are manifest in the assumption (perhaps true, but inappropriate to speak about today) that his remaining in the party was "valuable" for the communists.

This attitude was accompanied by Strzelecki's typical *inability to pass judgment*, as well as the disinclination to do so, resulting from tolerance and the twists and turns of his life. In my opinion, this inability was rooted in a peculiar intellectual makeup that does not exist among young people today and is even alien to my generation of 40 year olds. Recently this way of reasoning was expressed most clearly by Leszek Kolakowski in a public lecture after twenty years of absence from Poland.[37] In his lecture, "Norms and Prohibitions," he replaced the term *dialectics* with the term *God*, while at the same time retaining almost unchanged the vision of the world that he had had as a Marxist. In this vision "evil" (antithesis) is a necessary element for "good" to exist (dialectical synthesis). "Sin" helps "virtue" express itself: and so "the devil should be saved" and passing judgment is impossible. Platonism, which Kolakowski had rejected in his "revisionist" period as the archetype of a totalitarian utopia, returned here as a private, individual idea of "humanity." In Kolakowski's opinion—which is hard to disagree with—such Platonism on a small scale, which does not pretend to organize the world after it own mold and is an element of the encounter of the individual with the self, is a necessary condition for acting with integrity in the world.

While the last thesis is also shared by my generation, it is difficult to accept this dualistic (for it is based on the inseparable tangle of "good" and "evil") monism, which makes it impossible to pass judgments and searches for one explanatory principle (dialectics-God) for both of its elements. Brought up on the phenomenological vision of a multitude of worlds (and hence also arguments) created by ourselves, my generation does not search for such holistic constructions. Paradoxically, in spite of the appearances of relativism, this enables us to look at "evil" more categorically, as simply "evil" and not as a condition for the existence of "good."

Jan Strzelecki's last long work, *A Lyrical Model of Socialism*, shows that toward the end of his life he rejected his basic argument that "one has to participate" and that only "from the inside can one change anything." The reason for this transformation was not only the emergence of Soldarity (and a much more realistic possibility of change "from the outside") but also the awareness that in party thinking myth always swallows up empiricism. To put it another way, ideological interpretative frameworks incessantly reproduce "supplementary reality," regardless of knowledge of the facts. In this situation it makes no sense to point out negative facts on the empirical level (and "from the inside" so that one would be listened to, which was supposed to justify staying in the party) because it will not change the general situation and beliefs in the correctness of the "idea." At most it will give rise to the argument that "too little has been done to put this idea into practice."[38]

Continuing Strzelecki's line of argument, one can fight with a myth only by presenting another myth—that is, a new principle of interpretation. Only then will the helplessness that accompanies the collision of two unverifiable myths and that results from the impossibility of communication and mediation force both sides to come down to the level of articulation closer to real processes. The Solidarity myth of "moral right" played such a role in confrontation with the "myth of the avant-garde." It was only after this encounter and the abandonment by both sides (or rather, by their splinter groups entering the new center) of their myths that the present political negotiations became possible. Though Jan Strzelecki seems to have accepted the Solidarity myth of "moral right," he must have been put off by its fundamentalism and intolerance. The younger generation appears less inclined to accept any collective myths. The anticollectivism of young people is especially evident in the Orange Alternative movement, where even the crowd functions as a watered-down sum of individual countenances and rituals. This accounts for the clear feeling of estrangement from Strzelecki's need for belonging.

Equally anachronistic and strange (at least to some young people)[39] is the neo-conservative version of collectivism evident in the recommendation of Marcin Król,[40] a Communist party deputy, that "one should choose selectively from the tradition experienced" (whether one believes in it or not). In Król's opinion, in a polarized world the political behavior of individuals who assume that one can have support only in oneself (in one's own knowledge and ethical and aesthetic principles) leads to ambiguity and isolation (since one is rejected by all sides). Even if practice were to show that he is right in promoting such political collectivism (based on the assumption that in order to act politically one must associate oneself with an institution with a firmly rooted tradition in the society, e.g., with the Church), for me personally there is something beautiful and worth continuing in the belief that "one can be saved only individually." This is true even when it is accompanied by bitterness and the troublesome thought that, in spite of Polish anti-Semitism, it would have been easier to have been born Jewish: then "not belonging" to the "dominant tradition" would be forgiven.

Fortunately, the young generation seems more included to reject both socialist (represented by Strzelecki) and Tory (tradition as a substitute for ideology) collectivism, with all the latter's antiliberalism. To young people today collectivism without faith as a recipe for acting honorably in the world, in which there are political and moral divisions, does not seem attractive and intellectually safe. In the last years of his life Strzelecki became ever more skeptical (and ever more zealous in his search for a new faith).[41] He felt life to be a burden in conditions of disagreement about moral right while one is simultaneously faced with black-and-white choices. On this issue his counsel to the question asked during martial law is typical: should one sign a loyalty oath to the government? "One can sign, but one should have an uneasy conscience."[42] It is hard for me to agree with this counsel. In spite of what Jan Strzelecki believed, an uneasy conscience is not enough to justify oneself. Even more disturbing was the recommendation of Cardinal Glemp: "Signing under compulsion does not count." I believe that common to young people today is a greater need for adherence to principles—and not merely through symbolic gestures. It is no accident that, as studies have shown, the least popular people in their circles are "activists" (of all sorts).[43]

This rejection of collectivism and the politics of symbols combined with no sense of responsibility for real socialism (which we found as a ready-made system) considerably expands the range of political alternatives. This is why it is so important that the post–Polish Youth Union generation is now coming to power.

The last characteristic of strangeness between generations is the question of style. For most people of my generation the inclination to act as the "social conscience" seems pretentious. This feeling seems to be intensifying among young people. Although they are susceptible to manipulation (as was the generation of "revisionists"), the younger generation of the opposition sees itself with more irony and even displays bravado in laying bare its own weaknesses,[44] qualities which were lacking in the Polish Youth Union generation (and in their contemporaries from the then opposite camp).

I am aware that this *attempt to understand* Jan Strzelecki, an eminent and tragic figure (long before his macabre death), may be unacceptable to many. Perhaps this picture says more about me than about him. Perhaps, as someone once said who knew me well, I am unable to perceive greatness in another person, but can more accurately describe pettiness. Jan Strzelecki did the opposite.

The New Generation of Protesting Workers

While the break in generational continuity in the intellectual community (both in the circles of power and in the opposition) is not confined to Poland, the appearance of a new generation of protesting workers[45] with a clearly different way of articulating their grievances is a strictly Polish phenomenon. This is due to the specific nature of the Polish crisis, which brought onto the public scene considerably wider groups of the society than in other socialist countries.

This new, post-Solidarity mentality can be called *postmoderntic*,[46] if postmodernism is regarded as a special orientation toward the world and oneself. The features of this mentality are:

• disbelief in "progress"—in other words, rejection of the fundamentalist myth, which was so strong in 1980 and 1981, that "good must carry the day";

• uncertainty as to one's identity because one no longer sees the world in categories of "good" and "evil" and no longer attributes these features respectively to the society and to the authorities (as the fundamentalists[47] did);

• action as an independent value—a feeling of community built through common experience and not symbolic references.

Solidarity (in the sense of an organizational structure) is regarded by people of this mentality as something of a supplementary form for their own lack of solidarity, which is more important as a value that is experienced very strongly—such as in peer or prisoner groups. This is why they so dramatically experience the "betrayal" (in their feeling) of this value by the older generation of opposition activists, who did not defend them sufficiently after the strikes, even though the young workers called these strikes "representative" (conducted not in their own interest but for others).[48] The difficulties in defining their own identity are coupled with a typical "transferability" of symbols. For instance, they used on their protest signs and in their stories the same symbols (Smurfs from the fictional children's figures) to designate the constabulary (in blue uniforms) and also on envelopes handed out to strikers during the strike in August 1988. Perhaps they are aware of a certain accidentalness in the roles played. Most of the striking young workers—if their term in the army had come a little later—could have found themselves on the other side of the gate as draftees in the Reserve Force of the Civic Militia. This explains the basketball games strikers played with the militia outside the shipyard barricade and the ease of verbal contacts, in spite of the brutality of law enforcement units and the workers themselves when they met in direct clashes. It explains why strikers could relieve the boredom of the sit-in by playing the game of "ZOMO[49] (Regular Force of the Civic Militia) and strikers," with a symbolic battle at the end in which workers played both sides, including the role of constables. Such things would have been impossible during the strikes in 1980, when workers manifested their distinctness and their own symbols. The political language of this new generation is the language of children's TV programs[50] and fairy tales, which function as special myths that are supposed to express the nature and dynamics of the conflict. What is typical is that these are fairy tales in which none of the sides is categorically good or evil and no one wins all the time. The conflict consists in a never-ending—and in sum, absurd—free-for-all (action for the sake of action). There are also attempts to express the internal differences in the society itself which are so strongly felt in connection with the division of the opposition into the new center and one of the wings. Here this configuration of forces is expressed by means of a story taken from a folk tale, which is not surprising considering the low level of education and meager cultural and life experience of young workers from the countryside who "after the army" came to a big city but live apart from it. In this fairy tale[51] we have a "wise brother," who serves a lord and brings scraps from the lord's table to his sick mother (Poland). There is also a "stupid brother" (worker), to whom the "wise brother" (intellectual) tells fairy tales in the field to keep the former from becoming bored during hard work.

This new generation of striking workers, who are much younger and have a lower occupational and material status than the generation of strikers in 1980,[52] seems to be much more alienated than their predecessors were. The workers protesting in 1980 felt they were the equals of the plant owners while the machines were shut down, but the young workers in 1988 emphasized that during the sit-in strike they felt less homeless because they had more space for themselves than in their cramped hotel rooms. Low qualifications and unfamiliarity with the city and even with the immediate neighborhood (the residents of workers' hotels are regarded as an undesirable element) make it impossible for young workers to participate in the so-called second economy and adapt themselves to the crisis in this way.[53] Their only chance is to escape individually from the category of unskilled residents of workers' hotels; for them there is no group solution. They are just starting out in life, so inflation hits them hardest. They also will be the first victims of eventual unemployment in conditions of restructuralization, and the waiting period for one's own apartment now exceeds twenty years. The market rules give them no chance. This is why the political channel (including politics of the street) is so important for them, and the shutting off of this channel is one of the eventual concessions of Solidarity (in exchange for legalization). This explains the alliance of young workers with the Working Group (the populist wing of the opposition that is against part of Solidarity entering the avant-garde of the establishment).[54] This also explains the ever sharper conflicts, which become especially visible during elections of plant committees.[55] The economic conservatism of young workers and their support for state paternalism, weak "democratic restraints"[56] resulting from their disbelief in the institution of bargaining and in the possibility of reaching an agreement with the authorities and also from frequent contacts with brutality and law breaking on the part of lower-level state functionaries,[57] and finally their proneness to "politics of the street" make them an unpredictable element of the political scene. This is accentuated by their lack of generational identity, which they seek in common action, on the street.

Conclusion

The three processes described above—the emergence of the new center, the severance of generational continuity in intellectual circles, and the appearance of a "postmodernistic" orientation among young workers—are breaking up the identity and language of articulation from the previous phase of the crisis (that is, from 1980 and 1981 and martial law). The market-ownership reform is intensifying the differentiation of attitudes and interests. Moreover, the economic interests of specific social classes have made themselves felt on the political scene, whereas in the past the similar consumer needs of all citizens were felt politically. Fragmentary material claims and the total rejection of the system in moral categories have been replaced by a much more complicated matrix of interests and demands.

What is the relation between these forms of articulation and the transformation processes described in this book? Have the new owners (including those from the *nomenklatura*) found political channels that are open and influential enough to guarantee themselves the reproduction of their newly acquired status? Not yet, it seems. At present the forms of political expression are gravitating toward a peculiar borderland area[58] between what the society and the economy can no longer accept (the command system) and what the party apparatus and the populist wing do not want to accept (permanent ownership changes in the state sector). The latter is strengthened by the workers' self-management movement, which fears the loss of its position.[59] The members of the new center are guided by their own political interest (which favors stabilization, control, and the widest possible support). Such a configuration of forces may push the reform movement toward worker self-management solutions as being the least conflictive. This would delay the breakthrough in the socialist system for a few years, but it would be consistent with the Polish tradition.[60] An essential feature of the situation described here is that the formula (and identity) of Solidarity does not fit the new configuration of social forces and the rapidly intensifying conflict within the society itself.

The configuration of social forces sketched above does not seem stable and will probably change with the transition to the next stage of the breakthrough. The workers' self-management version of reforms may delay this evolution, but it will be unable to check the decline of real socialism.

Appendix. Elections to the Seym and Senate: the New Political Geography of Poland

August 1989

The elections of 4 June 1989 confirm the conjectures contained in chapter 3 on the social base of the oppositional part of the "new center," a new political geography of Poland.[61]

The social characteristics of forty-nine provinces were compared with three significant behaviors of voters in these provinces.[62] These behaviors are:

- absence (remember that only 62 percent of those qualified voted, and this figure ranged from 71.4 to 51.5 percent between regions);
- support for Wałęsa's Citizens' Committee (Solidarity) candidates. The percentages of valid votes cast for the most popular Solidarity candidate to the Senate in the first round ranged from 82.9 to 40, depending on the province; all other candidates got less.
- rejection of the Communist party candidates.

This comparison produces three important results. First, more important than the real power of Solidarity structures in a given province were regional-cultural differences and behaviors of the citizens that sometimes went back to the nineteenth century. Involved here are the traditions of patriotic and populist movements (in the southern provinces and part of Poznań province) rather than workers' and socialist traditions (e.g., one of the lowest rates of voting was recorded in Łódź). One can clearly see political differences that run according to the boundaries of the former zones of partition: the highest rate of participation and greatest support for candidates from the Solidarity list were recorded in former Galicia, followed by the former Prussian zone of occupation (which has a stronger tradition of citizen activity of the conservative type); the lowest rate of voting was in the former Russian-occupied zone (without such traditions), with the exception of Warsaw. The provinces of Lublin and Podlasie, with their traditions of peasant movements, were active.

Second, the comparison shows that candidates of the Citizens' Committee (Solidarity) received the most votes; non-voting was lower in provinces in which the rural population predominated over the urban population (i.e., regions that are industrially under-developed), in provinces with a demographically older structure and greater religiousness (as measured by church attendance), and finally, in more strongly socially integrated provinces (with a low crime rate). In other words, young people and the urban working class were less active in the elections than farmers, older people, and the intelligentsia.

Third, the presence of Solidarity structures was an essential factor but not the most important one. To be sure, in large cities, where in 1983 through 1988 there had been clear resistance to joining the new unions (and structures of then-illegal Solidarity existed) the number of voters was clearly greater, but in provinces where there really were no such structures and the social and cultural conditions mentioned above were evident (tradition, religiousness, dominance of agriculture) attendance at the polling booths was equally high or higher. The network of Citizens' Committees and Solidarity of Individual Farmers scored a success in the political sense (with the help of the Church). In the case of workers' Solidarity, the rift described in chapter 3 clearly left its mark on the election results. The populist Working Groups active in Kujawy, in the provinces of Łódź, Piotrków, Szczecin, and some of the northern provinces might have contributed to a smaller voter turnout in these area with their call for a boycott of the elections.

Other conclusions resulting from the new political geography show that the problems of national identity seem to be more important for voter behaviors (that is, *where* one votes) than the attitude toward the reformatory elite: Solidarity candidates who were not members of the national minorities lost elections. The above can explain, as well, voting behaviors in the borderland areas in Hungary, Slovakia, and especially in the Soviet Republics. Solidarity candidates also received relatively weak support in rich farming provinces (Leszno, Pile). In my opinion, this is evidence of the links between this agricultural elite and the local Communist party machine, as in access to the means of production, which were previously allocated in an administrative way, and with active members of the United Peasants' party.

Support for the opposition was also weak in western provinces with a large number of state farms, whose elimination was proposed by Farmers' Solidarity. This suggests the possibility of further divisions in the electorate of the opposition in the event it pushes more strongly for the privatization of the economy (which is supported, as I showed in chapter 2, by only some of the employees of the state sector).

A final conclusion is that the candidates of the coalition-government side who were elected to the Seym are:
- people not connected with the power apparatus (with the Communist party machine);
- people shown more often than others on television (which had no influence in the case of Solidarity, since people voted for

the entire "Wałşa team"; candidates from the Communist party, United Peasants party, and Democratic party were elected on the basis of their individual qualities.

• people active in the economy (e.g., in activity on their own account). Sometimes these are members of the ex-economic *nomenklatura* who have been made owners or organizers of the Union of Rural Youth or the Association of Polish Students and who are active in forms connected with the organizational ownership described in chapter 2.

Voting absence rates have indirectly confirmed the peculiar boycott of the elections by the power apparatus: there was no obvious compulsion forcing people to vote, and so the opportunists stayed home. The paradoxical consequence was that attendance increased where there had been a boycott in 1988 (during the elections to the National Councils), and where the attendance previously had been high (as a result of pressures, e.g., in the state farms) it now clearly declined.

Summing up, the new electoral geography is contributing to an identity crisis for all the participants in the public sphere, including the Citizens' Club of Deputies (see chapter 4).

Good supplements to the above remarks on the new political geography are the findings of studies on how the society perceived the first sessions of the Seym and Senate—now with the participation of the opposition.

The deliberations were followed relatively more often by men, by people between 30 and 60, by people with higher education, to a greater extent by employees of the private economy (handicrafts, agriculture) than of the state sector, and by members of newly formed or emerging social and political associations. At the same time, the deliberations were watched more often by members of the PUWP and UPP, organizations that—in comparison with the opposition—lost the elections.

The attitudes of persons interested in public events clearly differ. Hopes associated with the functioning of new institutions and satisfaction with the manner in which these institutions were formed were expressed by 32.5 percent (in relation to the Seym) and 34.6 percent of the respondents (in relation to the Senate), and negative opinions (fear of the future, mistrust, disbelief that anything will change) by 20.5 percent (in relation to the Seym) and 22.9 percent (in relation to the Senate). There is also a clear category of persons who, though pleased with the symbolic victory over the previous government coalition, are simultaneously pessimistic as regards the possibility of changing the situation and overcoming the economic crisis (16.7 percent of the respondents). The rest either have no opinion or express skepticism concerning the newly elected institutions and fear of the future.

What is striking is that more interest was shown in the deliberations by those who evaluated their material situation as better than average and by persons declaring activity in newly formed associations or organizations of a political nature (75 percent of this category) than by persons belonging to the trade union Solidarity (58 percent declaring membership were interested in the deliberations). Once again this is a clear continuation of the political public that made its appearance during the elections, when participation in the voting in a given province was determined more by the efficiency of the Citizens' Committee (identified with Solidarity but dominated by the middle class) than by the traditions (and presence) of the trade union Solidarity. Both during the elections and today, the residents of small towns show more interest in the deliberations of the parliament than the residents of bigger cities: in the category of residents of cities with a population of up to 100,000, 57 percent were interested in the deliberations; in cities with a population of 100,000 to 500,000, 51 percent, and the proportions were similar with respect to voting activity and support for candidates of the opposition.

Young people (from 18 to 22 years old) were less interested in the deliberations than older people: only 34 percent of this category followed the deliberations of the first sessions; in the 22 to 30 age category, 42 percent; and among older people, an even higher percentage.

Persons showing interest in the deliberations are a special political public. They are scattered in small population centers and are able to show their support in statistical categories (elections or a referendum) rather than by opposing "politics of the street" or strikes in large plants. Strikes take place in large urban centers and are organized by people from another age category (chiefly young workers). So we are observing two scenes that are isolated from each other. The first has the beginnings of a civil society that observes the activity of political institutions from the point of view of its economic interest (because these institutions determine the direction of the reforms) and is more ready to take part in political and social organizations than in trade unions. This civil society is found in small urban centers and in the countryside, and since the closing down of the Citizens' Committees (in June 1989 after the elections—a few months later these committees were recreated), it lacks coordinating centers.[63] Consequently, it is threatened with dispersal, unless it makes an effort to set up organs of local self-government and works to elect its people to regional offices.

The second scene—strikes in large plants and large industrial centers—is the scene of people who do not show much interest in the activities of the representative institutions that the opposition has entered. Perhaps this indifference and preference for direct ways of articulating their interests rather than through representative institutions is caused by the disbelief in "politics" and in the efficiency of mediating bodies. In other words, it was a signal of strong political populism.

What is characteristic is that even those who can be called the first fruits of the civil society are still in the initial stage of "raising their heads" and gathering up moral courage. For what appealed to them the most during the deliberations of the Seym and Senate were not discussions about the economy or local self-government but the attacks on the Ministry of Internal Affairs (license, lawlessness). These observations confirm a well-known historical pattern: the political public and base of support of institutions of parliamentary democracy are the "middle" classes (people working on their own; white-collar workers) rather than the large industrial working class. The latter, which is strong in numbers and concentrated in one place, prefers to fight for its rights directly. Conducive to this preference are deep-seated antagonisms toward "politicians," chiefly of intellectual origin. What is more, the working class is bored by and weary of institutional politics, whose drama, concealed by procedural debates, does not strike their imagination. The "politics" of this working-class movement is above all the fight for status—"who's on top"—with its clearly visible winners and losers. And this is precisely what, for tactical reasons, activists of the opposition wish to avoid. In this situation, however, it will be difficult for the new establishment to win the support of young workers in large urban centers.

Chapter Four

Stage Two: The Collapse of the New Center and Its Reorganization

June–August 1989

This chapter will describe a few factors pointing to the rapid breakup of the "new center" described in the previous chapter. All the phenomena discussed are taking place in Poland, and the description in this chapter of the breakup of the new center, of necessity, will focus on that country. These events, however, are a sign of broader problems that concern all of Eastern Europe. The differentiation of collapse of the new reformatory center is also taking place in Hungary and the U.S.S.R., and some processes (e.g., the conflict between the factions of globalists and populists in the Communist party) are taking a similar course. Also, the differentiation of the pro-reformatory elites as conflicts in the society intensify seems to concern (if not today, then certainly tomorrow) all the countries experiencing "revolution from above." And this is or will be attended everywhere by the same logic of revolutions of this type: the elite who have entered the public scene, which in the past had appealed to the society as a whole, will have to gain the support of a more specific social base and state precisely who their supporters are. This is necessary in order to establish identity in the pluralistic political process that is based on more complicated mechanisms than general support or rejection, which is often based on the politics of symbols, as in the June 1989 elections in Poland.

In this chapter I describe only some of the mechanisms working to break up the new center. First and foremost of these mechanisms are the divisions among party reformers and how these divisions left their mark on the "round table" talks; also important are lines of division in the opposition wing of the new center and signs of a crisis of identity among the opposition in the wake of legalization. Finally, I look at the "anarchy of the transition period," caused by, among other things, the disintegration of the administrative hierarchy, which refuses to obey the new center.

The Polish disintegration is due not only to pressures from the more radical wings, but most of all to the internal dynamics of a new field of political forces that coalesced as a result of the "round table" talks and the elections. In other words, the collapse of the center is chiefly due to its own dynamics. Not without influence is the differentiation of the society and the ever-clearer articulation of conflicts of interests and pressures. This is connected both with the deepening economic crisis and the consequences of changes in the system. In addition, there is the logic of democratization "from the top." The reformatory elite—after entering the public scene— begin to look for a more specific base of social support (which goes hand in hand with coming into conflict with another segment of the center that appeals to different interests: viz., the internal divisions in the power camp and the opposition in connection with the city–countryside conflict). After the opposition enters the public scene, it is also more difficult for it to say that it represents the "entire society," for it must create a coalition with other forces in the parliament—in exchange for concrete concessions—and must calculate what part of the present electorate will be lost in this way and what part will be permanently gained. It is also necessary to think about the future elections. The overall confidence in the opposition (expressed in Poland in the voting for "Wałesa's team") will probably not be repeated. Finally, putting into concrete form the previously general catchword "reforms" also leads to the disintegration of the new center: this concerns factional divisions against this background both in the power camp and in the opposition. This is attended by the breakup of the previous "ruling coalition" (gathered around the Communist party), caused by the eagerness of its members to become autonomous and establish their own identity.

The Conflict concerning the Future: Globalists and Populists in the Community Party

Western observers (as well as opposition groups in the countries undergoing transformations) do not appreciate differences between factions of reformers with different orientations in the camp conventionally called the "authorities."

These differences and disputes (suspended when there is a threat to the Communist party as a whole but continually resurfacing) express not only conflicts of interests of various institutions of power but also are a sign of more fundamental differences in ways of reasoning that result from, among other things, generational differences and different challenges (as well as training and information) in a given segment of the ruling apparatus.

The conflict in the camp of reformers that I call the "conflict concerning the future" concerns three matters:

• *Perception of the nature of the crisis* in real socialism. The globalists put the main emphasis on relations with the capitalist system which are based on the systemic subarticulation of the socialist mode of production to the capitalist world. The populists pay more attention to internal contradictions (also within the bloc) and to the "leadership" crisis, which was caused, they think, by following the "leading role of the party" formula in the past.

• *Visions of reform.* The globalists are supporters of the notion of "ontological opening" (see chapter 2), treating political reforms as a condition for making ownership changes and "introducing market mechanisms" smoothly. The populists, in turn, treat political reforms (such as the workers' self-management movement, reanimation of the party, better representation of interests) as an autonomous element, regarding privatization of the state sector as a temporary maneuver that will allow socialism to "catch its breath."

• *Guarantees of the permanence of reforms.* The globalists put greater stress on legal guarantees and a social contract with the opposition. The populists emphasize the role of the Communist party (reformed). Characteristic here is the statement of one of the party experts.[1] I quote it in its entirety because both in its language and argumentation it is a good illustration of the twisted thinking of the members of this faction:

I believe that most of the members of the M.F. Rakowski government are aware that the effectiveness of the government's actions requires a gradual departure from the principles of socialism. The new economic legislation has created rather honest rules of the economic game, in which state and socialized enterprises will be dislodged by more competitive private firms. Due to the workings of the market, in several or a dozen or so years the greater part of the economy will be in private hands, and Poland will become an ever more capitalist country. The right wing wants to speed up this process. . . . That is why it is perhaps better that such breakneck and dangerous changes were initiated by the PUWP, which has numerous, experienced, qualified, often intelligent cadres and the support of the Civic Militia, security force, and army.

To describe the differences between factions of party reformers in more detail, I start with the problem of the perception of the crisis. Most generally the interpretation of the globalists (in all the countries undergoing reform) can be called the "world-system perspective,"[2] which makes use of the vision of two-level dependency.

Socialism is seen as subarticulated and dependent on capitalism, and as "punished" twice: for being peripheral and for being unable (due to collective property rights) to follow the market logic. The second-level dependency, the politically imposed interdependency in the Eastern bloc (COMECON), is perceived as an *adjustment* to the first-level dependency. The main aim of this adjustment is to redistribute among the East European countries the costs of subarticulation (costs that are initially unequal, due to the uneven starting levels of the development) and to impose "import substitution specializations" (often in spite of local advantages) as well as politically administered transfers. Such adjustment makes possible the consolidation of the political empire, able to compete with the West in spite of socialism's economic subarticulation to it. But to have both empire and social stability in the Eastern bloc is more difficult. A solution to these problems, as reformers see them, is to build in each country a sort of *dual economy*, with one of its segments deeply integrated into the COMECON (and administered directly from Moscow)[3] and the other one radically reformed (with capitalist mechanisms, including privatization introduced into the state economy). The latter would eventually reduce the costs of subarticulation, while the former would make adjustment to it more rational from the point of view of Moscow. This plan goes in the opposite direction from the hypothesis of the rapid decline of regional hegemony.[4] Economic reform, based on the property rights shift, is unthinkable without *legal and political guarantees* (nobody would invest capital without such guarantees). Reformers "from above" understand this and see both the end of "revolutionary legitimacy" and the new relationship between state and society as functional imperatives for a successful economic reform that can save the empire. The basic features of real socialism are given up (including the leading role of the party and collective ownership) in order to accomplish this task. Reforms are based on a high degree of coordination of changes in particular segments, not de-correlation, as K. Jowitt sees it.[5]

The segment of the ruling group which is behind the new world-system interpretation of both the crisis and reform is linked—by its professional responsibilities and training—with foreign policy, counterintelligence, foreign trade, and the scientfic institutions behind these fields, not to the traditional party–police contingent. The latter not only have a local orientation but will be hurt by the reforms. With a dual economy, control over material resources will shift directly to Moscow or partly pass into private hands (through property rights reform inside the state economy). Their hope was that with political reforms, steerability from the top eventually would be restored (and bureaucratic anarchy overcome), but the direct control of the administration on the lower levels would be weakened.

In each country this first faction is confronted with a different vision of reforms represented by the *populist faction*, linked to a more traditional vision of both crisis and solution. And both of these groups have to fight with the bureaucratic faction, which is linked to the low-level state apparatus, the Communist party hierarchy, and more traditional (control oriented) segments of the police and army.[6]

The main advantage of the globalist faction is that it is insulated from local pressures; its main disadvantage, that it does not have an executive network of its own that has experience in dealing with domestic problems (especially with the economy). In the above conditions it is no accident that the Moscow globalists were able to make foreign policy more pragmatic, to reinforce reformist tendencies in parts of the Polish and Hungarian power elite, and to introduce a few new rules on the central level, but at the same time were unable to introduce basic changes in the Soviet economy.

The main ideological debate in Eastern Europe is going on in the triangle described above: two competing, reform-oriented factions —with different visions of reforms—confronting not only each other, but also resisting the Communist party bureaucrats. Before I move on to this debate, I would like to describe the different tracks of reforms in Hungary, Poland, and the Soviet Union which are rooted in the local conditions of each country (the factional struggles are only one element of these conditions).

The competing, reform-oriented factions in each country see new links between capitalist mechanisms and socialism in a different way: while the globalists seem to be interested in a more lasting and deeper transformation of the system, the populists support transformation only under the condition that it is a temporary relief (as the New Economic Policy in the U.S.S.R. was), not a lasting evolution. Political control by the Communist party as well as administratively controlled entry are—from the populists' point of view—the necessary framework of property rights reform. In a sense this is reminiscent of the approach of Gierek's team in the 1970s.[7] The populists also emphasize the economic reserves that could be put into circulation after renegotiation of obligations within the COMECON as well as after carrying out a branch restructuralization of the economy. In other words, they emphasize structural changes in the framework of the present model of ownership, while the globalists postulate the rejection of this model. Also the vision of the political structure that would serve as a guarantee of stability/control during the period of transition is different in each faction (as well as in each country, due to its specific, internal tensions). In other words, each country builds its own system of checks and balances.

Hungary is moving toward a multiparty system and tried (unsuccessfully) the revitalization of the Communist party (through its "socialdemocratization") *before* elections. The Polish experience, with its accelerated corrosion of the new center, seems to be a discouraging example not only for the ruling group, but also for the Hungarian opposition.

Poland, with its government crisis and problems with carrying out the political trade-offs of the "round table" (due to the collapse of the new center), seems to be moving toward a new form of prerogative state, with an extraordinary center of power behind the phony institutions of parliamentary democracy.[8]

In the Soviet Union the main obstacle to reforms is the middle-level executive apparatus (both party and state), and the main destabilizing factor is nationalistic pressures that are already present inside the power structure (and interpreted by Soviet globalists as a competition between elite groups). In an obvious way political reform in the Soviet Union is a sort of adjustment to these problems. The centralization of power in the hands of a reform-oriented leader (Gorbachev himself) on the one hand, and the new, populist-type activists on the other (activists who entered the power structure after the last elections to the People's Councils) should curb and limit the power of the middle-level apparatus. The two-level electoral procedure was intended (it is not yet clear if it worked that way) to limit access to the power structure at the republic level for people from the dominant nationality in order to make conflicts less visible. Also the recent introduction of some top dissident figures on the list of candidates to the Council at the national level can be treated as a kind of "politics of symbols" (when signs of deeper commitment to liberalization—such as A. Saharov and Roy Miedviedjev as candidates—are used as instruments of manipulation aimed at calming national aspirations that could hurt the reform process).

The patterns of change described above are advocated by the globalist faction in Hungary, Poland, and the Soviet Union and can be presented in a schematic way as follows:

The local conditions responsible for the above differences are as follows:

- stage of the systemic crisis,
- level and pattern of the society's mobilization,
- splits in the ruling elite.

The factional element in the Communist party is important for explaining both recent developments in the political system and its future dynamics. Remember, however, that conflicts between

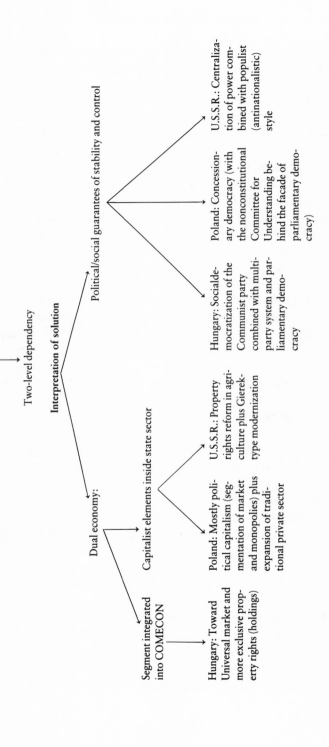

Interpretation of the crisis

Two-level dependency

Interpretation of solution

Political/social guarantees of stability and control

Dual economy:

Segment integrated into COMECON

Capitalist elements inside state sector

Hungary: Toward Universal market and more exclusive property rights (holdings)

Poland: Mostly political capitalism (segmentation of market and monopolies) plus expansion of traditional private sector

U.S.S.R.: Property rights reform in agriculture plus Gierek-type modernization

Hungary: Socialdemocratization of the Communist party combined with multi-party system and parliamentary democracy

Poland: Concessionary democracy (with the nonconstitutional Committee for Understanding behind the facade of parliamentary democracy)

U.S.S.R.: Centralization of power combined with populist (antinationalistic) style party factions are usually suspended when there is a threat to the party as a whole. This was clearly evident in Poland during the so-called government crisis (when signs appeared of a collapse of the exising coalition around the PUWP, and the Club of Deputies of the United Peasants' party declared a desire to form a coalition with the Citizens' Parliamentary Club). The newly elected First Secretary of the Communist party, Rakowski, who before this (as prime minister) had been suspended between the factions, brought into the party leadership advocates of the populist (antiapparatus) line—L. Miller, S. Wiatr—but also members of the apparatus— Manfred Gorywoda, Secretary of the Provincial Committee in Katowice, and Janusz Kubasiewicz, Secretary of the Warsaw Committee. At the same time, the politburu seems to support the conception of political capitalism as a method for the privatization of the state sector (an approach that in the past was more stressed by the globalists). This peculiar eclectivism of the program, coupled with signs of appealing to the old sources of power (the support of Moscow,[9] loyalty of the forces of law and order),[10] is an attempt to restore the political position before the "round table" and the elections. This strategy is accompanied by a return of ideological rhetoric.

A similar situation exists in the U.S.S.R. The crisis in China (and the clear politicization of the Soviet army, which is opposed to the globalists' maneuver of "ontological opening") has visibly increased the antireformatory mobilization of the Red Army. This tendency was accompanied by an increase in the number of conflicts over nationality and economic issues and an increase in social disorganization, as measured by a 30 percent increase in crime in 1989 (in comparison with the previous year). In this situation the reaction of the party (threatened with a real loss of power) was to suspend factional struggles and to enter into an alliance with the KGB against the danger of Bonapartism.[11] What is more, as in Poland, use was made of certain organizational proposals of the populist faction: for example, the formation of the Interregional Council of Deputies headed by Yeltsin,[12] which cuts across national representations and uses antiapparatus rhetoric as a substitute for separatist slogans (emphasizing what unites rather than what divides). Besides this apparently symbolic rhetoric, Gorbachev and Yegor Ligachev (the leader of a faction of the apparatus) moved closer together, united by the common danger to the party as a whole from the army.

In connection with the above, one should not overestimate factional differences within the Communist parties of the reformed countries. Yet these differences must be noted, for they had, and still have, an influence on developments in the political system. An example that clearly brings these differences to light is the recent debate between the Polish version of globalists and populists which took place at the Third Ideological Conference of the PUWP (February 1989), where both factions were present.[13] And before that there was debate at the Tenth Plenum of the Central Committee, where the moderate version of the globalists' proposal was presented as the thesis of the Political Bureau (prepared by M. Orzechowski, ideological secretary and former Minister of Foreign Affairs).[14] The main topics of this debate were:

• *the place of the Communist party in "reformed socialism."* Both factions agree that the Communist party is now one of the main obstacles to reform, due to its role as a transmission belt for local and branch interests of industry that oppose a deep restructuring of the economy. Such a role is unavoidable when, as in Poland, one-half of the 1.8 million party members are *nomenklatura* people, holding managerial posts in the state administration and industry. The solutions proposed by the factions are different: while globalists would like to withdraw the party from the enterprise level[15] (or at least to change the pattern of recruitment of party managers to one based on the selection of managers from their own enterprises),[16] the populists are much more radical. They propose abolition of the *nomenklatura* as a recruitment mechanism of the managerial cadre.[17] However, they want to keep the party on the enterprise level, close to its "class" base.

• *the place of "pluralism on the left."* Radical globalists speak about two parties on the left (reformist and "revolutionary"— whatever this second label means in the context of the ruling party),[18] and less radical globalists about one party but with the right to formulate dissident "platforms."[19] Populists advocate a lively, strong party movement: definitely one party on the left, but with the right to organize and keep "factions" inside the party.[20]

Generally speaking, the moderate globalists in Poland seem to be interested in a weakening of the Communist party, which would be transformed into a sort of social-democratic party with loose membership, active only during election time, but with a highly mobilized representation ("club") in the parliament.[21] The populists see the Communist party as the center of the power structure. But of course they want a different party, one that operates in a movement-type style (imitating some of the methods of Solidarity during its 1980–1981 state of development). Highly personalized leadership and a willingness to participate in the face-to-face confrontation with members of the opposition are elements of this new style. This has some consequences for the status of the opposition as well: while globalists are interested in the co-optation of the most moderate part of the opposition, populists reject such a development (and during the "round table" worked hard to prevent the formation of the "new center"). Populists, however, are not interested in victimization of the political opposition. They would like to use it as a "sparring partner," making it easier to build up the identity of the party movement. Gierek's "repressive tolerance" pattern seems to be the closest to the populists' vision of the status of the political opposition.[22] We have to remember that such a pattern is not only very dangerous for the legal system, but also corruptive for both sides—the apparatus as well as the opposition itself. The populists seem to be uninterested in both the rule of law (they prefer "substantial," not "formal," justice) and parliamentary procedures (too boring and not spectacular enough for the party movement). Yeltsin in the Soviet Union, I. Pozgoy in Hungary, or the much younger Miller (or A. Miodowicz) in Poland are the most characteristic examples of the populist style.

Both factions are in a deep conflict with the traditional power structure (each for different reasons) in spite of their tactical alliance to face the threat to the party as a whole. I will try to describe in a schematic way recent trends in Poland on the lower and district level of this structure to show the dilemmas that confront both factions.

On one hand, the *role of the Communist party is weakened*, especially on the local-authority and enterprise level. There is now a less intensive flow of members of the Communist party apparatus into the state economic administration: from 45 percent of those joining the administration in the 1970s to 15 percent in the late 1980s.[23] Also, the previous polymorphic role of the party is now being taken over by the domestic security network: officials close to the institutions of "justice" and law and order are now more visible in all voluntary organizations than party people.[24] But at the same time, the *negative selection* to the party apparatus (people entering the party apparatus to increase their chance for managerial positions are generally of lower qualifications than people starting in managuial jobs) is now even more obvious than before: What is more, it is (for different reasons) negative from the point of view of both factions of reformers (globalists and populists). And globalists, with less access to inner party affairs than populists, are without any influence on personnel policy on the low level of the party apparatus. The peculiar pattern of "politicization" as a substitute for "professionalization" exists on the low and middle levels of the power structure in Poland.[25] In spite of the fact that the overwhelming majority (73 percent) of the power holders on the local level are Communist party members and most of them (90 percent) have a college degree, two different career patterns can be observed:[26]

The first pattern is as follows: a person already has a college degree when he or she is picked up for a managerial job in the local power structure in administration or industry. On the average this happens ten years after graduation from college. Such a person treats Communist party membership as an unavoidable tribute to the *nomenklatura* mechanism and gets a party card about six months before formal nomination to the local power or managerial position. So the first pattern is a college degree combined with short-term rank-and-file party membership before moving to a managerial/administrative position.

The second pattern (followed by more than 60 percent of people in the local power apparatus)[27] is linked with early party membership, a low level of education (vocational or high school), and attending college after being picked up for the power position on the local level. Usually this happens twenty years after graduation from high school. So the second pattern is low educational level combined with work in the professional party apparatus as a start for a managerial/state career. During a crisis (or, as today, during the permanent crisis) there is an additional requirement: recruitment to a low-level post in the party apparatus is based above all on *loyalty* (or expected loyalty). Those who have waited for their first power position longer than others are now picked up, which is the best way to build a strong patron-client network that embraces the local and district levels of the party apparatus. And both of these levels resist both the globalists' and populists' visions of reform. Another characteristic feature is reinforced during a crisis: activists are less often promoted than quiet conformists and passive, early party members.[28] This puts the populist faction at a big disadvantage.

On the average, "professionals" in the local power structure are ten years younger than the members of the local party apparatus, and their social background also is different (more often they are from the middle class). They can be treated as a potential (but difficult to reach in organizational terms) social base for globalists. For them, party membership seems to be pure ritual. But those who made a career by using "politicization" as the entry ticket would resist above all a weakening of the party (because they do not have access to other managerial positions); they also resist turning the party into a social movement and are for keeping the *nomenklatura* mechanism of recruiting.

The situation at the *district party level* is different, but difficult as well. To get such a position one has to be both politicized (early party membership) and professional. Relatively young people are picked for these jobs, without even entering the lower level of the power structure; often they were active on the top level of a students' association linked to the globalist faction. In spite of the fact that dynamic overachievers are recruited, resistance to reforms exists on this level as well. Too early commitment (when the fate and pattern of the reform are unsure) can harm a brilliant career; passivity is the best tactic. According to recent Party Academy research,[29] 65 percent of all party secretaries on the district level are against reforms (they reject the four trade-offs that were already decided on the top level). Among the 35 percent who support the reform, more than half are ideological secretaries (75 percent of all district-level secretaries linked to the ideological department support reforms). This is not surprising, since they recently were selected for their positions by one of the leading members of the globalist faction (Orzechowski, Secretary of the Central Committee and member of the Political Bureau responsible for ideological matters). But the mainstream of recruitment to the district-level party posts goes through the Central Committee apparatus, not the Political Bureau, and again it is not surprising that the First Secretaries on the district level (decided at the Political Bureau level) are more sympathetic to reforms than the rest of the district apparatus. What is interesting is that the rejection of or support for reforms is not based on an alternative vision of the social order nor on loyalty to the party as a whole. It is very *selective rejection or support* based on personal experience and individual professional risk caused by reform. Those who in the past had contacts with the opposition (for instance, organizational secretaries who are close to the domestic security structure) are not as afraid of legalization of the opposition as are the others. Economic secretaries, who are more familiar with workers' self-management at the enterprise level, accept this institution but not liberalization at the top or the relegalization of Solidarity. And those with less experience with "pluralism" (party secretaries from the less industrialized districts, where Solidarity and the opposition are weak or absent) reject all proposals aimed at liberalization. It is worth underlining here that personal experience is crucial in the Soviet Union as well: globalists, by their training and experience, are much more familiar with the West and capitalism than the populists are. Globalists also have had experience with the "controlled pluralism" pattern: such a pattern has been used for years as part of the "communist solar system."[30] (A degree of autonomy that is yet under control, but which could be presented as a genuine liberalization, is a more familiar experience for the globalists than for the populist faction. In such a situation it is not surprising that one of the leading figures of *glasnost*, Fiodor Burlacki, has his political roots in circles that for years flirted with the idea of controlled pluralism.)[31]

Both the local and district-level power structure members are *uprooted*: they usually get their first position in unfamilar territory in order to prevent intermingling with the local interest groups and using party channels as a transmission belt of their pressures. Such a "preventive" arrangement is even more strange in a situation when local government is now being given more self-management possibilities.

As we see, the power structure in Poland is characterized by a *multilevel discontinuity*: the local apparatus is cut off from the society, while the reform-oriented elite in the Communist party is not only divided, but cut off from its own executive apparatus as well. The latter is recruited by the district party apparatus (hostile to reforms) and built into the patronage network.

The discourse between globalists and populists now going on in the countries of Eastern Europe is a sort of continuation of the debate on modernization at the peripheries of Europe initiated in Russia in the nineteenth century. I have in mind here the dispute of the Westernizers with the Slavophiles (later, narodniks) and also the model discussion of the 1920s. Then, as today, arguments were raised about the threat of colonialization by Western capital,[32] and collective ownership was seen as a safeguard that would make penetration more difficult; moral dilemmas were pointed out by the advocates of introducing capitalist relations in a deep crisis and with awareness of the social costs of such a transformation (before the social benefits became visible).[33]

This striking continuity of regional dilemmas and the constantly reappearing topics of discussion were already evident earlier. Moshe Levin noted these things when he wrote about the discussions of Soviet economists in the 1960s.[34] Today these similarities are even more striking. Paradoxically, even the importance of the so-called peasant question is repeated: the necessity for building political alliances with groupings representing peasant interests modifies conceptions of economic policy—both the government's version and the opposition's.[35] Other similarities of the present discussion between populists and globalists and the discussion of the "left" of the 1920s with the supporters of Nikolay Bukharin (and with Bukharin himself) are:

- The initially small differences on economic questions (more on the accents than questioning the general direction of changes, such as the role of the state or the type of guarantees of "equal chances" for the state sector under the conditions of New Economic Policy) quickly deepened and the polarization of positions became ever more clear. The reasons—then as well as now—lie in the political system, which leaves no place for factions to operate legally (and hence also no place for mediatory actions). In this situation, in order to survive, a faction must become the dominant line, destroying the others.

- In the course of the discussion all economic questions became politicized; through the radicalization of positions each of the factions built up its identity. Labels began to dominate over the substantive context of positions, and even with similar views on some questions (e.g., threats from the bureaucratic apparatus), an alliance became impossible: vide Trotsky's famous statement that he would not fight against Stalin from rightist (Bukharin's) positions.[36]

• Finally, then as well as now, in spite of a polarization of theoretical positions, the urgency of real problems (the budget deficit, inflation) brings the representatives of both factions close together on current issues. This also applies to many practical problems that are being discussed today in Eastern Europe by governments and their opposition. Remember that the pressure of immediate problems and the interest of the administrative apparatus (minimizing uncertainty caused, they thought, by the market, and maximizing control over resources) brought an end to the New Economic Policy. On the whole the ideologists of the "left" did not support the administrative methods that were used. They wanted only to create conditions enabling the state sector to compete with the private sector (which today is again the basic argument of the populists).[37]

Looking at the debate going on inside reformatory circles in the power elite (concerning the manner—and possibility—of introducing capitalist mechanisms into real socialism) it is worth emphasizing that the problem of social actors of market-type reforms keeps coming up. What is more, it comes up in the same context, in connection with the identity of the reforming elite—that is, the problem of who will be the elite in the reformed system. Because the necessity for reform is determined by the "theoretical interest," and the historial subjects interested in its continuation will appear only *after* ownership changes (e.g., the *nomenklatura* as owners, before which some of the more idealistic reformers recoil), peasants are beginning to be seen as the protobase of the reform. The latter are closest to the market orientation, though they also think partially in statist terms: vide the fight over parity of incomes guaranteed by the state. Such a shift in the vision of their own "social base" leads to a crisis of identity for people who previously perceived themselves as the "left." One of the attempts to overcome this crisis is the notion of "agrosocialism." Here is a statement by one of its supporters;[38] some elements of such reasoning are characteristic also of Yeltsin and Gorbachev:

"Real socialism"...came into existence thanks to the accession of the peasant masses and functioned largely at their cost. None the less, in this political system a gradual emancipation, above all an intellectual one, took place of the peasants, who through masses of their most able and active members fed the ranks of the intelligentsia, or, to put it more precisely—constituted from their own body a group of neo-intellectuals, who naturally differ from the traditional intelligentsia with its genealogy in the gentry and middle class. These are the basic facts. . . . These facts make possible a "third road" that I would call 'agrosocialism." In order to give a somewhat accurate description of this "third road," one would have to make a thorough analysis of the ethoses functioning in our society, especially of the ethos of most of the society, that is, of the peasants. Let us recall that when the war ended 80 percent of Poles were residents of the countryside. Even today countryfolk make up 40 percent of the citizens, and 80 percent of the workers—in the first and second generation (including Wałęsa)—are migrants from the countryside. Nowadays "new intellectuals" of peasant origin are dominant in positions of authority. . . . The peasant ethos also differs fundamentally from the nobleman's ethos of combat, the burgher's ethos of profit, and the worker's ethos of work. The ethos of labor is bound up with functioning in direct contact with nature, in small groups. . . . A fundamental element of this ethos is pragmatism understood as taking account of realities ("you can't fool the land") and such features as tenacity, patience, resistance to setbacks. The complete emancipation of this ethos should result in its sublimation, expressing itself in the spread of protective attitudes. . . . The organic process taking place in our country, and in the ambit of "real socialism," is a process of the total emancipation and sublimation of the rural ethos. What will be the form of the political system that emerges from this process? This probably will be a system based on different forms of ownership (small: private, medium: cooperative and communal, large: society-state) and institutions of one's "mates" [meaning that these institutions are one's own but not necessarily self-governed—they can be highly centralized: such an understanding of freedom as one's own sphere dominated in Solidarity—J.S.].

What is striking in this attempt to define the identity of party reformers is the rejection of the traditional Marxist philosophy of history—not so much by rejecting the category of the a priori progressive proletariat (is this an effect of the shock of the rejection of the Communist party by the workers?) as by giving up all thinking in categories of the philosophy of history in favor of categories from the world of ethics and culture.

The second fascinating element in the statements quoted here—statements made in the opinion-making circles that the authorities pay heed to (ones that supply them with expert's reports and time- and labor-saving expedients)—is the manner of justifying the necessity for introducing capitalist solutions into socialism. Paradoxically, these arguments are close to the traditional rhetoric of the "left." The manner of linking up this tradition with the vision of transformation is fascinating. I think the materials analyzed here (interviews conducted during a discussion organized by Col. S. Kinatkowski for party intellectuals in their thirties and forties) are just as important for understanding the mentality of party reformers of the 1980s as the statements collected in T. Toranski's book *Oni* (They), which describes the way of reasoning of Stalinists (who are today in their late seventies).

A striking feature of the rhetoric of party reformers is the continual use (as in the "dogmatic" times, the late 1940s and 1950s) of a peculiar dialectic and conception of the "objective laws of history" (except that now they read differently). Hence the necessity for political and ownership changes is justified as follows.

● The *borrowings are two-sided* (the chief merit of socialism is its influence on capitalism; in other words, we take from a capitalism that we ourselves have shaped): "Both types of systems . . . incorporated universal features and solutions . . . both of them can take positive examples from each other. For decades the capitalist countries have been carefully following socialist experiments and have accepted some of them. Now it is our turn to learn from the capitalists. The principle is simple: what is good for man is also good for socialism—even if it comes from hell."[39]

● Change is an *"objective necessity"*: "The rules of the market economy or political democracy have an older pedigree than capitalism and the use of them in this system should not limit their usefulness for the next one . . . what is recognized as 'capitalistic' is simply the result of recognizing objective laws and principles that are independent of the political system. Where the recognition and respect of these principles is involved, there is no problem of rivalry or the 'displacement of the socialistic by the capitalistic.'"[40]

• This is a *breakthrough that eliminates the effects of the previous breakthrough*; "progress" is interpreted in categories of the *continuity* of civilization: "Progress requires taking into consideration the advances of previous systems. . . . Rejecting the legacy of capitalism must lead to a crisis of socialism. Yet wiping out this legacy leads to regression. This is an objective law of development."[41] And from another statement: "Stalin rejected this law; and not having his own, positive conception of socialism, he recognized that socialism must be the exact opposite of capitalism."[42] Note: Imputed to Stalin here is what Alan Besancon already accused Lenin of.

Besides this continuity of rhetoric, however, which today is used in the service of new goals, there are also elements of rejecting certain themes from the past: Hence there are sharp attacks against the a priori superiority of socialism. One of the interviewers says, "Socialism in and of itself is no value—it is necessary only in so far as it becomes useful for the survival and life satisfaction of wider circles than in capitalism."[43]

A neccessity for departure from revolutionary "creativity" (Hoyecian constructivism) also is expressed. Development is supposed to be "organic." ("A normal tailor sews a suit to fit the customer. A mad tailor cuts the customer to fit the suit . . . changes are overcoming the barbaric, essentially mad way of ramming the society into discredited political forms and replacing this procedure with a civilized, normal, isolated, evolutionary, reformatory adaptation of the forms of social life to new social needs."[44]

The criticism of the way of reasoning of Stalinists that is formulated today by party ideologists of the period of transformation also goes deeper. Some of the criticisms are:

• hypostatizing concepts: "In the world today the traditional paradigms of 'capitalistic' and 'socialistic' have lost all connection with reality";[45]

• reasoning in dichotomous categories ("private" versus "social" ownership, "spontaneous" versus "guided" processes), whereas in reality there are numerous intermediate forms. What is more, they are permanent, not "temporary" or "incomplete," as they are called by the advocates of dichotomous visions (from various political camps);[46]

• fundamentalism: the belief that "pure" (polar) types of social relations in some sense are better than "intermediate" types, and hence that social relations should be "improved" (read: transformed into one of the polar forms).[47] I call this way of reasoning in politics taxonomic radicalism (the striving toward pure models), which is rather common among leftist (and rightist) ideologues of the older generation;

• totalism: in other words, "the belief that all types of human actions are connected with each other in an unmistakable way, and if this 'unmistakableness' is absent, a 'contradiction' appears that requires 'resolution.'"[48]

The supporters of transformation also use practical arguments. Hence it is asserted that "competition with capitalist forms will aid socialist forms, which hitherto have operated in a vacuum and in an incubator of isolation." And further: "Experience has shown that gaining advantages for the socialist sector with administrative methods and the elimination of other sectors brings harm . . . to socialism and the society." "The socialist sector becomes sluggish."[49]

Finally, the experts and ideologues of transformation from the ruling camp are aware that "the 'capitalist' institutions installed in real socialism are still only the appearances of capitalism." "Today we have to do with many attempts to install in Poland elements similar to capitalist ones, but which have few features in common with capitalism or only some inessential features . . . most of the economic institutions in our country that think they are capitalistic would not survive more than a few days there . . . this is the result of culling out from one cohesive system."[50]

What, in their opinion, ought to be introduced from capitalism? In a nutshell: private ownership of the means of production, incomes from the title of ownership,[51] an active market,[52] recognition of the opposition as a legal element of the public scene,[53] parliament as the main scene of the political contest.[54] It is necessary to "reject socialism as the ideology of the state and reduce it to the role of one of many political orientations."[55]

How to do this? One should "create local capital [a patriotic justification of political capitalism?—J.S.]. Otherwise we are threatened with economic dependency on abroad."[56]

In their opinion, what are the chief dangers? "The most important problem is to avoid economic dependency and what follows—political dependency on capitalist countries. We must always remember that he who has a strong economy has power (the experience of the 1970s)."[57] "Great stratification of the society will take place...polarization of opposites of wealth. Last year (*Polityka*, 18 March 1989) 61 percent of those employed earned less than the average monthly wage...40 percent of families live below the social minimum."[58]

They envision a feudal model of creating owners: "An old pattern is being repeated: royal land is being taken over by state officials (dukes, counts),[59] who regard their office as a title, but property as ancestral in nature." And the opposite argument on this question: "Notables are people with a function but without an occupation. . . . They will be absorbed by business not so that they can be effective there, but so that they will not stand in the way."[60]

On the strategy of the globalists, one opponent said, "Ideological confusion, collapse of the system of values."[61]

How do those concerned see the field of political forces within the power system—in which they themselves are actors? Here is one of the responses:

The procapitalist [globalist—J.S.] current coexists with an important faction in the PUWP that of late has been gaining ever greater influence, which sees hope of retaining the dominant role of the economic and administrative apparatus (the *nomenklatura*) in concluding a "pact" with part of the Solidority opposition. The natural ally of this faction will be the opposition that bases itself on the prospect of "freedom of actors," efficient administration on the basis of a "consensus of elites," and limiting the unproductive social consumption fund in order to reduce the "overprotective function of the state."[62]

And further: other opinions about the faction of globalists (linking up with the apparatus) were expressed by another opponent: "The political flirting of the PUWP with the social right, while at the same time (at least until recently) fighting sharply against the noncommunist left, has put the Polish left on the defensive.[63] ...Increasing pauperization...causes an increase of populist tendencies."[64] Supporters of the populist faction speak about the "restoration of capitalism as the preparation of a better stepping-stone to further socialist development. Here one can cite an idea of Marx's: to draw back in order to make a better jump forward.[65] "Though it is not called such directly, this variant is the real current of the Polish reconstruction movement" (as exemplified by M. Krajewski, M. Gulczynski). "The revival of elements of capitalism and intermediate forms does not create dangers, but conditions for the formation of a socialism better than the original version. Where state capitalism comes into being [temporarily?—J.S.], it should function in the interest of and under the control [political—J.S.] of people of work."[66]

In conclusion I present (in the form of a long quotation from the collection of texts discussed here) a vision of this state capitalism that is different both from the realities of political capitalism discussed in chapter 2 and from the liberal model of privatization that limits the role of the state in the economy. It seems that this vision was the target program of the Political Bureau in 1989 under the leadership of Rakowski (with two new secretaries from the populist faction and the economic secretary, M. Święcicki, defending the vision of ownership in the form of holdings, which also would be created by the state (see chapter 2), and finally with newly co-opted members of the party apparatus). Note well that, in the opinion of its authors, the proposal of "state capitalism" is directed both at "peripheral socialism" and "peripheral capitalism," as they call the program of the globalists, which, in their opinion, has insufficient guarantees far strengthening the role of the state in the economy. The greatest danger that they see is "an alliance of peripheral socialism with peripheral capitalism"[67] (e.g., in the form of political capitalism described in chapter 2, which will be harnessed to the colonial structures).

The strategy of building modern state capitalism in the interest of and under the control of workers assumes that:
  • in the economy we will make use of carefully studied and suitably adapted experiences and mechanisms of modern capitalism in all areas of economic life: production, trade, banking and fiscal activity, and foreign commerce;
  • in the reformed economy prices will be objectively shaped by market mechanisms;
  • capital will be under social control, which is crucial for development, and its functionaries will have no less power than modern managers and will behave like modern capitalists, which will be the basic criterion for selecting the cadre directing the economy;
  • in addition to pluralism of social and private ownership, pluralism of ownership in the social sector will become a fact in a double sense: (1)

as pluralism of various kinds of ownership (ownership of the Treasury, banks, workers' councils, municipalities, cooperatives, ownership of federations and associations, etc.); and (2) as pluralism of various forms of management (brigade system, workers' council, trusteeship, company, etc.); this is a solution that will ensure mobility and dynamic development of the social sector and at the same time will create a mechanism to counter state-controlled and bureaucratic totalitarianism;

- a strong workers' self-management sector will be portioned out;

- state bank capital will appear, which in symbiosis with big, modern industrial-productive and commercial capital will make up state financial capital and become a new center capable of steering and overseeing the policy of Poland's structural, technological, and technical development;

- we must be aware that without a suitable policy of structural development we will waste every effort, even the most efficient and honest one, of individual workers and enterprises;

- conditions will be created for the mobility of capital, for its socially beneficial shifts;

- in addition to income from work, income from capital will become recognized, also in the state sector (ownership of the Treasury, a cooperative, a municipality, etc.), and both kinds of incomes will be socially controlled and regulated:

- The banking system will develop under the control of workers, thanks to the socialization and capitalization of hitherto nationalized funds: housing, insurance, retirement, and so on. These funds should not be the property of the state, because the state wastes them and steals them. They should be taken from the hands of the state and put under the control of their owners, shareholders of banks, and financial associations and holdings, which would buy shares in the most modern, profitable sectors of the economy. This would create the foundations of a capital market. Flows of capital will speed up the development of modern sectors of the economy, supply credits to build a new society by younger, more energetic and productive generations. The measure of humanism of a given society is its attitude toward old people. In the new society they will become rentiers, owners of financial capital, living from constantly increasing interest revenue, multiplied by the work of the young, productive part of the society;

- social but competent control (chiefly by trade unions, workers' councils, the movement of partnership brigades, professional associations, etc.) will be created, and this control will extend to economic mechanisms, leading to the formation of a system of political verification of the economic process—so that the system could function effectively in the interest and under the control of workers;

• a modern political system will arise based on socialist pluralism, i.e., on a system in which at least two parties exist with a definite socialist orientation, capable of governing the country in turn; (1) pluralism in socialism will be created; i.e., it will be possible for nonsocialist parties to operate, capable of entering into a government coalition or being a parliamentary-constitutional opposition; (2) opposition within the party may appear, or a coalition of the opposition outside the actual government coalition may form, so that a change of the leading party could take place; (3) elections to the Seym will be elections between at least two programs, two election lists of parties with a clearly socialist orientation; (4) the socialist parties can form coalitions, and then in elections people will vote for such a coalition list.

These are—in our opinion—the initial slogans of a strategic conception of Poland's development toward modern socialism. We do not want an artifically contrived system, however, but one that grows out of real experiences and is socially better and economically more efficient than developed capitalism. Such a socialism will become a reality only when the young part of the society takes over the helm of the state.

The long quotations presented here are not regarded as intellectual revelations, but as characteristic of changes in the consciousness of the party elite during the period of transformation. I preferred to quote this document word for word instead of summarizing it in order to illustrate the language used by the power elite in speaking about the changes taking place: they justify the changes while retaining the previous ideological rhetoric. The authors of the statement are people of the middle and young generation of party intellectuals and sometimes are a reference group for the party leadership, even though some of them are no longer in the party (e.g., the former activists of the horizontal structures of 1980 and 1981). The argument cited here is repeated at meetings of the party leadership with its apparatus, with functionaries of departments crucial for stability (the army, police), and finally, in the internal party debate between the two factions of reformers described here and in contacts with communist parties of other countries of the bloc. As the program of reforms is made more precise, the differences noted in these statements deepen, which is an essential element of the breakup of the new center. Understanding the reasoning of these people makes it easier to grasp the pattern of thinking of the people who now support Gorbachev in the Soviet Union.

The Opposition: Crisis of Identity after Legalization

August 1989

The legalization of Solidarity and the entry of part of the opposition onto the official political scene (legislative activity in the Seym, participation in forming a new government) caused a serious identity crisis in opposition circles. The new situation not only laid bare the lack of a program (and difficulties in moving from protest to joint rule) but also the lack of clarity as to who really is the social base of the opposition. These doubts are intensified by a clear hiatus between the real political geography that was revealed during the elections of June 1989[68] and the symbolic workers' base of 1980 and 1981, which today remains indifferent and deaf to the calls of the opposition to desist from egalitarian strikes.[69] Already in the first weeks of the deliberations of the new parliament with the participation of the opposition, in tackling concrete problems (such as indexation of wages, the state budget, introducing "market mechanisms" in agriculture) it became clear that the society is divided and that the representation of "everybody's" interests (as in protest situations) is not possible.

What is more, when the opposition enters the orbit of real politics (with very limited freedom of maneuver, chiefly on account of Poland's materials barriers and indebtedness) there is an unintended *effect of continuity* between successive ruling teams—even if the opposition is in power. For this does not change the essence of the dilemmas and limitations, and as a result the choices of successive teams are similar[70] (especially when material limits exist), in spite of different initial declarations and different systems of values and final visions.

Another essential element of the identity crisis of the legalized opposition is the ever clearer discrepancy between the egalitarian trade-union orientation (rejecting political "wheeling and dealing" and joint responsibility for the economy) and the orientation of a quasi-political party (Citizens' Parliamentary Club). This is accompanied by a conflict between the structures corresponding to these orientations, most clearly in the stance of the National Commission of Solidarity, which calls for the abolition of the Citizens' Committees.[71]

This discrepancy is all the more dangerous in that it is not entirely clear where the decision-making center of the legalized opposition is: Solidarity's National Commision (NC), Wałęsa and his circle, the Citizens' Parliamentary Club (CPC), its Presidium, the group from the opposition participating in the Committee for Understanding,[72] or the combined presidia of the CPC and the NC.[73]

The identity crisis of the legalized opposition also is linked with the hitherto unknown problem of joint responsibility for the future of the country and divisions due to different approaches to solving this problem: from "being exclusively an opposition" (not entering the government, but participating in the Committee for Understanding, where the real decisions would be made) up to "dyarchy" (the other extreme of creating a government by the opposition in a coalition with the United Peasants' and Democratic Parties). Other divisions concern the degree to which this government should be a trade-union government, one that represents the interests of wage earners and not the interests of various types of new owners of the means of production. The vision of a trade-union government, which seems close to the notion of Prime Minister Mazowiecki, contains unavoidable contradictions, while his vision of "appealing to public opinion in such a case" (interview in *Gazeta Wyborcza*, 22 August 1989) does not seem very promising politically. These contradictions are of two kinds. First, a contradiction with the program of the reforms, which require a branch and ownership restructuralization of the economy as well as a stabilization policy that in many cases will be painful for workers. Second, a contradiction with the nature of the new coalition that made it possible to form a Solidarity government and is based on an understanding with the peasants' party (with simultaneous fundamental differences of interests between the city and the countryside as to the manner of distributing the costs of the crisis and the reforms). Both of these contradictions might make the new coalition a shaky one and create dilemmas in introducing market reforms.

An essential element of the present identity crisis in the opposition is the problem of continuity. A clear break has taken place from the formula of Solidarity as a social movement. This formula closely linked trade-union activity per se with a peculiar understanding of politics and contained a moment of mass mobilization, with clear accents of a cultural revolution.[74]

Today we are observing a clear separation of trade-union work from political activity, which is now understood differently and is engaged in by professional politicians, who often have several years of experience as opposition activists. There is also clear pressure for demobilization (abstinence from strikes) rather than for activity at the plant level. This is part of the first version of a Solidarity government, which is represented by a political current of the opposition (Michnik, Jacek Kuroń, Bronislaw Gieremek) that is aware that perhaps a government formed by the opposition will be forced to suspend for a time the activity of all trade unions—including Solidarity—in the name of the reforms and stabilization. This policy of demobilization—together with disbelief in the durability of the changes now taking place,[75] the lack of space for responsible trade-union activity in conditions of a severe economic crisis, and the exodus of Solidarity intellectuals of 1980 and 1981 to other activities—is the reason for the striking sluggishness and lack of enthusiasm in setting up trade-union structures.[76]

Also contributing to social apathy is the special climate in which the transformations are taking place. For the actual assumption of part of the power by the opposition is occurring with the acquiescence of a president associated with the Communist regime (Jaruzelski) and with the playing up by television of signs of satisfaction of part of the previous establishment (such as the hands raised in triumph by Wałęsa, M. Malinowski, and J. Jóźwiak as they left the offices of the president to the accompaniment of the friendly greetings of the departing Kiszczak). The dramatic struggle for power is taking place in the convention of parliamentary voting, institutional horse trading, and discussions behind closed doors and not in an open confrontation understandable to and perceived by the fundamentalistically oriented masses. For tactical reasons the hidden drama of the enture operation is carefully hushed up by the interested parties. But in turn the lack of this drama (and the material limitations about which I wrote earlier) make it difficult to create the feeling of *discontinuity*, which is indispensable for electrifying the society. There is a possibility that the maneuver will be interpreted as a shift among the various elites, with increasing tensions and resentments toward all elite, regardless of their origin. This is promoted by the increasing threat of poverty and the increasing anarchy of economic life and by the peculiar "trash of understanding"[77] that is flooding the official press. Like the ideological pap of the Communist party in the past and the moralistic rhetoric of Solidarity later, this "trash" makes it more difficult to express the nature of social conflicts. A secretary of the party losing power calls those who call for countermeasures "stiff-necks."[78] A Communist party commentator speaks about a "more normal situation, though unpleasant for the party."[79] In the consciousness of the man in the street this debases the importance of what is taking place, and it is happening in the name of creating the impression that the society is finally "on its own."[80] The surrealistic impression of continuity is deepened still further by the tone of communiques from Moscow, where commentaries on the nomination of Mazowiecki as prime minister stress the continuity in this way of "the broad coalition of all proreformatory forces," thereby—presumably for fear of repercussions in its own apparatus—covering up the loss of power by the Communist party (which obviously does not mean a loss of power by the former center of the prerogative state which is centered around the Committee for National Defense: Jaruzelski, Kiszczak, Gdula). Also, the former *nomenklatura*'s adept adaptation to the new circumstances (managing directors are leaving the Communist party[81] and keeping or improving their position through political capitalism) creates the impression "on the bottom" that nothing really is changing.

The surrealistic impression of continuity in change is also coupled with a striking similarity, in some respects, of the present political class to the previous ruling teams. In particular this concerns thinking in terms of state control on economic questions[82] and treating the law as an instrument of politics bent to present needs.[83]

As a note to the above, one can say that the rupture in the unity of European culture is the deepest in legal culture, and where the opposition seems to be on the same side as the previous ruling group. For both of them the decisive factor is not right but political convenience,[84] as in the recent experiments of "natural law, right" (contra formal law) used when Mazowiecki's government introduced lessons in religion in the schools without the necessary legal proceeding in parliament. One of the aims was to get Catholic Church support for Mazowiecki in his conflict with Wałęsa (August 1990). Yet one cannot fail to see that such a disrespectful attitude toward the law *facilitates* transformation (which is also the case, as I showed earlier, in the privatization of the state sector). To a certain degree this justifies the above-mentioned selective attitude toward the law that is demonstrated by the opposition. However, the consolidation of such an attitude (which is advanced by the complexity of the political and economic situation) would be very dangerous. Sometimes the opposition ignores legal regulations, and sometimes—using the tactic of a "paper revolution"—it calls for enforcing the rules of parliamentary democracy, which are based on governments of law. In the decisions of the "round table" the opposition consented that in the transition period it would treat the institutions created as a kind of phony, defective democracy. In turn the present change of position emphasizes the extralegal nature of the "round table" agreements; this argument, however, was used by the opposition only after the opposition had exhausted all the benefits that these agreements gave and in a moment when the Communist party began to reach out for such benefits (such as participation in forming a government, in spite of having lost the elections).

Generally speaking, the experiences of the prerogative state and the philosophy of law rooted in revolutionary legitimacy promote the breakthrough in the system. The "continuity in change" described above is irritating, but it is probably necessary because the agreements with an unclear legal status (and contacts in extraconstitutional structures) made it possible to move to a new situation. What is more, the past experiences of the ruling group, which taught it that the law is only a facade and everything depends on the balance of forces, dulled its vigilance. The first alarm was the breakup of the coalition, and then it was already too late, for the facade began to be treated by the political forces (outside the PUWP) as the *only reality*. Serious treatment of the institutions of the president and the parliament combined with refusal to listen to the entreaties of the Central Committee of the Communist party to all intents and purposes means an end of the "leading role" of the party. For there are no formal and legally guaranteed political instruments that could prevent the formation of a government without a prime minister from the Communist party (if this is what the president and the parliament want), while Moscow clearly regards the president (and the Committee for National Defense, and officials keeping the departments of the Ministry of Internal Affairs and Defense in the government) as sufficient guarantees that Poland will remain in the empire. That freedom of economic maneuver is limited not only by agreements with the U.S.S.R. and within the COMECON but also by the noncompetitiveness of the Polish economy in Western markets enhances this view. Hence "disloyalty" of the coalition (as it is called today in Communist party ranks)[85] and the opposition's tactic of a "paper revolution" sufficed to carry out—with the acquiescene of the faction of globalists (Jaruzelski, Orzechowski)[86]—a clear change in the system (under the fundamentalist rhetoric of continuity). All of this is taking place with both sides clearly tempted to use Leninist tactics: the Political Bureau headed by Rakowski would probably like to dissolve the Constituent Assembly (but how?), while the opposition is reaching for power without a program, without a clear base of social support, and with clear inclinations toward the role of a Leninist avant-garde.

A good test of traces of Leninism in the ex-opposition mentality is the attitude toward the present nonparliamentary opposition, which considers the following possibilities:

- to give this opposition the right to act, in spite of illegality;[87]

- to oust it from the political scene by creating political parties from above (with CPC deputies selected on the basis of loyalty to Wałęsa but representing different program options). Suggestions of such preemptive actions from above, which would create structures in competition with parties forming spontaneously at the grass-roots level, were made by J. Onyszkiewizc and A. Wielowiejski;[88]

- to co-opt part of the nonparliamentary opposition by bringing it into the work of the Citizens' Committees of lower levels in order to prepare future elections to the Seym together and, in the immediate future, elections to local self-government bodies;[89]

- to destroy it by discrediting it in the eyes of society or cutting it off from financial and physical (such as printing) resources.[90]

In this chapter I take up only some aspects of the multidimensional identity crisis in the legalized opposition: in particular, the dispute about the Citizens' Committees, which is a good illustration of the conflict between the trade-union and political segments of the opposition; and the identity dilemmas of the trade union Solidarity.

The problem of forming a government by the opposition (and discussions against this background) are presented in a separate section. For this problem is a good illustration of wider events on the political scene. Not without influence here are the earlier described factional divisions in the Communist party or tensions between the authorities of all parties (including Solidarity) and their parliamentary representatives. Also, the characteristic evolution of the position of Moscow (and differences of opinion in various segments and at various levels of the power apparatus) has wider implications for systemic transformations in all of Eastern Europe.

The Dispute about Citizens' Committees

The Citizens' Committees of Solidarity[91] were set up in order to prepare for the participation of the opposition in the elections to the Seym and Senate, a task that they performed with great enthusiasm and efficiency.[92] About two thousand Committees were formed in cities and communes as well as forty-nine Provincial Citizens' Committees. Some of them sprang up spontaneously (around parishes that since martial law have gathered many Solidarity activists and around Clubs of the Catholic Intelligentsia). Others were formed only at the call of Wałęsa's Citizens' Club or were even set up by the Central Election staff. The lack of democracy was justified by the necessity for haste, but not without conflicts over this issue. In some provinces two Citizens' Committees were formed under the sign of Solidarity (Łódź, Suwalki) because of deep divisions in the structures of the opposition.[93] The purpose of the Committees was to prepare lists of candidates for deputies, to conduct their election campaigns, and to organize the participation of the opposition in State Election Committees in order to control the course of the elections. In turn the four-man Election Staff appointed by Wałęsa's Citizens' Committee had the task of offering substantive and financial help to the Citizens' Committees of a lower level and also to mediate in local conflicts. This staff, however, quickly seized the initiative in determining the list of candidates by preparing the so-called national list of Solidarity, which contained names of candidates for deputies from which the Provincial Citizens' Committees could draw (later, from which they had to draw if they had no strong counterarguments). This list contained the members of Wałęsa's Citizens' Committee (including the members of the Election Staff) and also candidates put forward by the Temporary National Council of Farmers' Solidarity, economic associations, and the Chief Council of Attorneys— and a strong representation of lawyers working for the Catholic Episcopate. Missing were many names of opposition activists who, for various reasons,[94] were overlooked in the formation of Wałęsa's Citizens' Committee (even before the "round table" talks). The manner of drawing up the national list of Solidarity was criticized even within the Citizens' Committee.[95]

According to a member of the Election Staff, H. Wujec,[96] "at the initial meetings most of the regions stated that they had complete lists or clearly announced that they wanted to fill in the gaps with people from their own area. There were also those who from the outset cried: give us someone well-known..." (as in small cities like Chełm, Krosno). Soon, however, as H. Wujec continues, "drawing from the same pool became ever more common."[97] It should be added that between the first stage and this "soon" stretches a region of dramatic conflicts (with pressures on the local Committees and even attempts to dissolve them by members of the Staff or public condemnation when they refused to support a candidate from the national list).[98] These pressures and the shortage of sufficiently well-known candidates in their regions (along with a general lack of faith in the possibility of winning the elections)[99] were not the only reasons for drawing candidates from the national list. This was also furthered by local conflicts between various factions of the opposition, conflicts that often went back to the period of underground activity. These conflicts—and the rule that one candidate is put forward for one seat (allocated to the opposition as a result of the "round table" talks)—promoted taking someone from the outside.[100] In addition to conflicts between Citizens' Committees of various levels over putting up candidates, tensions appeared in this period with Farmers' Solidarity, which thought it had been given too few places on the list.[101]

The spectacular electoral success of Solidarity candidates was also a success of the Citizens' Committees: attendance at the polls and support for candidates of the opposition depended not so much on the power of local Solidarity trade-union structures as on the activity of the Citizens' Committees, and sometimes this success was the greatest where the trade union Solidarity to all intents and purposes did not exist.[102]

Most of the Citizens' Committees wanted to continue their activities[103] in various forms, from discussion clubs and bases of support for local deputies and senators to the embryos of a political party. Problems appeared, however, in finding a legal formula and financial sources and—what is more important—in a conflict with regional and national authorities of Solidarity, which had financed the Committees during the elections and had lent them its name. The fear of dyarchy appeared among trade-union organizers: in some regions the newly emerging trade-union organizations in plants registered themselves with the local Citizens' Committees and not with the regional trade-union authorities.[104]

In this situation the National Committee of Solidarity passed a resolution[105] to thank the Committees and disband them at the provincial level, where they were in competition with regional trade-union authorities, leaving them intact at the level of cities and communes—but without the name Solidarity and without trade-union financing. The task of these loose, local bodies was to be preparing future elections to regional self-government and to coordinate local public initiatives. After a stormy discussion,[106] fearing a conflict with the National Committee, Wałęsa's Citizens' Committee made a decision that went in the same direction, but which was couched in less drastic words. It proposed setting up a commission to prepare the future form of action of the committees (which for a time put off the conflict over this with the NC) and leaving the final decision to the trade-union authorities in individual regions.[107] The inconclusiveness of the statement of the Citizens' Committee increased the bitterness of the activists of the local Committees and clearly took the wind out of the sails of the newly emerging movement.

In press debates and during the deliberations of the National Committee and Wałęsa's Citizens' Committee, the following arguments were made for eliminating the Citizens' Committees:

- the fear that the Citizens' Committees would transform

themselves into a party structure on the lines of the British Labour Party;[108] that this would result in a rejection once and for all of the post-August formula of Solidarity that combines socio-occupational and political matters in one organization;[109]

• that the movement would split into a network of Committees dominated by intellectuals and the trade union Solidarity dominated by workers, which would slow down even more the formation of the union and impede its operations;[110]

• that a breach would take place in an organization using one name—Solidarity—and made up of such diverse elements.[111] This would be especially dangerous if the political current of Solidarity, working toward the formation of a government by the opposition, began to promote the reforms (introduction of market mechanisms, privatization) and techniques of stabilization (e.g., suspending all trade unions in the name of social peace). The sharpness of the conflict with the trade-union current and simultaneously the ambiguity resulting from the use of the name Solidarity by both currents could weaken the readiness for social activity, which was already smaller than in 1980 and 1981;[112]

• the desire to create a clear structure to which opposition deputies and senators would be responsible. The trade union should retain direct and exclusive influence on deputies, without the mediation of the Citizens' Committees, whose makeup is often fortuitous: "The voters voted for Solidarity";[113]

• the fear of dyarchy in regions, which would weaken the trade union;[114]

• the fear of continuing a bipolar situation, where all political actions and social activity are taking place in the name of Solidarity. Retaining the Citizens' Committees as bodies gathering various political groupings, including part of the nonparliamentary opposition, would blur such diversity.[115] In such a situation Solidarity's reach for power would lead to surrealistic situations. The use by all elements of the name Solidarity would impede the development of a civil society[116] and the establishment of their own political identity by individual groupings. "This would be Bolshevism";[117]

• on account of their political orientation the Citizens' Committees of Solidarity are not "marching in step."[118]

And here are the arguments in favor of retaining the Citizens' Committees:

• their elimination would mean wasting a great potential of activity and organizational talents. In places where it is difficult to form a strong trade union (in the countryside, towns without industry, small plants) the Committees are the only place for social activity;[119]

• the existence of the Citizens' Committes and their electoral success plucks up people's courage and even promotes the establishment of trade-union structures in plants;[120]

• the Citizens' Committees could become the base of a movement in support of elections to organs of local self-government; work in this direction ought to be started now in order to avoid situations such as—for lack of time and preparation—occurred in elections to the Seym. Stripping the Committees of the name Solidarity or, as Gieremek suggests, suspending the decision on their fate until a special committee could settle this matter would destroy their impetus, discourage activists, and to all intents and purposes would mean their end;[121]

• this would destroy the information base for deputies and senators, which is especially dangerous in a situation when many of them (from the national list) do not come from the region they represent and do not know its problems;[122]

• disbanding the Committees would increase social passivity and check the development of citizens' initiatives. The very fact that Solidarity candidates competed with representatives of opposition circles who did not enter into "Wałęsa's team" (and who lost) contributed to the breakup of many political circles and the bitterness of their activists. Abolishing the Committees could lead to a further exodus or activists;[123]

• with the closing down of the Committees the intellectual base for trade-union activities in plants would be erased. The belief that activists of the Committees would return to activity in the plants— after whetting their appetites for public activity on a wider scale— is illusory;[124]

• in this way a movement would be wiped out that could be the seeds of a civil society, making possible the real replacement of the *nomenklatura* and "taking over the state";[125]

• their elimination would mean stuffing Solidarity into the same fundamentalist rhetoric rejecting any political mediation as in 1980 and 1981, whereas both activists and the situation have changed and "one never enters the same river twice."[126]

This debate ended with a compromise. In some cities (Wrocław, Warsaw) Municipal Citizens' Committees were formed, which continued activities without violating the decision of the Solidarity's National Committee (forbidding structures at the regional and provincial level). These Committees hold regular meetings (of the nature of regional councils)[127] and have the ambition—now without using the name Solidarity—of coordinating actions of the nonparliamentary opposition as well (e.g., the Warsaw suggestion of convening a Congress of the opposition).[128] In small localities, however, the Committees disbanded and disappeared from the public scene, often in spite of the protests of Farmers' Solidarity, for which such a base is indispensable and whose representatives were not invited to the meeting of the NEC at which the decision to abolish the Committees was made.[129]

The identity crisis of Solidarity after its legalization (though it put off attempts to articulate this crisis until the Second Congress of Solidarity)[130] combined with the monopolistic aspirations of regional trade-union authorities to put an end to the social movement before it really began to act and after its first spectacular success.

The Dilemmas of Solidarity as a Trade Union

The reasons for the present passivity and very slow revival of the trade-union structures of Solidarity in places of work are multiple and complex. The most important of them is the present lack of faith (so powerful in 1980 and 1981) that one's own union is a panacea for the difficult economic situation and that any trade union at all can provide a cure for the economy.[131] Ever more widely perceived is the collision between reformatory and egalitarian activity (and the awareness that owing to its very nature—wage demands, the plant-branch perspective—a trade union may even become a barrier to the reforms). This is especially the case when it is radicalized in its trade-union activity by competition with another trade union such as the All Polish Association of Trade Unions.

Reasons for the lack of enthusism include:

• the fact that the trade union is being formed from above, so to speak, by administrative methods, without the experience of fighting for the union that brings together the crew (as in August 1980). The present strikes are chiefly quite unheroic extortions of wage hikes that are criticized by the National Committee of Solidarity. Missing is the solemn atmosphere of 1980. At that time this atmosphere was coupled with the euphoria of discovering values in oneself that are worth defending (such as dignity) and solidarity with others. Today the taste of victory is absent (paradoxically, in spite of the opposition's real and successful reach for power). For this is not accompanied by the impression of real control over anything: the crisis and anarchy of economic life are deepening continually. There is also no vision of how to overcome the crisis, except nebulous expectations that now the West will help.[132] At the same time the press and TV are creating the impression that everything is taking place with the acquiescence of General Jaruzelski and Moscow ("we have agreed to the Finlandization of Poland and Hungary.").[133] Everything is drowning in the "trash of understanding," blurring conflicts of interests and differences so evident in places of work (based to an ever greater extent—owing to the anarchy of the transition period—on client-clique relations). What is more, the sense of victory is being spoiled by the migration of the *nomenklatura* from the Communist party to the private sector, often by changing power over goods in short supply into basic capital (see chapter 2).

The formation of the union is also made difficult by the outflow of energetic people to other forms of activity, such as the parliament, Citizens' Committees, publishing houses, political parties, clubs, the private sector.

There are also no strong and mobilizing accents of a cultural revolution as in 1980, with its educational actions and plant bulletins edited by workers. Then Solidarity had a monopoly on criticism, but today the official press is full of it and words have become devalued.

Finally, there is no chance of a quick "trade-union success"[134] in the plants. On the contrary: putting central decisions (such as indexation) into concrete form may only worsen what was decided upon at the "round table" (e.g., there are no funds for indexing wages in the proportion of 80 percent of the inflation rate). What is more, an agreement must be reached in the plant on indexation with trade-union activists belonging to the All Polish Association of Trade Unions. It was impossible to reach such an agreement at the "round table," and the conflict was thrown onto the shoulders of Solidarity structures at the plant level. This leads to a situation in which workers in the plant ask What have we really gained? For it turns out that there are no binding decisions, and their legal status is unclear. At the same time, those shop-floor Solidarity activists who, heeding Solidarity's National Committee, stopped their crews from striking, found their authority undermined. For as it turned out, in the Seym the Citizens' Parliamentary Club supported the formula of general indexation (also for those who on their own—by striking—had won wage increases, in defiance of the stance of the National Committee). Paradoxically, the same National Committee later on changed its opinion on indexation (which before was radicalized by competition with the populist All Polish Association of Trade Unions) and put pressure on the Citizens' Parliamentary Club[135] to limit annexation.

Activists at the plant level are also complaining about the lack of help from activists of the regional and national levels, who are absorbed with politics and personal rivalries. For instance, no one from the national authorities of the union came to the first all-Polish training session of Solidarity trade-union activists. The lack of preparation for trade-union activity (e.g., in labor law and labor safety) and the shortage of trade-union funds are more reasons for the lack of enthusiasm in reactivating Solidarity structures at the plant level. And finally, Solidarity set high membership dues (1 percent of wages), while the OPLL does not charge dues to its members and has considerable financial resources.[136]

The above situation is attended by divisions and disputes over the conception of Solidarity and an ever clearer breach between the majority loyal to the National Committee (but passive) and the active minority gathered around Working Groups. Attempts at mediation have not been successful.[137] Opponents of Wałęsa and the National Committee often refer to things that cause the real dissatisfaction of crews (the disengagement of NC activists from matters of vital concern to workers for the sake of engaging in politics; the lack of a plan of action; the lack of democracy in the trade union, since some of the regional leaders were appointed by Wałęsa).[138] Also emphasized, and irritating to many, is Wałęsa's "bossy" style (also demonstrated by the Citizens' Parliamentary Club).[139] Wałęsa in turn accuses his opponents of "betrayal."[140] All of this furthers the passivity and demobilization of rank-and-file members. The rise of "neo-Solidarity" (as Wałęsa's opponents call solidarity, legalized in 1989) is accompanied by a peculiar atmosphere of collectivism, where loyalty is more important than initiative.[141]

The consequence of the above is a very slow increase in membership in the union. For example, in Zamość (a provincial city) fifty-two plant committees are active with a total of 1200 members (in spite of the fact that this was a region of great electoral activity). There are cases of people repudiating their membership declarations—people are afraid to have trade-union membership recorded in their personnel files and the atmosphere is reminiscent of the situation before 13 December 1981. In the Slaśko-Dąbrowski region (mining, metallurgy) there are about 600 committees (in 1980 there were 1000). At that time 80 to 85 percent of the crew belonged to Solidarity; today, 10 to 30 percent. The Masurian Lakes region (like Łódź and Szczecin) is divided: about 8000 people belong in the entire region. In Częstochowa there are about 15,000 members—considerably fewer than in 1980 (in one plant alone—the Bierut Steel Works—1000 of the 12,000 employees belonged to Solidarity in 1980). These statistics are from *Gazeta Wyborcza*.[142]

The Government Crisis and Its Dynamics

August–September 1989
The history of the government crisis in Poland is brief but exceptionally important. Not only did this crisis end with the appointment of a person from opposition circles to the post of prime minister, but during this crisis and evolution took place in the assumptions on which the political system is supposed to rest in the first phase of the breakthrough in the system. What is more,

the reaction of Moscow to such an evolution was "tested" (for use by other countries of Eastern Europe).

The political agreement of the "round table" turned out to be not only not precise enough (especially on the question of forming a government) but also out of date after the defeat of the Communist party at the polls and the breakup of the coalition around this party. The formation of a new coalition on the appeal of Wałęsa[143] and the acceptance, though with numerous limitations, of the principle that "who won the elections forms the government" considerably outstripped the pace of the political changes that had been assumed by all participants of the "round table." What is interesting is that the dynamics of this evolution surprised not only observers but also the actors on the political scene.[144] For this evolution was propelled by unappreciated and, on the surface, secondary factors.

One such factor was the tensions appearing in all political parties (including Solidarity) between their leaderships and their deputies in the Seym. These tensions were connected with the fight over where the decision-making center should be located and resulted in the leaderships and clubs outbidding one another in the radicalism of their proposals. Wałęsa, through his proposal of a new coalition, restored his top position, which clearly had been lost to the Citizens' Parliamentary Club. A continuation of this process is the working out of the political platform of the new coalition in the triangle of the National Committee of Solidarity, the Secretariat of the Democratic party, and the Secretariat of the United Peasants' party,[145] and not in the clubs of deputies. In turn the rapid and surprising consent of the leaderships of the United Peasants' and the Democratic parties to the proposal to break the coalition with the Communist party and form one with Solidarity also can be explained by tensions between the parties and their clubs of deputies. The entry onto the political scene of the chairman of the United Peasants' party, Malinowski, in a new role (at the call of Wałęsa) saved him from political death, for some members of the rural party and the Parliamentary Club of this party were calling for his resignation. A similar, though perhaps not as severe, situation also appeared in the Democratic party. In turn this "saving" by Wałęsa of the existing leadership of the United Peasants' party gave rise to protests on the part of Farmers'

Solidarity[146] and undermined the unity of his base of social support. For in order to recapture the political initiative (with his staff)[147] from the Citizens' Parliamentary Club, Wałęsa sacrificed the political identity of Farmers' Solidarity, which had formed in opposition to the United Peasants' party in its present shape. However, when Wałęsa approached political activists from the old establishment (Malinowski was a former Marshal of the Seym; J. Jóźwiak, a minister in the Z. Messner government), this largely determined the positive reaction of President Jaruzelski: the political risk of the new situation seemed to be less than would be the case if Wałęsa formed a coalition with radicals from the clubs of deputies.

The second factor was an identity crisis in all parties, once again including Solidarity. The latter had to react to the election of General Jaruzelski as president (with the indirect support of deputies from the opposition)[148] and respond to the complaints of the voters that nothing had changed after the election victory. In turn the Democratic and United Peasants' parties—indicating readiness to leave the coalition with the Communist party[149]— waged a fight for their image in the eyes of future voters. And in the future elections no parties would be guaranteed a specific number of seats in advance. What is more, the Communist party several times reminded the other two parties that their deputies were in the parliament only thanks to the Communist party.[150] This warning was supposed to hold the coalition together, but it had the opposite effect and only hastened the fight of these parties to mark out their own political profiles. This was especially so when serious competitors appeared among the emerging parties, competitors who appeal for support to the same social groups. It is no accident that Malinowski responded positively to Wałęsa's appeal on the day after the formation of a new peasants' party that goes back to the traditions of the Polish Peasants' party, and during the "peasants' round table" that had the aim of uniting various factions of the peasants' movement (but no longer under his leadership). Similar anxieties were experienced by the representation of the United Peasants' party in the Seym and by the Democratic party, whose place in the political spectrum (appealing to private trade and the handicrafts) easily could be taken in future elections by newly formed parties (labor, liberals, etc.).

A third factor influencing the dynamics of the government crisis was the intensifying conflict in the Communist party between the faction of populists (co-opted by Rakowski to the politburo together with—which sounds surrealistic—representatives of the party apparatus) and the faction of globalists, whose influence in the Central Committee he removed in the course of personnel changes at the Thirteenth Plenum.[151] The surprising support of the Club of Deputies of the Communist party for Wałęsa's initiative ("the Club receives with satisfaction the wish of the opposition to take joint responsibility for the future of the country"),[152] which came during the same time when in the Central Committee words were spoken about "breaking the 'round-table' agreements, the entry of the opposition into the intense phase of the fight for power, treachery of the former partners of the coalition,"[153] can be explained by the fact that the globalist Orzechowski heads the Club. A sort of catalyst here could have been the attacks on the Club of Deputies of the Communist party by some of the new members of the politburo[154] and the attempt by Rakowski to execute the "leading role of the party" and recommend to the Club the candidacy of General Kiszczak for prime minister even before President Jaruzelski himself formally presented it to the Marshal of the Seym.

This increasing support for Wałęsa's proposal, which was motivated by the interests of organizations, reasons of prestige, and competition for status, had a snowball effect that gave new force to the entire process, to the surprise of its participants.

Not without influence was the failure of the maneuver of "introducing market mechanisms to agriculture" and the uncontrolled inflationary spiral,[155] which in July and August led to a new wave of strikes (among railroad men and miners as well as farmers). It seemed that only a "government of national confidence" would be able to control the situation, especially as talks were approaching with the International Monetary Fund, which called for further sacrifices, and when a new element appeared: the spectacular Sachs plan for saving the national economy through shock therapy.[156] Neither the expectations of the IMF nor the proposals of Sachs can be carried out without the willingness of the society to endure sacrifices and without the confidence that this time these sacrifices will not be wasted. And this eventually could be assured (though there is no certainty) by a government formed by Solidarity. These calculations are somewhat complicated by the fact that in the end the initiative of forming a government came from the trade-union section of Solidarity, which is least ready for ownership and market reforms.

Essential for the countries of Eastern Europe observing the Polish experiment was the evolution of the Soviet position: from general assent (we won't interfere in the matter of forming a government in Poland),[157] through anxieties expressed in a rather cautious tone[158] (only one commentary spoke about the "influence of the government crisis in Poland on destabilization in Europe" and was quickly toned down),[159] to the argument that "the entire process is legal"[160] and even the open declaration of consent to pass from a formal to an informal empire. Here I refer to a publication stating the possibility of the Finlandization of Poland and Hungary,[161] if this would increase the influx of Western credits and technologies. Economic ties would still remain in place (in the form of cooperation in production and specialization within the COMECON); these ties would not be threatened by political changes, since today they are based on civil law (e.g., joint ownership). Simultaneously warnings began to appear—this time addressed to the Communist party—for it "to remain calm and enter the new government on a constructive basis."[162] The Communist party had "threatened" that it would remain in opposition (while at the same time retaining control over the Ministry of Internal Security and the army) because the cabinet posts offered to it in the new government "do not match its state and political potential."[163] The Soviet warnings considerably, though not entirely, mitigated the position of the Communist party; its main concern became "saving the cadres," and it announced that it would defend the *nomenklatura* (the people and not the principle).[164]

Returning to the reaction in the U.S.S.R. to the government crisis in Poland, it should be emphasized that it varied in different segments of the Soviet state: it was most calm in the Ministry of Foreign Affairs and its agencies[165] and most sharp in circles closest to the party apparatus. This is important for predicting future changes in the U.S.S.R. itself, where the globalist faction once again seems to be strengthening.

In my opinion, the calendar of the government crisis should begin on 4 July 1989 when Adam Michnik stated, "Your president—our prime minister."[166] Michnik spoke then about "a new order that would be acceptable to all the main political forces." The proposal of appointing a prime minister from opposition circles (in exchange for the acceptance by the latter of a president from the Communist party) was made in the context of a presidential crisis (when General Jaruzelski for various reasons, including the fear of not being elected, withdrew his candidacy for the office of president). The reactions to Michnik's proposal varied considerably, but skepticism prevailed even in the Citizens' Parliamentary Club: "I believe that . . . the time has not yet come."[167] A sharp attack was lauched by A. Wielowiejski (deputy marshal of the Senate from Catholic circles).[168] He charged Michnik and his supporters of "being tempted with playing the role of an avant-garde" (though the expression *Leninism* was not spoken, the context of the statement suggested its possibility). In Wielowiejski's opinion, taking power without a program and without one's own executive apparatus (for the old one has to be ousted) is a "revolutionary tactic," but "we want an evolution—we already know the effects of revolutionary actions."

Michnik's proposal was supported by Jacek Kuroń,[169] who pointed out that without a loyal executive arm the influence of the opposition via the parliament would be illusory. He indicated, however, that it would be necessary to gain the consent of at least part of the existing coalition (in order to acquire a majority in the Seym). This theme was taken up by the staff[170] preparing "Wałęsa's statement" on the new coalition. Surprisingly enough, greater enthusiasm was shown by deputies from outside the opposition. The head of the Club of Deputies of the Democratic party, J. Janowski, called it "highly interesting."[171] Karol Modzelewski came out sharply against Michnik's proposal,[172] emphasizing that its realization in fact would mean a "government of a big coalition": the Communist party would have the Ministry of Internal Affairs and the army, while the Solidarity side would bear the exclusive responsibility for the results. Solidarity, however, has no program and cannot count on the loyalty of the state administration. Kuroń summed up the discussion by pointing out that a Solidarity government would speed up ownership and market reforms, for carrying out these reforms requires public confidence.[173] If the formation of such a government will not be possible, one should not enter a government formed by the Communist party but remain in opposition instead. Kuroń's stance became obligatory in the Citizens' Parliamentary Club,[174] especially after the unsuccessful attempt to build a coalition with United Peasants' party deputies in order to block the candidacy of Kiszczak for prime minister.[175] At the same time it was decided to take up actions to set up a "shadow cabinet,"[176] to establish an "independent agency of foreign investments," and to strengthen efforts to "limit the Leviathan."[177] On the last question the suggestion was made to establish—under auspices of the parliament—a "board of trustees of state property" (supervising ownership changes) and a Senate-Seym committee with which the government would have to coordinate important economic decisions. Both of these proposals violate the division of powers into executive and legislative. Compromise solutions also appeared; e.g., Deputy J. Rokita of Kraków (legal adviser of the Episcopate) proposed a government that is not "ours"/"yours" but coalitional—after previously negotiating the foundations of this coalition. These compromise solutions went further than the agreements of the "round table."[178]

The tactics of the Citizens' Parliamentary Club to remain in opposition lasted up to Wałęsa's declaration of 17 August about forming a new coalition with the United Peasants and Democratic parties and together with them forming a government under a prime minister from Solidarity. After this declaration Wałęsa met with the heads of the United Peasants' and Democratic parties, and this was followed by their joint visit to President Jaruzelski and putting forward the candidacy of T. Mazowiecki for prime minister.[179]

Only on the surface is this variant similar to the proposals of Michnik and Kuroń, for in the meantime the initiative, for the moment, had shifted to the trade-union segment of the opposition. This undermines Kuroń's argument that it would be easier for a Solidarity government to carry out ownership and market reforms. This trade-union segment, which seems to be more clear on the principles it wishes to observe (the law, truth) than on its economic goals (especially as concerns the final economic model), probably would not handle such reforms well. Moreover, this government is hampered by a difficult coalition of the trade-union segment of the opposition with an aggressive and egalitarian peasants' movement, with a considerable divergence of interests between the two of them (and with very limited funds). Happily for economic reforms (especially the stabilization plan), Mazowiecki's government acted in an autonomous way, not following its trade-union genealogy. This, in turn, is the reason for new conflicts: their outcome (summer 1990) will probably be a shift in decision-making and consensus formation from political elites to economic elites and their corporative representatives. This government has to act in a surrealistic situation, in which—in spite of the formal acceptance of the principle "who wins the election forms the government"—one still feels the strong presence of the principle of "the leading role of the Communist party." The party states that "responsibility for the nation" does not permit it to remain in opposition.[180] According to its own declaration,[181] the formula of its presence on the political scene was to be "having an influence on the efficient functioning of the state," which requires leaving the Departments of Defense and Internal Affairs in its hands. At the same time, however, there is a further warning, which amounts to blackmail: the party states, "as much responsibility as power" (ironically repeating the former rhetoric of Solidarity). This means that not giving the Communist party more than the two cabinet posts mentioned would turn it into a "constructive opposition." Whether this means rejecting the first formula is not entirely clear, though Miller, Secretary of the Central Committee, threatens this outright if Solidarity begins to eliminate party members from the executive apparatus.[182] The latter in turn (though without the atmosphere of witch-hunting) is to some degree necessary in order to move to governments based on competency and to create the impression of change in the public consciousness.

The only way out of this vicious circle would be for President Jaruzelski to take resolute actions, but that would mean a further acceleration of the evolution of the political system which is not without risks. Jaruzelski could take a clear position that, by virtue of the "round table" agreements, it is he (or rather, the office of president)—and not the Communist party—who is the guarantor of continuity and stability. And using his powers, he could order the depoliticization of the armed forces and the Ministry of Internal Affairs.

It is interesting that the Hungarians—foreseeing the possibility of such a stalemate—already have started to close down Communist party cells in the army and security forces and the Department of Justice.[183] Generally speaking, the Polish experiment opens up to the Hungarians (and in the future to political forces in the U.S.S.R.) a modification of the rules in such a way as to make the transformation as smooth as possible. Hence after the parliamentary elections in Poland it was already clear that the proportional rather than the majority formula (as applied in Poland) is safer for the party. One can also observe a characteristic imitation by Hungarian Communist party reformers of some of the moves of the legalized opposition in Poland, especially in the symbolic dimension, as in the declaration on the anniversary of the Soviet invasion of Czechoslovakia in 1968 condemning it. Other problems that are being "tested" with the help of the Polish experiment are: from the point of view of Eastern Europe, the reaction of Moscow, and from the point of view of the Soviet Union, the impact of political reforms on economic reforms and the chances of overcoming the economic crisis. The Polish example, for the time being, shows that this influence does not have to be completely positive, and that alliances formed in the course of political transformations may even impede such reforms (e.g., the Polish shaky coalition of trade-union populism with the peasant movement that was formed during the government crisis.

Anarchy of the Transition Period

September 1989
The striking lack of state control over real processes (inflation, introducing "market mechanisms" in the food economy), the disintegration of hierarchical ties in the economy and the administration, and the loss of horizontal cooperative and financial links are only some of the signs of the increasing anarchy in daily life in Poland. These signs were visible in the period of political and economic transformations described in this book. In addition to the spontaneous anarchy, there is also anarchy introduced consciously as an instrument of political struggle[184] that is connected with a regrouping of political forces and the loss of political power by the Communist party.

Many of the sources of anarchy lie in the systemic features of real socialism:[185] the crisis has only sharpened them and brought them to the surface. Some of them result from the methodology of rule of the previous power center that assumes the unsteerability and weakness of the state. This assumption functions as a peculiar self-fulfilling prophecy. Hence in drawing up the state budget for 1989 the budget-makers assumed that businesses would disobey government regulations and exceed financial limits (anticipated fines for exceeding wage limits make up about one-third of the expected income tax revenues from state enterprises).[186] This sum is an absolute condition for balancing the budget (which from the outset is "in the red" in planned expenditures). The anarchy and inflationary behaviors at the level of enterprises are even becoming functional for the budget—without fines it would be out of balance. Thus the system of management, which even so is inconsistent and based on exceptions and horse trading, is going to pieces. Another anarchizing influence is the instability of economic conditions in the COMECON due to a deepening economic crisis in all countries of the bloc.[187]

In this chapter, however, I am interested only in the reasons for anarchy which are directly connected with the breakthrough in the system currently taking place in the domain of rule and ownership relations. In my opinion, five groups of such reasons can be cited. It can be surmised that they appear, though perhaps in different proportions and intensity, in all the countries of real socialism entering onto the track of a similar breakthrough as in Poland.

1) Political inflation connected with "buying" social peace in the period of transformation[188] and also, as just before the "round table," increase of prices of agricultural products (indexation) at parity level, with attempts to shore up the disintegrating old political coalitions (government–Communist party–United Peasants' party).[189]

2) A crisis of obedience and control appearing at all levels of the administrative and economic hierarchy, which is rooted in inability of superiors to supply their subordinates (managers of a lower level) with the means to construct a strategy of survival. And it was precisely this—the principle of reciprocity—that was the source of the obedience of the latter.[190] The general feeling of uncertainty concerning the power apparatus after the defeat of the

Communist party in the elections, the rise of a new coalition, and the formation of a government by a prime minister from the ranks of the previous opposition is moving down to ever lower levels. It is also certain that administrative managers at the provincial and commune level will not be elected to local offices in the next elections (for even the "reformers" from the central level were not elected to parliament). The future role of the provincial Citizens' Committees (and lower) of the Communist party is not clear: dramatic questions are coming up as to whether (and how) the party will protect people from the *nomenklatura* (an army of about 900,000 managers of various levels).[191] The lack of answers to these questions and the vagueness as to the intentions of the government formed with the participation of the opposition (in spite of assurances of the new prime minister that he is not interested in a "witch hunt")[192] have prodded managers of all levels to begin looking for new ways of surviving (read: maintaining their present standard of living and status) without relying on their superiors. These strategies often boil down to the ostentatious demonstration of disobedience toward their present superiors or a sudden reversal of their political orientation.[193] Sometimes people from the *nomenklatura* attempt to set themselves up in the private sector by using their previous connections. From time to time these are organized actions: they seek platforms of survival for the entire previous elite of a town by utilizing the remnants of rapidly corroding relations and connections. This is often at the cost of the individual strategies of people from the executive apparatus or at the cost of organized strategies but on a lower level of the hierarchy. The most spectacular example is the duty-free zone in Biała Podlaska.[194] The limited liability company The Duty-free Zone Malaszewicze-Terespol (the main transshipment station and border point with the U.S.S.R.) was formed in August 1989 by fifteen partners, each of whom put in 1 million złotys (then equivalent to about $140 U.S.). Among the shareholders are two representatives of the Ministry for Cooperation with Foreign Countries; the governor of Biata Podlaska, the automobile factory from Warsaw; the shipping company Hartwig, Polam of Warsaw; and a number of other legal and physical persons. The chairman of the board is the head of the social and economic department of the Provincial Committee of the Communist party. This company will take over the entire highly profitable so-called border trade with the U.S.S.R. (which in the past was a source of profit for many private persons and about 120 companies set up in the form of organizational ownership by the lowest level of *nomenklatura* and the apparatus of agricultural circles—see chapter 2). For simultaneously with the establishment of the "duty-free zone" company, a decree of the Ministry for Cooperation with Foreign Countries[195] has limited the freedom of border trade, from which the previously mentioned small companies had benefited. As of 1 September 1989 permission is required for the export and import of every group of commodities; this also applies to the so-called manufacturing cooperation of enterprises in which small private companies had been set up to engage in mutual trade. This decree gives the shareholders of the "duty-free zone" a clear advantage over those who had built their survival strategies on their own.

Not all the members of the *nomenklatura* have ideas and the opportunity for such spectacular actions, but all of them— uncertain of the future criteria of evaluation—are holding up decisions and refraining from taking action while waiting for the situation to clarify. This paralyzes many institutions and deepens the general economic collapse. Today the networks of reciprocity that have been built up over years in the administration and the economy, which have made it possible for many of the elements of the economy to function in spite of severe shortages, are being suspended. For no one knows who will remain in a job or for how long, or whether people will be called upon to make a strict accounting of the property entrusted to them. Enterprises are no longer "lending" each other workers, capital, and materials.

Here it should be added that the makeup of the state administration changed considerably after 1982 (especially on lower levels). The removal of people infected with Solidarity and at the same time the desire of the martial law ruling group to avoid a specific feudalization of the state (such as existed in the 1970s) resulted in the replacement of the managerial cadre of the low and middle levels and the promotion in the administration of new subservient people. According to the studies of W. Staskiewicz of the University of Warsaw, about 80 percent of the managers at the level of communes and small provinces are newcomers in the administration.[196] Though most of them have higher education, two-thirds of them got it after their nomination in evening administration courses on a very low level. People with no roots in a given area were selected, people who come from other places, in order to prevent the formation of cliques. But the reverse has happened. The new people, who were often inexperienced and many had complexes due to the strong status orientation of Polish society (79.6 percent came from families of blue-collar workers), quite often were unable to resist the pressures of local interest groups. Split between loyalty toward the higher level and local interests, they became involved in the latter as soon as loyalty ceased to pay off (with a change in the political landscape and institutional criteria). Today this helps them to find individual strategies of survival (most of the private firms—also with foreign capital—are being set up in smaller centers for tax reasons), but at the same time this has resulted in the atrophy of hierarchical relations and in often flagrant disobedience toward and disrespect for their present superiors, who now lack influence. An atmosphere of cynicism and saving one's own hide overshadows all other considerations. The remnants of influence are used to create a new position, and attempts are made to make capital of the small power that is left.

3) The third reason for the presently observed strange bureaucratic anarchy (combining chaos with helplessness) is the particular culture of law (or perhaps lawlessness). This is a permanent factor, but in a situation of a breakthrough in the system and the passage (in theory) to governments of law this factor is taking on a new qualitative meaning. This particular attitude toward law is derived from the prerogative philosophy of rule that is professed at the top of the power hierarchy. There the law is regarded as an instrument of politics; here, at the bottom of the hierarchy, as a flexible instrument that is bent to local (and personal) requirements. According to the research of J. Jabłoński of the University of Warsaw,[197] only about 25 percent of the managers of the state administration make use of the advice of qualified attorneys. So it is hardly strange that every year a few thousand decisions are appealed as illegal to the Administrative Court. The Court upholds this charge in about 30 percent of the cases, a figure that has not changed over the years, which indicates that knowledge of the law among managers of the state administration has not im-

proved. The rest of the managers either follow the principle that in unclear questions are should refer the matter to one's superior (in order to avoid responsibility), or—again 25 percent—they accept the principle of substantial and not formal legality. In other words, they hold that one should not abide by regulations that make it harder to solve local problems. "I'm supposed to act—and not abide by impracticable regulations"; "Adhering to the letter of the law would paralyze the economy"; "The spirit of the law counts—not the letter"—these are the common arguments. This 25 percent admits to a special tactic: an interpretation of a regulation that is convenient for themselves (and the region); this interpretation is agreed upon with managers of a similar level in their own environment. Solidarity and the principle of reciprocity are supposed to ensure safety, and the higher level will not cause trouble for everybody (besides, it uses a similar tactic). A disrespectful attitude toward the letter of the law is also promoted by a particular political climate, in which successive ruling teams repudiate laws and decrees—still valid—of their predecessors. Such an approach was common during martial law, when people were even encouraged to disregard regulations that were formally still in force but, as it was said in ruling circles, "accepted under pressure" (of the society—J.S.).

4) The fourth reason for the present anarchy is linked with the scenario of the economic reform, which, as I showed in chapter 2, is based on segmentation of the market and fragmentation of economic structures, while at the same time leaving the distribution of scarce productive factors in the hands of the local authorities (because of compulsory employment exchange and control over credits and materials). This facilitates the legal absorption of the reform (read, neutralization): the formal equal rights of sectors of ownership and branches ends with the actual privileged position (through the allocation of a productive factor in short supply) of one of them (depending on local conditions). By virtue of a decree of the Minister of Finances,[198] the low level of the adminsitation—e.g., a local tax office—has the power to arbitrarily exempt economic subjects from taxes (to an amount of 20 million złotys). This has made it possible to create on the bottom of the power hierarchy tie-ups that today are enabling individual members of the executive power apparatus to survive and to refuse to obey superiors without a threat to their material status, because for some time

now the foundations of their material existence have been outside the administrative hierarchy.

5) The last reason for the unpredictability and zigzags of behaviors (e.g., in legislation)[199] is connected with the logic of democratization from above. The elite appearing on the political scene (in the parliament) are not representatives of structures with a clear base of social support (perhaps with the exception of the United Peasants' party). The social base of each of them is fuzzy and made up of groups in conflict with one another (as is certainly the case with workers' and farmers' Solidarity, which are the social base of the Citizens' Parliamentary Club). In this situation loyalty to one's own club is being continually (and in a difficult-to-predict way) corroded by submitting to one of the interest groups. Most often one submits to each of them in turn: first full indexation was passed and then indexation for farmers (who receive supplements both as producers and as consumers, which fuels inflation). Added to this is the atmosphere of the spectacle (radio and television broadcasts) and the frequent subordination of legislative behaviors and the manner of voting to the desire to win over future voters (when the number of seats per party will no longer be fixed in advance). All of this, together with the government crisis, increases the feeling of uncertainty in the executive apparatus,[200] and all the processes described above contribute to the characteristic anarchy of the transition period.

The Emerging Type of State

Changes in political structures can be analyzed in several dimensions, taking into consideration respectively:
- the manner of formation of the government;
- transformations of internal solutions in the state;
- changes in the political line of the state;
- reformulation of arguments legitimizing domination.

The transformation in the domain of power taking place in Poland today (and, in a somewhat different variant, though the general direction is similar, in Hungary and the U.S.S.R.) is not proceeding uniformly in all these dimensions. Looking from this angle at the Polish phenomenon of a prime minister who comes from the previous opposition, one can make the following claims.
- The manner of formation of the government certainly has

changed. The myth of the avant-garde has been rejected. This myth accorded the Communist party the "leading role" and, if no longer a monopoly on power, in any case an exclusive right to decide who could be on the public scene. Replacing this (with certain limitations about which more is said below) is the principle "whose electoral success—his government."

• Institutional transformations have taken place and are still taking place in the state, but, as I will show later, it is hard to pin down their nature if one wants to go beyond the generality of democratization or reconstruction.

There are rather slim chances, however, of a dramatic change in the policy of the state; this is made nearly impossible both by material barriers (indebtedness, severe disequilibrium on many levels, obligations toward the U.S.S.R. and COMECON) and the fact that future terms will be made facing the same dilemmas and dramatic decisions concerning the manner of distributing the costs of the crisis and the reforms.

Finally, the change in the principle of forming the government did not change in a spectacular way the language of power: reformulation of the latter already had taken place earlier, during the formation of the new center. For at that time the party recognized that it was no longer able to replace or fully control social subjects and acknowledged the real presence of the opposition on the public scene as a legitimate one. The opposition, in turn, abandoned the fundamentalist myth of moral right and the notion of freedom as its own exclusive sphere, separated from the world of politics. Both sides began to use a similar language of control, for the sake of the reforms. The present stage of transformation, however, is attended by the earlier mentioned "trash of understanding," when both sides appeal to the same symbols and arguments. In the public consciousness this creates an irresistible (though false) impression of continuity.

Besides, even the obvious change now taking place in the principles of forming the government escapes public attention because often the same people enter the government who were offered these positions when the previous principle[201] was in effect, except that this time someone else is nominating them. This is still a government of a "grand coalition" (with participation of the Communist party in the politically crucial ministries)—except now someone else is forming it.

Important, though difficult to conceptualize, are internal changes in the state. Some of these changes are obvious: e.g., the end of the previous tie of the Communist party and the state (linked in the past through the principle of *nomenklatura*). Today even if the same people remain in executive positions of power, "loyalty to the state and government"[202] is required of them and not loyalty to any party. Future promotions and new recruitment to the power apparatus are supposed to be based on the principle of competency (though the opposition also shows a tendency to make use of a peculiar principle of the *nomenklatura*, which is more of a hybrid of combatant services and loyalty than preparations to solve complicated economic and legal problems).

Clearly a new element in the political system is the phenomenon of dyarchy, which is a kind of shock absorber of the transformation. The changes in the institutional forms of this dyarchy, however, depend on the stage of the latter.[203]

These are only some elements of the new situation in the domain of power. Now I would like to attempt a more comprehensive description.

How can one describe the form of the state rising before our eyes? This is by no means a modern state of government of law (Rechsstaat) and parliamentary democracy. Neither is it a state based on corporational articulation of interests that mediate between representations of clearly specific groups divided according to economic and occupational criteria. The type of government presently being formed in Poland in certain respects is close to consociational democracy,[204] in which elites representing well-defined segments of the society (e.g., nationalist or religious groups) reach a compromise and from a government on the principle of proportionality.

In my opinion, however, the formula that best fits here is the estates' state (Standesstaat).[205] This form of state appeared historically in Germany between the last phase of the feudal state of the Carolingians and absolutism.

The characteristic feature of the estates' state is a segmentation of the structures of domination. Moreover, each segment arises in a different way and has different functions. There is no universal rule that defines and is binding on all actors. These actors are collective subjects (estates), which only superifically resemble corporations. As in the corporative system, certain agreements and mediations take place between them, but these are group ethoses, "centers on which the solidarity of individuals crystallize,"[206] which are distinguished on the basis of different genealogy and tradition (such organizational loyalty is occurring today) and not, like corporations, representations of clearly defined groups with specific economic interests. Unlike corporations (which are created from the bottom, so to speak), these political estates are in the process of looking for their social base, often competing with each other for the same groups, and sometimes gaining the support of groups with conflicting economic interests.[207]

In such an estates' state (as in Poland today) different political principles embodied in particular segments crisscross. So we have a segment aspiring to become the embryo of the Rechsstaat (in Poland, the parliament, government) limiting itself to the benefit of the segment from the previous system (the Communist party) and incorporating the previous system into the coalition on account of the geopolitical situation. The Communist party, however, has already ceased to be the center and source of power (just as the monarch in the Standesstaat changed roles in comparison with feudalism, though the monarch was still present). The Communist party today is beginning to function as one of the estates (and hence, according to a new principle), though its presence in the new coalition is still based on the old principle. The seeds of a third principle also are appearing: namely, representations of the corporative type (in Poland the closest to this are the United Peasants' party and the All-Polish Association of Trade Unions, with its populism). The emergence of each of these segments of the political system is based on a different political rule, and each limits and modifies the actions of the others. The corporative state is no longer, like the feudal state, a collection of individuals (and vassals) and no longer serves merely to organize support for the center (king or Communist party) but is made up of collective actors. These actors represent different systems of values and ethoses, though when one looks from the perspective of economic interests, differences between estates often become blurred. Thus in comparison with feudalism (or the Communist party of the monocentric state), the distinguishing feature of the Standesstaat is assumed duality: the king/Communist party and the estates recognize each other as separate (and based on different principles) centers of power, each with its own domain (sphere of domination).

Other features of the historical Standesstaat are similar to those of the type of state appearing in the first phase of the breakthrough in the system of real socialism.

- The roles of individual segments are established and reified on the basis of political agreements (e.g., the royal privilege for a given estate) and not through the effects of a law that is the same for all segments.

- The individual segments in the system of domination of the Standesstaat are not organs of a modern state: each of them appeals to different (specific to itself) sources of power. The functions of each segment are also different: the "small coalition" (Solidarity, Peasant party, Democratic party) appeals to the results of the elections; the late Communist party to the "round table" agreements and the geopolitical situation (including real control over the army and the Ministry of Internal Affairs), while President Jaruzelski and his "shadow," Wałęsa, stabilize and regulate conflicts and are a guarantee of the direction of reforms (as a tandem, they can be for both Moscow and the West at once).

- In the Standesstaat there is no automatic regulating principle: though the opposition formed a government after winning the elections, this happened after additional, extraconstitutional interventions by the stabilizing segment (Wałęsa–Jaruzelski). What is more, in forming a government the opposition limited itself to a principle other than the "victorious elections," one that is a modification of the principle that was in effect before the elections. As a result of this self-limitation and the crisscrossing of several political principles, a division also took place of the spheres of influence of particular segments of the political structure: the army and the Ministry of Internal Affairs were left under the control of the Communist party.

The above points fully bring out the differences between the estates (as collective political subjects) and corporations. The political importance of corporations unmistakably comes from the power of the social groups whose economic interests they represent. In the Standesstaat the hierarchy of "political estates" (or characteristic political elite groups) comes not only from the power of their social bases, but also from a certain a priori vision of the state, guaranteeing, so to speak, the political principles according to which individual segments are formed and function. What is more, as opposed to corporations, the social base of political estates as a rule is ill defined, and these estates (as ethos groups) often compete for the support of the same groups. In contradistinction to corporations, there is no exclusiveness of the represented section of the society in the Standesstaat. There is less mention of "representation" and more talk about the realization of a particular vision of the social order.

What further evolution of the structures of domination can be expected? It is useful to take a look at the historical development of the Standesstaat. For then and now we are dealing with characteristic transformations in the society itself (with the development of market relations and exclusive property rights and the breakup of various forms of collective and nonexclusive ownership). An evolution is taking place from a state of social atomization (where the masses, excluded from rule, support this or that estate, being guided either by similar material needs or emotions that spring up around symbols) toward individualization of the society. Different, though interrelated, economic interests of individuals are appearing (connected with various elements of material production), and the political and civil rights of these individuals are becoming ever more clearly defined. In the historical Standesstaat (as is happening in its modern version in real socialism) this evolution led to a gradual breakup of the political estates (collective political bodies operating on the base of group ethoses). In Poland today, their place is being taken by corporations. At the same time this will be the next stage in reducing the scope of state control of the political sphere: the first stage, as I wrote earlier, was the collapse of the revolutionary legitimation of power (or of traditional authority in the historical context).[208] This shift from the "politics of ethoses" to the "politics of economic interests" will have further consequences:

• a characteristic "deficit of legitimacy" will appear, which will be filled by greater pressure for legal legitimation;

• politics will become a vocation (as it became with the evolution of the historical Standesstaat). The public scene will no longer be characterized by the physical presence in political institutions of persons belonging to a given estate (a presence regarded as an element of their "honor"); instead, these persons will watch over the rules of the political game behind the scenes and put into this game "political functionaries" of particular interest groups. For domination and politics no longer, as in the Standesstaat, will consist of the unregulated settlement of individual cases and situations but in a more routine and legally regulated action. Reducing state control of politics will contribute to such a separation of social and political elites.

In the historical Standesstaat all of the aforementioned changes paved the way for the evolution to absolutism and then, to the modern state. A similar evolution is in store for the version of the Standesstaat that has appeared today—in the first phase of the breakthrough in the system of real socialism—in Eastern Europe.

The Discrete Revolution: The Role of Society in the Transformation Directed from Above

September 1989

The first stage of the breakthrough in the socialist system described in this book is still an open situation, for this stage can lead either to a change in the system or to a mutation of it (with the retention, and even strengthening, of its basic features, while only their institutional guise changes).

What is striking here is the similarity to the situation in Russia after 1905. Then also it seemed that a breakthrough was beginning toward parliamentary democracy and production relations based on clearly defined, exclusive property rights in industry and farming. After several years of intensive self-organization of the society and efforts to create a middle class in the cities and countryside, however, World War I and the 1917 revolution brought political and economic collapse. The revolution revitalized (in a radical form) the basic features of autocracy (monocentrism, the prerogative type of domination, ownership without separate shares, and an economy without a capital market, in which the state replaced absent economic mechanisms and interests).

In Russia after 1905, in a period reminiscent of the first phase of the breakthrough described here, associations appeared,[1] and Czar Nicholas II recognized the right of the society to participate in government through its representatives in the Duma.[2] Citizens revealed their aspirations, and discussions broke out on the future shape of the political order.[3] The atmosphere of freedom was apprehended as "transitory liberty,"[4] with the awareness that one was participating in history. After 1905 trade-union activity also developed, which passed through three stages.

- Period One, in 1906 and 1907 was characterized by dynamic trade-union activity that often copied the forms of action of Western European trade unions.[5] Government authorities were aware that the presence of legal trade unions with a certain amount of autonomy was a condition for achieving the rationality of control reformulated after the shock of the eruption of 1905.[6] This period ended with Stolypin's coup d'état,[7] after which trade-union liberties were considerably limited.

- Period Two, after 1907, was coupled with the next reformulation of the philosophy of rule. Now it was recognized that limiting the trade-union movement was in the interests of stabilization, speeding up economic reforms and bringing more rapid economic growth. And this growth, it was believed, required limiting the powers of the trade unions and betting on the middle class and initiative. This period lasted until 1912. Poland now seems to be entering this second phase, but recession induced by government's "stabilization" can prevent it. It is possible that, if populist pressures increase and make reform more difficult, "Stolypin's coup d'état" may be carried out—in the name of economic reforms—by a government formed by Solidarity itself or by Wałęsa as a strong president. Rationalizations in this direction, which recall almost exactly the arguments used to limit trade-union activity in Stolypin's time,[8] are already appearing.[9]

In Russia this period ended in April 1912 with the so-called massacre on the Lena, after violent outbursts of protest by desperate and poorly organized workers.[10] After pacifying this spontaneous movement, the authorities once again returned to the idea of trade unions as a necessary form for institutionalization of the conflict.

- Period Three saw workers' frustrations continue to increase: this time on account of the obvious contradiction between the impressive organizational potential of the trade-union movement and its meager results. The latter were due to the economic crisis and the increasing pauperization of the society. The crisis was attended by the collapse of the traditional defense mechanisms that enabled workers to survive (traditional forms of security), which inexorably resulted in a radicalization of the public feeling.[11]

In Poland today we see elements of Period Two (the demobilization of trade unions steered from above and, as part of the strategy of "self-limitation," coming from the command center of Solidarity) and Period Three (lack of visible effects of trade-union activities, in spite of the reactivation of Solidarity and its formation of a government; liquidation of the traditional niches in the illegal second economy, which allowed the working class to survive. Their place has been taken by the legal small private sector, and deep recession has canceled the possibility of adjustment on an individual level.

In Russia in this phase there was a sudden politization of trade unions and competition between mensheviks and bolsheviks for influence. In Poland one may expect similar tendencies, with the role of the more radical bolsheviks—ironically—being played by activists of the All Polish Association of Trade Unions, which was established during martial law as a substitute for Solidarity.

Is Poland in this situation threatened with a revolution in the name of "ethical socialism"—rejecting reforms of the market type, privatization, and opening to the West? In my opinion, this is possible. Signs of an "ethical socialism" mentality are already visible in attacks on "making owners of the *nomenklatura*," in the forms of political capitalism[12] described in this book, and in the resistance of crews to having their enterprises form companies with Western capital.[13]

Such a "revolution," however, would spell the end of the breakthrough in the system and revitalize the remaining socialists in both structure and mentality. That such a course of events is possible can also be seen from an argument carried out with another type of concept. Let us look at two sequences of events, leading— each in the name of different premises—to the idea of "ethical socialism." The first sequence, which was analyzed by Max Weber[14] and R. Kosseleck,[15] is:

- the collapse of the traditional legitimation of power in the course of the religious wars, which made the association of royal power with divine right and the Church politically troublesome;
- absolutism: "naked power" and a legitimacy vacuum;
- the intellectual and political revolution of the Enlightenment

in the name of the idea of the formal equality of citizens (as in civil rights and legal guarantees of individual property rights). This produced legal legitimation as the solution of the absolutist crisis of legitimation;

• the rebellion (intellectual: through the construction of leftist utopias) against formal justice and the social order based on it (governments of impersonal bureaucracy; capitalism) and in the name of substantial justice and "ethical socialism."

And here is the parallel sequence, which is perhaps taking place in Poland:

• the collapse of revolutionary legitimation (based on the myth of the historical mission of the party) in collision with the workers' rebellion in the name of the fundamentalist myth of moral right;

• the social energy of the rebellion used by the political elite working toward an order based on formal justice, rights of the individual, and guarantees of private ownership. This is linked with the passage from the language of values to the language of politics and economic interests (or rather, their theoretical vision, for the elite themselves have no economic interest in change). Fundamentalist collectivism evolves toward individualism. There is an upheaval (of the Reformation type against the Church) in both political camps—the Communist party and Solidarity—for their elites reject the previous a priori myth of the "right" of their own organization in favor of individualized practices based on pragmatism;[16]

• a rebellion from below (as an eventuality in the future) in the name of substantial justice and the collectivism of "ethical socialism." "Politics" is rejected (especially when it appears as "naked power," without control over real processes). Collective security and egalitarianism are valued, as opposed to the political capitalism, privatization, and individualism of the first phase in the breakthrough in the system.

Characteristic for the course of events in Eastern Europe is the break in continuity between the ethos of a mass movement (fundamentalism with strong collectivist accents) and the political actions of the elite. This leads us to reflect on the general problem of the role of society in the transformations in the system described in this book.

A reading of the previous chapters leaves the impression of the absence of society in the changes taking place. I might even be charged with using a state-centered paradigm, for even the division of the first phase of the breakthrough into periods (the formation of a new center, its subsequent breakup, and reorganization in a new coalition) is made from the perspective of the dynamics of political structures. And yet R. Kasaba is right when he writes:

We should remember that how a temporal continuum is divided reflects a distinct way of viewing not only time but also the very historical context that is under scrutiny. This means that when we adopt a periodization we also adopt a viewpoint that may shape our entire approach to the subject matter.[17]

After all, the periodization of the breakthrough and the stages of its dynamics (together with turning points) might be comprehended in an entirely different way by the society itself. What is more, events other than those emphasized in this book in fact might determine the chances of the breakthrough taking place or not. For the society, certain events (the "round table," the formation of a government by Solidarity) might not "exist" because they are draped in the "trash of understanding" and do not cause spectacular changes in everyday life or social relations (power relations included) known from citizens' everyday experience in their places of work and residence. Yet the real turning point for the society in the changes taking place might be the unsuccessful maneuver of "introducing market mechanisms and a stabilization plan" (from August 1989), resulting in uncontrolled inflation and revealing a crisis of the structures of domination that was deeper than only political. In other words, a crisis that showed that the authorities were not in control of real processes. This changed social attitudes toward reforms of the market type and undermined the authority of the political leadership (including the leadership of which the former opposition is now a part). Both of these moments might decide the chances of the breakthrough in the system and increase populistic pressures (and thus put a stop to the breakthrough). For the experience of the unsuccessful "market operation" might become the catalyst for a mass rejection of property rights reforms and privatization.

The "openness' of the present phase of the breakthrough is that one still does not know whether "ontological opening" will take place and whether the new political structures will not simply carry out (with new methods, with the help of authority and not force) what the old elite unsuccessfully attempted to do. What is the real scope of changes and continuity under the cloak of spectacular personnel changes? It seems that from the perspective of the society the aspect of continuity is more strongly experienced than the sense of change, and this perception itself (regardless of whether it reflects the real state of affairs) may take on the features of a self-fulfilling prophecy, inducing social apathy and feelings of revolution for the elite only. And finally is it correct to take as a measure of change either the pace of moving toward the model of Western democracy and economy or the degree of moving away from the "classical model" of real socialism? Perhaps what is regarded as manifestations of anarchy and disorder is the germ of some new, permanent way of functioning? We often forget that societies can remain in a state of limbo for quite a long time. Progressive segmentation (as a result of the crisis and reforms), disintegration connected with the collapse of former command techniques of management, and the failure of new techniques to take their place on an equally general level (when the market does not operate yet, due to lack of a capital market), and finally, the collapse of former strategies of survival on all levels might be a sequence of events similar to those through which the Ottoman Empire passed in the course of unsuccessful Westernization: regress, unsuccessful reforms, disintegration, and further peripheralization in relation to the world system, though on somewhat different principles than before.

The dynamics of the breakthrough in real socialism are often explained (as I also do) by "the string of absences"—absence of a middle class (in the Western sense) and a civil society. Such a vision also is held by part of the political elite,[18] leading to the Stolypinist temptation to limit existing collective subjects and create new ones.

For we still know too little about the silent majority of the society on which successive elites project their own visions of "theoretical interest." In this respect nothing has changed, and the strange vacuum in which rulers uncertain of their social base move is a permanent feature of the situation, in spite of the institutional and personnel changes taking place. A deeper regularity is reflected here: in a society enslaved and under state control through collective ownership, it is not only key economic interests that have been liquidated but also interests in change that could reconstitute the economic interests. Interest in supporting the process of change first has to be created "from above" in the name of a theoretical vision—with all the dangers accompanying this type of revolution from above.

This does not mean, however, that the role of the society, which is not present directly on the public scene, is not crucial for the dynamics of the breakthrough. Before I outline its presence, I wish to say a few words about the historical relation of state to society, a relation that is different in the individual countries of real socialism and, in my opinion, determines the manner in which the breakthrough is taking place in each of them. Most instructive here is the comparison between Poland and Bulgaria. In Poland, as has been emphasized many times, during the partitions the society demonstrated that it was capable of enduring for more than one hundred years without its own state, thanks to unity of culture, religion, and language. As a consequence, informal institutions ensured continuity of the social bond. This made it possible in the 1970s to articulate the notion of a "substitute society" (which—as self-organizing—was supposed to take over the functions of the state). This notion was the ideological foundation of the actions of Solidarity and turned out to be an effective instrument of political struggle. Its rejection (and the entry of the opposition elite into the new center) was a necessary next stage, but it caused tensions and an identity crisis in the opposition. This entire sequence of events would be inconceivable, however, without the strong awareness of a social identity that is separate and independent from the state.

In Bulgaria there are no conditions for developments of this kind. The state there, including the communist state after World War II, was a factor integrating and constructing the Bulgarian nation (e.g., a national language was developed and disseminated by the state educational system). Without the state even today the Bulgarian society might fall apart and disintegrate around national, religious, and linguistic divisions. What is more, one of the myths integrating the Bulgarian nation is the myth of the historical alliance with Russia against Ottoman captivity. In this situation political articulation in categories of a society independent from the state (as in Poland) is impossible. In Bulgaria the state still determines the very existence of the society. Also, anti-Soviet feelings (as in Poland) are inconceivable. When one looks from a similar perspective at the struggle going on today in the Baltic republics and others (the Ukraine, Moldavia) for their own language, it turns out that this struggle has deeper roots than it appears at first glance. For this is preliminary action that is a prerequisite for all future political actions. The aim is to put republican institutions in charge of the educational and cultural institutions that determine national identity and not institutions representing the imperial level. For only this will make it possible to articulate the political conflict (against the ownership and political structures imposed after World War II) without falling into anarchy. Integrated state institutions at the republican level will still remain, and they will make it possible to articulate national identity. In this situation the rebellion against the "colonial state" will not be a rebellion against the state in general, which will be a big help in carrying out the reforms.

Similar, but more thorough, analyses of the society's tissue are necessary in Poland and Hungary, though in the present book I must limit myself to merely pointing out the need for them. What is really happening in the working class? What are the aspirations of the anti-Wałęsa movement? What part of the working class, if any, has a chance of participating in privatization of the state sector? Will new niches come into being for the rest that will enable them to survive the crisis, or will only blind rebellion remain? Finally, was I wrong in concentrating mostly on the structures of the state-party and oppositional elite, and not on massive processes? To what extent does my analysis depict the real course of the breakthrough in the system of real socialism that—in my analysis—is taking place in the form of "revolution from above"? What is the impact today of the phenomenon that I called elsewhere[19] a lifeless (inert) structure, asserting that the society in fact is active (striking) but absent as a transformational force (and perhaps even impedes this transformation)? For the fundamentalist rejection of the system in 1980 and 1981 was coupled with the acceptance in fact (in the name of material needs) of the unregulated presence of the state in the economy and socialist state control.

It is no accident that during the hearings before the Seym Commission, T. Syryjczyk,[20] candidate for Minister of Industry, said, "I represent subjects that do not yet exist." Indeed, the specific feature of the breakthrough taking place in real socialism is that the present political elite is not economically interested in its success and refers to "theoretical interest." In other words, it has a vision of an efficient system, which to be sure is rooted in science rather than ideology, but a vision that brushes dangerously close to the latter on account of the lack of precision and the magical approach of many slogans, e.g., the "market." What is more, this elite does not know which social groups make up its social base and are interested in such a transformation. All that is known is that such groups certainly will appear once the reforms have reached an advanced stage (e.g., in property rights) but that the beginning of these changes will take place in a strange vacuum and in an atmosphere of resistance from part of the society and without the clear support of any organized groups. So this is the reverse of the situation from the times of the bourgeois revolution, when the emerging political elite articulated the political interests of clearly established and visible groups/classes for which change meant pulling down the barriers to their economic expansion. Moreover, part of this base was the former social base of the ancien régime (landowners entering into the structures of finance and commercial capital). In Poland such a group could be the new owners from the *nomenklatura*, who are building new economic foundations to maintain their high social status. This group, however, is being attacked by the nascent political elite and as a consequence is throwing in its lot with the former apparatus and not releasing its transformation potential. Another group with clear economic interests (peasants, owners of private farms) is politically represented by an elite (United Peasants' Party, Farmers' Solidarity) that appeals to the state-controlled ideal of incomes based on parity and not efficiency. Thus part of the society still seems to be operating within the egalitarian schema of "dead structure." Most of it is blocked through an "exclusionary corporatism" pattern. But some (peasants) are politically represented in a way that can harm the breakthrough.

So what is the role of the society in this entire process? Here, in my opinion, three aspects ought to be mentioned.

• The initial impulse to the transformation from the mass workers' rebellion of 1980 and 1981 and the crisis of revolutionary legitimacy (also in circles of the Communist party itself) not only called into being oppositional political elites that (as part of the revolution from above) joined the reform process but also became an argument for party reformers interested in "ontological opening" (in the name of a better accomplishment of imperial interests).

• A continual—lasting to this day—general danger of a new social outburst breaks down the resistance of the Communist party establishment to sharing power (in the name of stability) and forces it to renew reform efforts, even though reforms themselves are a source of tensions.[21]

• The danger that society will join the hypothetical future rebellion (as a force blocking the transformations) conducted in the name of "ethical socialism" against elites, politics, individualism, formal justice, and privatization is constant.

In this context it is worth pointing out the specific climate in which the revolution from above described here is taking place. Apathy and lack of enthusiasm or widescale interest (in contrast to the euphoria of 1980) were attended by the increasing sense of danger in connection with the apparent inability of the government to control the inflationary spiral until very harsh measures of stabilization were introduced in January 1990; since then recession seems to be out of control. Another striking element is the discrete (hidden) nature of the changes and the ennui accompanying them, which is felt even in such turning points as the "round table" and which results from a simultaneous political fight waged in the mass media to capture the public mind. It is worth emphasizing that in his diary the poet Alexander Blok in 1917 complained about the ennui and cultural trash of the revolution, and the fundamental nature of the changes taking place at that time eluded even professional historians.[22] The masses (especially the young generation of workers for whom August 1980 is now only a myth) would like a visible revolution, one that in one leap would change power and status relations in their immediate environment and clearly identify who "we" are and who "they" are. In the meantime, the aforementioned "trash of understanding" is already accompanying the changes and the former *nomenklatura*'s remarkable adjustment to the new situation, such as their success-ful attempts to retain their former privileged status by becoming owners. Also spoiling the taste of victory is the acquiescence of the Communist party (obviously only in the propaganda dimension) to an auto-da-fé (such as when the Communist party deputies made the initiative concerning removal of the "leading role of the party" from the Constitution). What is more, the phenomenon of "making owners of the *nomenklatura*" is perceived by the general public as one of the aspects of the reform, while at the same time the reform destroys workers' strategies of survival (e.g., by elimi-nating the second economy, which is dislodged by the new legal private sector).

The legal, dry language of the institutional changes taking place and of most of the Seym debates as well as the fact that the oppo-sition deputies, in spite of opposition and under the pressure of time and circumstances, are ratifying measures initiated by the Rakowski government, are effectively destroying the sense of rev-olutionariness of the changes taking place. This is especially true when the mass media highlight (as happened when Prime Minister Mazowiecki took over the government) the moment of common celebration by the old (Jaruzelski) and the new elite during a period of numerous state holidays and celebrations.[23]

Finally, the festive mood is effectively destroyed by ambiguity connected with the sense of guilt for uncommitted deeds. The wave of accusing Polish society (and especially the Catholic Church hierarchy) with anti-Semitism in connection with the con-flict over the convent of the Carmelite nuns in Oświęcim coincided with a fact that clearly shows the absence of anti-Semitism, name-ly, the election by the Polish society of many Poles of Jewish origin as political representatives. The wave of accusations was touched off by a tactless address by Józef Cardinal Glemp, Primate of Po-land. It contains clear elements of overreaction, for it is above all an expression of his frustration connected with the fact that the Church supported the elite put forward by the Citizens' Commit-tee, often against Christian Democratic candidates closer to the Church, but even this support did not protect it from the label of anti-Semitism. That one cannot openly discuss the layout of polit-ical forces in Poland in nationality categories—without fear of acquiring such a label—functions as a special instrument that

hampers criticism of the political behaviors of the new establishment.[24] The frustrating awareness of the impossibility of articulating the conflict completely, intertwined with the bad taste left
by the dispute between victims of World War II—Poles and
Jews—destroys the joy from the changes taking place and makes
it hard for the man in the street to lift up his head. In this dispute,
even the German press felt entitled to admonish the Poles, and
there was obvious overreaction on both sides.

The feeling of strangeness and "standing aside" is especially
evident in the case of young people. They use their imagination
to comment on the changes rather than to participate in them
creatively. Here are samples of the often beautiful style of this
commentary taken from Warsaw walls. "Cold corpuscles of small
pancakes" (this about oneself). "Freedom = free" (with the drawing of a house, for "dom" in Polish means house)—this is about
homelessness, when the waiting time for an apartment is twenty
or more years, with the price of a square meter of an apartment in
the free market about $300 U.S., while an assistant professor at a
university earns about $120 U.S. a month at the currency rate at
which the government buys dollars. "Down with down with"
(about the excess of "politics" that no one any longer controls).
Finally—a comment on the defeat of the Communist party at the
polls, expressed in Church symbolism (in June the traditional First
Holy Communion of children is held, which coincided with the
elections): "First Communion with a cross of bread" (the cross
meaning the specter of hunger).

In analyzing the social climate in which the transformation in
Eastern Europe is taking place, it is worth emphasizing, in my
opinion, that it is not accompanied by an ideological debate. The
latter is taking place within individual camps: in the Communist
party between globalists and populists and inside the opposition,
which is experiencing an identity crisis. The elite are debating
(most often behind closed doors), while para-ideological measures
are being used against society, as in the campaign in the mass
media to create a particular definition of the situation in the public mind. The crisis of revolutionary legitimacy of power also
occurred in a para-ideological way (in collision with the fundamentalist myth) and not through ideological discourse.

I want to devote this concluding part of the book to these two problems. I begin with an outline of the dynamics of the crisis of revolutionary legitimacy in the context of the fundamentalist, workers' myth. This is a fascinating phenomenon, not only for its importance for the future but also for its references to the past and the analogy with the dynamics of the breakup of the traditional legitimacy of power. At the same time this is an example of irrationality on a mass scale (the fight with a myth not by means of arguments taken from reality but with the help of another myth), which turns out to be historically rational. For this irrationality makes it possible to initiate the transformation: the social energy released by the myth became the substance of the revolution from above ingested by the reformatory elite. Their actions create the chances (though they do not yet give any certainty) of getting out of the absurdity of real socialism.

Changes in the Sphere of Ideology

New configurations on the public scene are accompanied by transformations in the ideological domain. The latter are much less spectacular, however, than the actual transformations of political institutions (in particular, the clear limitation of the role of the Communist party). Most of these changes are taking place without ideological justifications. We are observing a discourse on many planes, of which the ideological debate constitutes only one of the dimensions, chiefly concerning communication of the reformatory power elite inside the Communist party with its own executive apparatus, which started before the "round table." Other dimensions of this discourse are:

• a discussion that appeals to standards of rational control and organizational arguments (the actors—from the opposition and the old regime—entering the new center during the stage of the "round table" communicate primarily in this language—see chapter three);

• communication effects that can be called *para-ideological*: ideas and emotions created at the level of common consciousness which will serve to stabilize the system (in spite of the crisis and complicated reforms upsetting the feeling of security).

The above phenomena were preceded by a characteristic sequence of steps that repeated themselves (though in a somewhat different pattern) in all the countries of Eastern Europe undergoing transformation.

Thus, first the revolutionary legitimation of the leadership broke down in the circles of its own apparatus. In Poland this took place conclusively in 1980 and 1981 as a result of the collision with the mass workers' protest. In the U.S.S.R. this crisis of legitimation was coupled chiefly with the disintegration of the imperial myth with the widening of the civilizational gulf in relation to the West and the "discovery" of the dependency of the socialist bloc on the world capitalist system. In the U.S.S.R. it is no accident that the faction called globalists, who look at the situation of the country in categories of the world system, was the chief initiator of reforms. The disintegration of the ideological construction based on the revolutionary myth of the "avant-garde" was speeded up even more by a shift of the decision center from the Communist party to a center closer to the security forces and the army (in connection with the adjustment of the power elite to governing in conditions of permanent crisis).

The next step was the departure in official statements in the mass media from always being in the right; of making arguments in categories of necessity (geopolitics), and a sort of cynical "realism" (one governs because one has power). In Poland the beginning of this stage was martial law (December 13, 1981). This was accompanied by greater pragmatism in decision processes, which now are directed toward rationalization of rule (the greatest effect with the least cost, in the broad sense) and not the carrying out of a priori ideological formulas. Yet at this stage there was no open rejection or change of these formulas, and also no formalization of new procedures in the system of rule. Changes were spoken about in categories of the "good will" of the rulers, which in Poland in 1984 through 1986 boiled down to:

• the announcement by the communist leadership that alone (without the society) it is unable to carry out the program of reforms; thus the myth of the "avant-garde" was rejected, but without drawing institutional consequences of this;

• allowing more open discussion in the Communist party, but without creating the statutory possibility of fighting for alternative programs.

This phase has two separate parts: pre-Gorbachev (1981–85)

and after Gorbachev's installation at the Kremlin. In the second part we observed the beginning of "transformation through transactions" that started in 1986 with the unofficial contacts of the reform-oriented officials of the communist regime with members of the opposition. Such contacts were often arranged with the help of the Catholic Church.

At this stage "transactions" deal with the possibility of "liberalization" (limited autonomy for society), not "democratization" (with new electoral rules and legalization of the opposition and the multi-party system).

The rapid acceleration in the movement toward democratic reforms was connected not only with the new wave of strikes in Poland (May 1988) but also with a new perception of the crisis (and reforms) in Moscow. This changed unofficial negotiations into the open "round-table" process (February–March 1989). The "round table" was the last accent of this stage of para-ideological discourse between the opposition and the Communist elite.

The third step of this sequence is connected with the acceleration of transformation in Eastern Europe in 1989 and 1990 (after the "round table" transition-through-transactions stage) and the entrance of the ex-opposition into the government.[25] All dilemmas of transformation are more visible at this stage, and new political/ideological divisions in the ex-oppositional camp are more obvious. The communist ideology is at this point irrelevant, but that does not mean the role of the old *nomenklatura* is irrelevant as well.

In the case of Poland, one year after the June 1989 elections, two conflicting sides in the Solidarity camp exist. One is the Wałęsa camp, which includes the alliance called PC (Porozumienie Centrum), a few center-right parties, and the farmers' party PSL (Polskie Stronnictwo Ludowe. The other side is the Mazowiecki/ Gieremek camp, an alliance called ROAD (Ruch Alternatywny Akcja Demokratyczna), part of the Citizens' Parliamentary Club, and the so-called Forum Demokratyczne organized by J. Turowicz from the Catholic weekly *Tygodnik Powszechny*.

Five axes of conflict are the most characteristic here. They cannot be presented simply in terms of "right" and "left." They deal with the following problems.

First, the methodology of the "revolution from above." Both

sides agree that the role of the state is crucial and that the policy of the latter has to be based on some sort of consensus. Differences deal with the pattern of consensus formation. Wałęsa's group asks for moving from the rhetoric of Solidarity's ethos, which is less and less relevant to current choices, to more explicit debate on new conflicts in society and between state and society. It means moving the consensus/policy building from the present political elite to a social-economic elite (some of them created by the transformation itself). This could not only improve the quality of decision making but reduce the present contingency factor in decision making. In other words, it would introduce elements of representation of the emerging civil society in the Hegelian sense. It also means the end of the political role of the East European intelligentsia-type politicians, with their claim to a special role in history as social conscience and source of norms, representing the interests of the whole society. The new, emerging elites connected with Wałęsa's camp are different: middle class, professional, provincial. The esthetics of the new politics will be different as well.

The second axis is connected with economic policy. Both sides apply liberal rhetoric, but with different interpretations. In the case of the Wałęsa camp, it is John Rawls's contractual "presumptivism" with Hayekian undertones. The Mazowiecki/Gieremek camp is closer to J. S. Mills's liberalism with its strong elements of distributive justice. Indexation introduced during the "round table" and recent (June 1990) Seym legislation on "unjust profits" represent such a pattern of thinking. Paradoxically, it is the Wałęsa camp that will reinforce the Balcerowicz segment in government and make possible an acceleration of privatization and structural changes. The only difference between this camp and the Balcerowicz proposal is the problem of capital formation and actual rigidity of fiscal/tax policy: the Wałęsa camp is for special treatment of the most promising—from the growth point of view —groups and segments of the economy.

The third axis of conflict within the Solidarity camp is connected with the "acceleration" claims of Wałęsa's side versus the "evolutionary changes" presented by the other side. Acceleration means revision of the conditions of cooperation in COMECON, such as in the terms of transfer ruble exchange and imposed specialization in production. Polish participation in the Warsaw Pact is also questioned by the Wałęsa camp. Both aspects of the Mazo-wiecki government's present policy isolate Poland in Europe and make structural changes more difficult: Poland has to subsidize production connected to COMECON agreements, and access to the most modern technologies is cut off.

The fourth axis of conflict is a different vision of the state. Both sides are somewhat contradictory here. In Wałęsa's camp we observe a mixture of political populism (with its vision of unity of state and society, without mediation of civil society institutions) with genuine claims for the "opening" of the public stage and a place for the new political parties. On the Mazowiecki side, there is a strong statist orientation (strong state as an autotelic value) but at the same time there is an unavoidable anarchy and weak-ness of the state machine connected with evolutionary political strategy prolonging an existence of Standesstaat. Wałęsa's claim to the presidency would also mean an end of the presidential seg-ment of Standesstaat built around Jaruzelski. Both sides are some-how ambiguous in respect to legal culture: both overestimate special instruments and institutions. Mazowiecki's camp, for in-stance, introduced religion into schools against procedure, using "natural law" arguments. The recent proposal for a new "round table" illustrates the Mazowiecki camp's tendency to use extra-ordinary procedures without changing routine decision making. On the other side, Wałęsa is talking about a strong presidency (which increases the ambiguity of the political process when he supports at the same time a multi-party system) and ruling with the help of decrees.

The fifth difference is cultural rather than ideological but has important political implications for the future. This conflict is somehow acted in a triangle: neo-traditionalization, modernism, postmodernism. The two camps differ in their vision of what to do with the neo-traditional pattern of popular political mobilization of the Solidarity type, with its strong accents of neo-collectivism and its ethical vision of politics. The Mazowiecki camp sees it as useful in the past but now to be demobilized. Some of the political parties on the Wałęsa side see such neo-traditionalization as the base of the new postmodernist type of society.

The ambiguities in the conflicts listed above are rooted not only in inconsistency but also in tactical coalitions that are changing the pattern of articulation, underlining some elements and putting into shadow others. The role of the Catholic Church is also full of ambiguity: the reform-oriented Church absorbed some modernist values, while the new movements, based on the de-privatized concept of religious life, are closer to the millenarian tradition of the pre-reforms Church.

Summing up: the Wałęsa side can be labeled as corporatist-liberal, in contrast to the social-democratic–liberal character of Mazowiecki's camp. Interestingly enough, the same inconsistent ideological syndromes were formulated in Eastern Europe after World War I. The historical challenges were to some extent similar: difficult entry into the world division of labor, development of a dependent capitalism structure, and conflict over the model of the state.

The new map of conflicts, as described above, is rooted in the two dilemmas for transition: the dilemma for democracy (contingency of "revolution from above" versus representation of the emerging civil society, a consensus that is increasingly less relevant versus participation) and the dilemma for capitalism (economic stabilization leading to recession versus capital formation for systemic transformation).

To sum up, three elements are characteristic of the indirect ideological change (or para-ideological phenomena):

● the disintegration of the revolutionary legitimacy of power, reminiscent of the disintegration of traditional legitimation;

● the "round table" as the para-ideological phenomenon, which created impressions on the level of popular consciousness (with implications for the stability of the system) and was as important as changes on the institutional level;

● the new para-ideological debate, loaded with not only political but cultural differences, inside the Solidarity camp (now in power).

In many respects the disintegration of the revolutionary legalization of power in real socialism recalls the crisis of traditional legitimation as described by Kosseleck.[26] On the surface these were diametrically different processes, for whereas the disintegration of traditional legitimation (and the transformation of monarchy based on divine right into absolute monarchy justifying rule on the basis of a configuration of political forces) had its source in religious wars (when the close link of the state with the Church turned out to be troublesome), in Poland a massive, fundamentalist workers' protest became a challenge to the idea of the ruling party as the revolutionary "avant-garde." The similarity is clear, however. In both cases the status of those in power, which they had ascribed to themselves a priori, was questioned with a line of reasoning based on equally a priori assumptions. And as a consequence, in both cases it became a logical step to base rule on principles of "naked power" (absolute monarchy, martial law), resorting not to right (which had been shaken) but to force. Other similar elements also appeared in both situations:

- the separation of politics ("reasons of state") from the ethical argument formulated from the perspective of the individual;
- the severance of earlier bonds (obligations) in the power apparatus;
- a sharper separation than before (and even opposition to each other) of the sphere of power and the sphere of social life.

Finally, both in absolute monarchy and martial law there appeared the problem of a specific "deficit of legitimation" and as a consequence a further evolution seeking justifications for rule in its formalization and relatively stable procedures. Such an evolution in the direction of the rule of law took place both in the passage of enlightened absolutism and in the next phase (after the open crisis and the rule of force) of the transformation of real socialism. The domain of politics, however, continued to be strictly separated from socially accepted ethical principles, and the society itself, excluded from influence on government.

An important element of further transformations of enlightened absolutism (in its original as well as figurative sense, in relation to real socialism) was protest action undertaken in the name of civil liberties. This revolution (and sometimes only a situation containing revolutionary potential) was accompanied by a return of the idea of natural law. Yet whereas in the past (traditional monarchy, the orthodox phase of real socialism) this law applied to the rulers (the "natural" connection with history, past or future), today it is a question of the "natural," inalienable rights of the individual.

There also appear demands to restore the ethical dimension to politics (not supra-individual ethics connected with "reasons of state" but ethics rooted in those same standards of dignity, truth, and reciprocity as the principles that govern interpersonal relations).

It is a paradox that the ideas of citizenship and the call for interlacing the sphere of politics with the social sphere and with ethical responsibility would not have been possible without the earlier separation of politics from "absolute right" (both in its traditional and socialist versions) and without stripping it of the ethical dimension relating to the rights and duties of the ruler. The situation of "naked power" followed by the rule of conventions and procedures somewhat equalized the status of all individuals in relation to the state. This made possible a return of ethics to the sphere of power, but this time it was ethics that relate to the ruled, the ethics of citizens equal before the law.

The second para-ideological phenomenon, the "round table," can be analyzed as yet another *spectacle of power*. In the Polish case its aim was not so much to conclude a particular agreement between the authorities and part of the opposition (for the real trade-off had taken place earlier), but to *create at the level of popular consciousness impressions of para-ideological significance* that would help to stabilize the system. In speaking of this as another spectacle I have in mind the largely ritualized "regulation through crisis" in 1956, when the authorities succeeded in separating the stage of real changes (1954–1955) from the stage of the formation of social actors and the "thaw" on the public scene (1956). The above, combined with elements of steering directions of social activity from above (e.g., designating "scapegoats" in the power elite), enabled the ruling group to retain control and at the same time to create the impression that a near-revolution had taken place. Then in 1970 such a para-ideological event was the visit of E. Gierek, the first secretary of the Communist party, to the Gdańsk Shipyard. This visit contributed to the re-creation among workers of the feeling of hierarchy that is a fundamental element of all rule. Gierek, by using slang mixed with apparatchik "newspeak" (incomprehensible to workers on account of their limited competencies in using such abstract concepts), made the shipyard workers aware of their helplessness in spite of their strength (by forcing them to make only concrete, local demands). He also made them aware that nothing had changed in the relationship of rulers and society and that the latter still recognized the right of the rulers to classify social roles: the workers spontaneously accepted as a "victory" Gierek's calling them "proletarians," thereby removing from them the odium of the label of "hooligans" pinned on them by the mass media. Thus in the popular consciousness the relations of rule were reproduced and even revitalized. In 1976 another such "spectacle of power" was seen in Poland when the faked delegations of workers apologized to Gierek in the name of the strikers. This humiliated the strikers and made them wish to forget the whole event. In this way this episode of the workers' protest (events in Ursus and Radom) fell out of the explicit, spoken workers' tradition and did not return in their conversations until 1980, when the authorities—in the general feeling—in their turn were "humiliated." Martial law also had its variety of "spectacles of power": it was, among other things, propaganda— ostentatiously wide of the truth and offensive—used to show that the authorities could take such liberties and to let people know "who was on top." And finally, there is the "round table," in which real negotiations are hardly more important than reporting about them in the mass media and thereby creating certain impressions.

The deliberations of the "round table" can be analyzed on three planes.

• The deliberations are an element of internal factional struggles that are to some extent an echo of the balance of forces between the faction of globalists and their opponents in the U.S.S.R. The success or failure of the "round table" was treated as an argument in this struggle, and at the same time is a derivative of that struggle (for it depends to a great extent on the current climate in Moscow).

• The "round table" is an important step in the process of disintegration of the old political classes and the formation of a new center (see chapter 2). This somewhat changes relations between institutions in the power structure and also determines the "rules of the organization of the society into a civil society" (and "ways of incorporating this society into the socialist state").

• The "round table" is a specific *communication ritual* with para-ideological functions. Its aim is to create certain effects in popular thinking. For instance, one of its goals is to reformulate in the popular consciousness the idea of the state and to create the impression that now the state has become the property of the society and not only, as before, of the *nomenklatura*. What is interesting is that both the ruling group and the opposition—for different reasons—are keen on creating such an impression. It lies in the interest of the ruling group to create the impression of an increase in the domain of social activity, without big institutional changes, which would be possible if the society recognized the already existing institutions (e.g., regional self-government) as its "own." The opposition in turn wants to create the impression of success to counter strong attacks from its populist wings. That is why it stresses the term "senate" (higher chamber) in discussions on the new shape of the Seym (whereas the ruling group speaks of a "second chamber"). The ruling group, in turn, tried to minimize this impression of victory by pressing for a final declaration: "What Unites Poles."

This battle over symbols does not end there: another essential element of the para-ideological effect is the creation in the popular consciousness of the impression of the *formation of mutual obligations* and the increasing similarity of the sides, which would stabilize the system. An example is the authorities' pressure on the opposition to sign the so-called "educational consensus" card. The contents were not important—the consensus contained generalities on "education for participation in the civil society"—but rather it was the impression of a common stance on such an important question as education that the authorities desired. They also tried to emphasize—with the use of incomprehensible terms—that "an elite is coming to an understanding with an elite." Finally, the public presentation of the arguments of the two sides in a dynamic way—in discourse—has the aim of *recreating the argumentation* through which the elites of the two sides had already passed before they decided to sit down at the table. It was to be re-creation, I might add, with the intention of convincing opponents on both sides. The organizational measure of multiplying "sub-round tables" (undertaken by the "round table" directors from the communist regime side) also has a para-ideological effect: its aim is to draw into the talks as many people as possible from both sides and thereby make them jointly responsible for the outcome of the negotiations.

Controlling the process of producing ideas is an essential element of the factional struggle, for the picture of negotiations painted by the mass media sends out signals about the actual configuration of forces. Often control of the picture of negotiations was just as important as influecne on the negotiations themselves. We are observing here a kind of self-fulfilling prophecy: sometimes it suffices to send out a signal indicating the ascendancy of one of the factions (through key words and symbolic persons and arguments) in order to cause a reorientation of the conformistic low levels of the apparatus and in fact to strenghten the factional position.

The struggle for control over the "production of ideas" (waged simultaneously with the struggle for control over the negotiations) was going on both between the authorities and the opposition and within the Communist party. This resulted in a number of surprising inconsistencies and contradictions in the TV portrayal of events.

Summing up: the "round table" talks can be divided into four stages. Dominant in phases one, two, and four was the aspect of "creating impressions," and only in phase three did the aspect of real negotiations (and not the ritual of communication) dominate. In addition, phase two differed from the others by being filled with the "politics of identity," since the sides—uncertain of their social base (in a situation of the pluralism of elites in atomized society)— were merely attempting to define and present to the public their identity, most often as the reverse reflection of the opponent and not a projection of their own clear vision for the future.

The main result of the "round table" (obtained mostly during the real negotiations conducted behind the stage) was a triple trade-off: legalization of Solidarity in exchange for stabilization; the president as a new institution, taking the role of the balancing force and guarantor of some sort of continuacy vis-à-vis Moscow; a semidemocratically elected parliament (with open competition for the Senate but not the Seym) but with some of its powers ceded to the president.

Not only reformers from the Communist party were divided during the "round table" and after; the political opposition in Poland was divided as well and unsure of its constituency. The joyless victory (surprising only for those not watching Polish affairs very closely) after the "round table" talks is partly rooted in a deep split in the opposition that developed around two issues: democracy from above and the direction of economic reforms. Four factions in the opposition today are important, and only two of them participated in the "round table" talks. A fifth—the national faction (KPN)—is in a way irrelevant when looked at from the "round table" perspective. The KPN vision is "independency first," whereas the "round table" used as its silent assumption that *political and economic reforms were to be undertaken in a colonial situation.* Both the strange political coalitions among these factions as well as the prevailing mood in the public mentality are responsible for the observed lack of support for the "round table" outcome.

For Polish workers Solidarity of 1980 and 1981 was not just a union but, above all, leverage in the *status competition*, in their everyday contacts with the local authorities. The relegalized union ("neo-Solidarity," as workers themselves call it) that was given from above, not won (taken from below), cannot serve as a symbol of status elevation. On the other hand, the need for such symbolic elevation is overwhelming in the society, where the chances for Communist party members to get managerial posts are thirty-five times higher than those of non-party members.[27] Also the new formula of parliamentary elections (with candidates nominated mainly through the corporatist structure of professional associations, based on middle-class membership) hardly can be seen by workers as a useful instrument in status competition. The above is combined with a strong *anti-elitist* orientation among workers. Looking at the "round table" outcome from this perspective, one has to remember that the "round table" was not only a bargaining place but also a proto-ideological phenomenon. In other words, it was also a communication ritual aimed at creating certain politically relevant images and emotions. It was no accident that the populist faction (which had greater control over the mass media than the globalists) underlined the theme of *"elites talking to elites."* This was an important element of the atmosphere surrounding the "round table" talks.

Regarding strange coalitions in Solidarity, four factions should be mentioned here:

- The *social-democratic faction* (the Committee for the Defense of Workers, ex-revisionist experts, and the generation in its mid-fifties) combined with lay Catholics who advocate the "moral economy" vision (Clubs of Catholic Intelligentsia). The most characteristic features of this faction are overestimating the impact of political participation in the establishment and underestimating (even rejecting) the necessity for changes in property rights in the state sector as a basic impulse for the development of a genuine civil society. This faction now is the most influential one around Wałęsa, and its domination of the "round table" talks produced workers' self-management in industry, a council dominated by Solidarity experts supervising the economy, and proposed indexation of incomes as a cure for the economic crisis. All these proposals have less potential for transformation and seem to be less radical than the previous government's own proposal included in the "consolidation plan."

• The *neo-conservative faction* (Young Poland Circle, *Respublica* journal) is reminiscent of English conservatives connected to the "Salisbury Journal," rather than of American neo-conservatives. Its main features are a strong, explicit elitist orientation; statism, with the state as the most important institution; and a peculiar collectivist orientation that can be labeled as "prefigurative politics." Its main elements are the imperative to participate in one of the main traditions of one's own society, combined with a vision of the Church as a political leader of the masses (giving them a value orientation that can serve as a substitute for ideology). Ideology is seen as something dangerous, as a form of reasoning abstracted from its content and the intentions that are behind it. Neo-conservatives strongly support private ownership, but are interested in a slow, evolutionary expansion of the traditional private sector. At the stage of the "round table" they did not advocate experiments with introducing exclusive property rights into the state sector.

Both factions agree that entering state institutions at this stage of the crisis is risky, but cannot be rejected as an offer. And both agree that the pattern of *democracy built from above* (with oppositional elites unsure of their social base, but already co-opted into the establishment) is unavoidable. The Social Democrats accept it for pragmatic reasons (as the only realistic possibility); neo-conservatives, as a result of their elitist orientation.

Two other factions, liberals and populists, were excluded from the "round table" talks by the Wałęsa circle (for different reasons in each case). The *liberals* (Gdańsk *Przegląd Polityczny* circle; economic associations in Kraków and Warsaw) were rejected as being too radical in their economic proposals, demanding a sweeping shift in property rights inside the state sector. The liberals are ready to support even the political capitalism pattern, provided that it increases productivity and accelerates the above ownership changes. Privatization through only private savings and stock buying seems to be too slow: all of the savings in złotys would be able to buy no more than 4 percent of all of the fixed capital in the state sector. Dollar savings (with a value 50 percent higher than złoty savings) would add another 6 percent.

The *populists* in turn (Working Groups in Gdańsk and Łódź) were excluded as too radical in political terms and linked with the rebellious young workers. Populists are highly critical of the development of political capitalism and unsure what type of economic reform they would like to support. At times it seems that they would like the traditional statist socialism as a framework in which they would fight with the state/owner using the Solidarity-1980 formula of a trade union operating as a political party. They also invoke the deep administrative redistribution. Populists are against the depoliticization of Solidarity, which is a crucial outcome of the "round table" talks that shifted politics from workers to the middle-class elite (Citizens' Committee).

Both liberals and populists are (for different reasons) against the democracy-from-above pattern. Liberals prefer democracy from below and sweeping economic reforms (leading to a new aggregation of the atomized economic society that eventually would constitute itself into a genuine civil society) as a necessary first step. The presence of the social-democratic faction of Solidarity in the parliament is no guarantee that future economic reforms will go in the above direction. Only after the formation of Prime Minister Mazowiecki's government did the influence of the liberal faction markedly increase. Liberals are much less optimistic about the potential of Solidarity to keep the social peace than are the Social Democrats. In general liberals are much younger than Social Democrats and slightly younger than neo-conservatives. Populists are also against the democracy-from-above method: they prefer movement-type activity and in many ways remind one (in their mentality) of the populist faction inside the Communist party. Populists present themselves as the legacy of Solidarity. This is not because they are fundamentalists to such an extent as Solidarity was in 1980 and 1981, but because they keep a value orientation in their debate on economic interests. In other words, *they follow Solidarity's identity* not by repeating its statements but by continuing its semantics. The latter was rejected openly by all other factions but was kept on the level of the popular working consciousness.

Strange political coalitions in the above situation (with the Social Democrats and neo-conservatives together facing an alliance between liberals and populists) are linked above all to the *democracy from above or from below? issue.* A deep split, however, exists in each faction over economic matters, and the pattern of political forces described above is a very unstable one.

The characteristic shift of Wałęsa himself in 1990 from the "round table" coalition to alliance with forces excluded from the "round table" reinforced the political forces described above. The result is the split in the ex-opposition in the form of five axes already described. Three other phenomena that occurred between the "round table" stage and the current, open split in the Solidarity camp should be mentioned here. They are responsible for the great unstableness (openness) of the transformation. Though the example of Poland has been used here, these phenomena are also appearing (with varying degrees of intensity) in the other countries of Eastern Europe. And in each case they create a peculiar aura of being in a sort of limbo situation—between two systems (when socialism's arrangements no longer exist but a new system is not yet created). These phenomena are:

- signals of "authoritarianism with authority";
- departure from the matrix (mediated by the administrative redistribution) model of social structure to the new type of structure without any institutionalized pattern of conflict mediation;
- tensions between the short-term stabilization (anti-inflation) policy of the government and its actions to transform property rights.

Authoritarianism with Authority

September 1989–January 1990

More and more voices are warning of the danger of authoritarianism, not so much from the return of the "old" as from the new forms of political life developing before our eyes.[28] This is accompanied by features of social life typical of authoritarianism. For example, one gets the impression that the dramatic collisions of economic interests (i.e., connected with the struggle to form capital in a severe recession period) remain unexpressed and manifest themselves in hidden forms (accompanied by a flood of verbiage and the helplessness of the uninformed parliament). Social support for the government is based not so much on the participation of public opinion in shaping its policy as on blind confidence. Thus, this is the not-so-rare phenomenon of authoritarian rule with authority (as opposed to the previous ruling group, which was regarded as alien). An expression of this blind confidence is the fact that, as the November 1989 polls of the Center for the Study of Public Opinion (CBOS) show,[29] about 70 percent of the society supports the economic policy of the government, though two-thirds do not know its assumptions. When respondents are asked about their own preferences, they go in the other direction (more government intervention).

This is accompanied by passivity and stagnation in all forms of social life, from trade union to party organizations.[30] Such passive acquiescence suits many members of the present ruling team: They erroneously assume that social activity would work solely to strengthen egalitarian pressures. Though efforts are being made to breathe life into the movement of Citizens' Committees (suspended in a vacuum in July under the pressure of Wałęsa and the National Committee of Solidarity), this is being done selectively. Only some of the Committees were invited to the meeting on 8–9 December 1989, and there was no time for a discussion of the concrete problems they face. Instead the meeting prepared the background for a ritual together and prepared the nucleus of an election machine.

There are various reasons for this typically authoritarian blockade of articulation: from the nature of the coalition behind the government (which suppresses conflicts between the city and the countryside) to the strict political discipline in the clubs of deputies.[31] For example, neither a liberal (Economic Action: about fifty deputies) nor a populist wing can form in the Citizens' Parliamentary Club due to the decreasing relevance of the myth of "Unity." False identity is another barrier to articulation: Many Communist (PUWP) delegates, for instance, are representives of the dynamic *nomenklatura* of new owners, but they have to act like leftists. The most essential element of the articulation blockade, however, is the strategy of *"exclusionary corporatism,"* which is made up of a tangle of mobilization techniques (e.g., support at the polls), but in such a way as to prevent differences of interests within the society from coming to light.[32]

Thus a sort of Non-Party Bloc for cooperation with the government, which some have recently attempted to form from the Citizens' Committees, would compete in the May 1990 elections to local offices along with candidates from political parties (those from the parliament and outside it) that express the more specific interests of concrete groups of the society. This concerns only a small part of the presently emerging political parties; most of them are still immersed in hazy symbolic references and appeal to the "general interest." We already had such elections in Poland—a supraparty bloc against parties—in 1935, and this was more of a plebiscite (for the government) than a democratic, conscious election of programs and people. The plebiscitary nature of the elections in June 1989 was justified by haste and necessity to cut off the candidates of the Communist party, but the price is the present quality of the parliament. To repeat this situation, however, would be a mistake that would increase the apathy of a society that is not being represented in its diversity. The plebiscitary nature of the elections also retards the coming to light of the political identity of opposition (and ex-opposition) elite. Neither does it help to rationalize the political articulation of the emerging political parties which today are turned more toward the past than toward the future. The formula of "exclusionary corporatism" (impeding the expression of differences of interests within the society) causes apathy and weakens social activity; it also hides the identities of political elites. For instance, it is still unclear whether the Presidium of the Citizens' Parliamentary Club is for or against radical privatization of the economy (without which we face a continuation of authoritarian statism with appearances of a market).

The above phenomena influence the special nature of the emerging state, which recalls the construction of the historical Standesstaat. The latter state was made up of segments, each of which was constituted differently and had different justifications. Political agreements and not universal legal rules determined the role of particular segments. These segments were specific ethos groups with different values and traditions and not representatives of clearly defined interests. The binding agents and stabilizers of the system were extralegal "institutions": in Poland, Wałęsa and the extraconstitutional KOK (Committee for National Defense).

An additional element is the blockade of information. Both the intentional blockade—e.g., about conflicts over the conception of the trade union, about differences among delegates within the Citizens' Parliamentary Club, about the real expository visions of the elite—and the unintentional one. An example is the soothing language of the new propaganda, which presents what really is a choice as something "with no alternatives" and does not reveal its often debatable assumptions, such as the upsetting assumption on which the government strategy of the fight against hyperinflation is based—namely, that when state enterprises reach the "demand barrier" (goods are not purchased by consumers because they are too expensive) prices will come down. This assumption fails to take into consideration another scenario: output will be reduced and prices stabilized on this lower level of the firm's production. And one also doubts whether the government is doing enough to fight inflation through an increase in production (e.g., coordinated, cooperative import and radical structural cuts in the economy from above). But the above dilemmas are not discussed openly in the mass medie and society is as excluded from the influence on options as before.

The New Map of Social-economic Conflicts

Four facts (the withdrawal of the state from setting prices; reducing subsidies to the economy, and hence the redistribution of funds through the budget; bankruptcy of the state sector, and hence an end to the role of the state as the accumulator of capital; and privatization by the method of political capitalism) sufficed to radically alter the map of conflicts in Poland. In the past the material position of all social groups depended on the administrative decisions of the state, which in most conflicts was regarded as the major opponent.

We are presently observing a dramatic fight over the formation of capital within the society itself. Thus this fight is simultaneous with the end of the matrix social structure (mediated through the state) described in the fourth chapter of my *The Ontology of Socialism*. This is a spontaneous struggle (though even here one can perceive a certain logic about which I say more below), for its course is not determined by a plan or by laws of the market (the latter does not yet exist).

Two things make this a dramatic struggle. First, there was a deep recession even before serious measures were undertaken to fight inflation, which in the first phase might even worsen this recession. Already today production is lower than before the recession of 1979 through 1982, and national income is about 95 percent of what it was in 1978. At the same time, investments are one-third less than in 1979 and indebtedness has doubled in comparison with 1978. The second thing is uncertainty whether the techniques for fighting inflation contained in the stabilization plan will prod producers to raise their output. Instead, is it not possible that given the physical barriers (supply bottlenecks) and absence of competition (monopolies, the lack of many economic interests on account of ownership relations) inflation will stabilize on a high level with lack of demand (due to lack of money) and leaving basic social needs unsatisfied?

In barest outline, here is how this struggle over nonequivalent exchange can be presented. It is taking place in the triangle: the state sector, *nomenklatura* companies built into this sector, and agriculture. As I showed in chapter 2, these companies are throwing part of their costs onto state enterprises, which increases the profits of the former and accelerates the formation of capital in this mode of production. The instrument of this nonequivalent exchange is not the market but the dual position of the new owners, who at the same time are managers in the state sector. This situation accelerates the decapitalization of the state sector and causes a peculiar shift of capital without a capital market. What is more, it may (though not necessarily) promote further, more rational (that is, not capitalizing political leaders) privatization.

Today Eastern Europe seems to be entering the stage of renewed primary accumulation. For the state sector is no longer able to create the capital necessary to make technological leaps. There is even a lack of capital for simple reproduction, and this sector is rapidly decapitalizing. Thus the formation of capital is also an initial condition of privatization. Alternative ways of capital formation are limited: Funds at the disposal of the traditional private sector are being consumed by inflation. An exchange of part of the debt for property rights causes controversies. Savings in the hands of the society suffice for only a very slow and limited privatization. From this perspective one should look differently at the model of political capitalism described in this book, for what has been presented here (and is so regarded by public opinion) as the drawback of this mode of production might be regarded as its advantage from a historical perspective. The point is that the *nomenklatura* companies in this mode of production have the possibility of passing on part of their operating costs to the state sector and the state budget. While the initial primary accumulation took place at the cost of agriculture, the second one is taking place at the cost of the state sector, even further accelerating its decapitalization. If it is recognized that privatization is the right path and the formation of capital is its condition, then the opinion here cannot be entirely negative. The litmus test of the rationality of the model of political capitalism will be the future of this capital—in other words, in what it will be invested, the degree of openness of the economy, and how diversified this capital will be. Historical analogies (e.g., Japan of the 1880s, where openness of the economy determined the economic rationality of political capitalism) show that there is a clear danger of the transformation of political capital into finance capital, especially when there is growing political resistance to this mode of production. So paradoxically, the greater its success in the first phase (the accumulation of capital), the greater the danger of the political and social blockade of the second phase that can give economic sense to this accumulation.

The above comments serve to underline the ambiguity of opinions about political capitalism. Its particular forms also should be looked at from this angle. This mode of production, which has become a Trojan horse in the state sector, must be analyzed not only as the preparation (often in the military-economic interest of the Moscow center) of channels for controlling the penetration of foreign capital (and so it is probably not by chance that most of the companies are being set up in branches producing the means of production rather than in consumer goods industries) but also as an instrument of accelerated accumulation and a stage before real privatization.

The state sector is defending itself against decapitalization by raising the prices of its products, which is facilitated by its monopoly position in most fields. In other words, it is passing on part of the costs to consumers, including agricultural costs. The peasants are also defending themselves by fighting for administratively guaranteed purchase prices of agricultural products (where the laws of supply and demand would call for lowering them). In this way farmers wish to avoid the necessary, though painful, adjustment processes through which all countries passed which today have a profitable and economically efficient agricultural sector: the bankruptcy of inefficient farms, the formation of larger farms, greater productive effort, more rational (e.g., common) use of the means of production, and the stratification of country property (according to the criterion of efficiency) and not "leveling" via parity. The paradox, however, is that farmers also lack the conditions for economically rational adaptive reactions. So the peasants are exerting political pressure (and are part of the ruling coalition). They are also using food blackmail (we won't sell!). And the state gives in because it has no food reserves that would allow it to wait out the farmers and make them sell through economic necessity.

Taking the necessary steps to make agriculture efficient would require not only strong nerves but also releasing peasant-workers from industry. The circle closes: agriculture is subsidized before it has begun to be economically efficient; it has nearly the lowest labor productivity in Europe. The costs are borne by consumers. Inflation increases. The methods of combating inflation (e.g., hard credit, higher taxes) stifle economic initiatives (apart from political capitalism) and deepen the recession. Pressures also build up for wage increases in the state sector, increases which through costs are passed on in prices. No one behaves rationally—and the situation of primary accumulation of the forties and fifties seems to be repeating itself. At that time capital was formed for the development of the state sector at the cost of private agriculture by decapitalizing it. Now the state sector is attempting to repeat this situation by defending itself from decapitalization (by promoting political capitalism) and from the effects of the recession. But today the peasants have powerful means of defense.

And so the vicious circle closes. How to break out of it? The answers are simple only on the surface: create a real market (the game described above is not a market) by immediately moving away from administratively guaranteed minimum prices in agriculture. Further, speed up privatization in the state sector and fight harder against monopolies. Finally, discuss openly the problem of indexation, which was framed in an irresponsible way at the "round table" and ratified by the Seym. A silent withdrawal only worsens the matter.

Paradoxically, implementation of the above measures is blocked by the political organization of the society itself. Thus none of the newly emerging peasant parties is willing to give up the fight for parity (even before agriculture becomes efficient), because otherwise it will lose its electorate. Privatization of the state sector has reached a standstill: the paths to it still have not been laid out and there are no legel regulations. The leftist faction of the Citizens' Parliamentary Club is calling for the creation of a National Property Fund in the parliament; a body of venerable professors would slowly decide the future of enterprises. The Ministry of Finances, which has suggested the sale of shares through a commercial bank (e.g., Bank of the National Economy, which is a sort of agency of this ministry), is blocked not only by this faction, but also by the Ministry of Industry, which fears giving excessive power to the minister of finances. Workers' councils (or rather, their political representation) also are firmly opposed to privatization in the state sector in forms other than stockholding by employees (which, in my opinion, is sensible but not as the only or chief form, for it is highly impractical in a situation such as in Poland, which calls for deep structural changes in the economy and where a certain concentration of ownership rights and interests is necessary in order to throttle the power of the bureaucracy in the economy).

Stabilization Policy and Transformation

Three elements are characteristic of the "stabilization plan" undertaken in the Polish economy starting in January 1990:
- a balanced budget, tight money;
- "internal convertibility" of the złoty;
- wage restrictions.

The government is cutting the list of subsidized goods by two-
thirds and liberalizing most prices (energy prices, for example, are
expected to rise by 650 percent). Interest on credits will rise to the
level of inflation (for January, planned at 50 percent but by the
third week of January reaching 65 percent). Both taxes and penal-
ties for tax evaders will be increased. At the same time the złoty
has been devalued (to an official rate of nearly 10,000 złotys per
dollar, when only three months earlier it was 2300 złoties). The
government will defend the new rate with the help of a $2 billion
reserve plus the so-called stabilization fund of $1 billion offered by
the IMF. The wage restrictions are expected to cause at least a 25
percent drop in real wages. Production also will fall: the government plan speaks of a 10 percent drop, but independent economists expect a much deeper recession. Unemployment will rise to an
expected minimum of 5 percent of the labor force. Gloomier economists expect at least three million unemployed (see *The Economist*, 23 December 1989). The program also has some shock
absorbers: lowering the exchange rate and raising import taxes;
this is aimed at increasing the competitiveness of Polish industry
vis-à-vis Western imports. The last measure has already been implemented, starting from 1 January 1990. An extension of import
taxes to raw materials and components for production would add
to the recession, however.

The effects of the above stabilization policy may hinder the
transformation of the economy and its evolution toward some
form of capitalism. The high taxes on the private sector as well as
expensive credit and high import duties on components for production considerably reduce the formation of capital that later
could be used to buy up property rights in the state sector (in the
event of its privatization). These factors largely determine the nature of this privatization in the future, though at present privatization is retarded on account of the social-democratic orientation

dominant in the Citizens' Parliamentary Club and differences of opinion on this subject in the government itself. Without domestic capital eventual privatization could take the form of state capitalism (companies owned by the Treasury and foreign capital). This could increase the dependency of the Polish economy on world capital and also impede the development of a civil society.

Also important is the sequence of measures undertaken in the stabilization maneuver. Originally this maneuver was supposed to consist of three simultaneous steps: liberalization of prices, demonopolization, and privatization of the state sector. For various reasons (among others, the organizational and political resistance to the last two measures) these steps have become separated. This can not only increase the social and economic costs of the stabilization maneuver but also increase the resistance to evolution toward the capitalist mode of production. Socialist and populist tendencies might be strengthened.

Conclusion

To sum up: the dynamics of the first phase of the transformation described in this book can be grasped in the following sequence: (1) an attempt to restructure the relation of the socialist bloc to the world capitalist system through "ontological opening," (2) political reforms as a way of achieving stability through the rule of popular government, and (3) changes in the network of dependencies inside the bloc (modification of the COMECON, which after successful "ontological opening" will no longer have to play the role of administrator of subarticulation); as a consequence, the Eastern bloc countries will pass from a formal to an informal empire, in which the directions of dependency will result more from the logic of the division of labor and the natural peripheral status of the Eastern bloc than from the use of political and military complusion.

Additional elements are influencing the ambiguity (fluidity) of the situation.

● First, the present "revolution from above" is a "discrete revolution" (invisible). This is true even though it has all the features of breakthrough in the system (though retaining the imperial framework), for it is accompanied by the rhetoric of "stabilization and control for the sake of reforms" which is used by the new "avant-garde" of the establishment. At the same time, there are no visible changes "at the bottom"; on the contrary, the former *nomenklatura* is adapting itself quite smoothly to the new situation. So there is no "status elevation" of the members of Solidarity in the work place, as was so important in August 1980. What is more, the tangle of engaging in politics and trade-union activity that was so characteristic of the 1980–81 social movement Solidarity has been severed, while the channels of political activity are open today mainly to the intellectual elite.

• Second, the revolution is taking place "from above" in the name of theoretical interests. Social actors interested in change do not appear until after it has been carried out. In time "ontological opening" will improve the material situation of everybody, including workers. The latter, however, will lose in the relative sense, for others will gain more. But workers will be the first to bear the costs of the reform, especially of the stabilization plan with induced recession. The reform also will destroy the traditional niche that helps workers to survive the crisis, for the small private sector is dislodging the illegal "second economy."

• Third, the former "power without politics" (of a post-totalitarian state) has yielded to "politics without power" (that is, without control over real processes). The anarchy of social life is felt painfully, especially by a society accustomed to authoritarian government. Some of the causes of anarchy are rooted in the crisis, others in the political reforms (when all levels of the administration, unsure of the future, are building survival strategies no longer based on loyalty and obedience to superiors but on their own foresight).

What is striking in this is the falseness of the situation: a trade-union movement for which it is ever harder—in the face of hyper-inflation followed by deep recession—to support reforms induced by the Solidarity government. An emergency solution, imposed by political activists of the former opposition, is to demobilize the trade union. This, however, would frustrate activists, swell the ranks of the All-Polish Association of Trade Unions, and in the next elections threaten a takeover of the union by Wałęsa's opponents.

This false situation is attended by changes favorable for the former power elite, namely:

• the separation of power from responsibility. The latter burdens the government formed by Solidarity, while a large part of the real control is concentrated in the hands of the president and extraconstitutional institutions (such as the Committee of Social Order led by Kiszczak or the Commission for Implementation of the Round Table Agreement, involving direct participation of Church officials as well as Inner Security officers). What is more, freedom of maneuver for the new government does not exist: the government is carrying out what the former elite had wanted but could not do on account of social resistance;

• rapid development following the model of political capitalism, which not only allows the former *nomenklatura* to retain its privileged material status but works toward modernization of the empire by using the market mechanism and individual interests in profit;

• weakening of the coalition standing behind the new government due to the city–countryside structural conflict, as well as five axes of new conflicts described above.

This is accompanied by changes in social configurations characteristic of the transition period. Certain subjects (the *nomenklatura* as well as the opposition that is now becoming the base of support for the government—or even the government itself) are disappearing or changing rapidly the base of their own social status. The question is who will replace them and how? New actors (*nomenklatura* as owners) are also appearing and old ones (the newly legalized economic underground) are coming out in new roles. What form will their relations with the state take?

Finally, the first stage in the breakthrough in the system is attended by speculations on the crisis and Poland's indebtedness, which adds to the ambiguity of the situation. Thus the undulations of conceptions for overcoming the crisis (including the nonpayment of debts) causes a decline in the value of the debt (bought up for a dozen or so cents on the dollar). In turn, information suggesting the possibility of Western aid for Poland raises the value of the debt. The possibility that those who bought up the debt will make money results in the artificial creation of a favorable and unfavorable climate around Poland. One can also analyze in this context the misrepresentations by some Western press agencies concerning the conflict over the convent of Carmelite nuns of Oświęcim.[33]

This analysis of the first phase of the breakthrough in the socialist system presents more questions than answers. My aim was not only to attempt an interpretation of the outwardly chaotic flow of events but also to work out conceptual categories and theoretical references for their analysis.

Conclusion: Dilemmas for Democracy in Eastern Europe

The term *democracy* belongs to the vocabulary of ideology, but it also has an analytical content. Contemporary Western visions of democracy are linked to the complex institutional and legal framework through which those who "rule" are checked by the "ruled," and conflicts that occur among the latter are mediated. The concept of mass democracy executing a mythologized "general will" is rejected and treated as remote and dangerous. However, it is worth remembering that these two models are also linked to the different patterns through which community/society constituted itself (or, defined itself) as a political entity.

Five such patterns have appeared during the recent transformation in Eastern Europe, bringing obstacles that could prevent the development of representative democracy based on the rule of law. This leads to the first dilemma for democracy in Eastern Europe. It is caused by the fact that during the first stage of transformation society formed itself (in order to start the whole process) into a peculiar type of political entity. And now, in the second stage of transition, the *very same form of political articulation has to be demobilized from above* by the new elite, which is composed of some ex-oppositional leaders. The dramatic paradox of this stage of breakthrough in real socialism is that popular, massive political mobilization is possible only in a nationalistic or fundamentalist way when the economic base for a genuine civil society does not exist. It is worth mentioning that I use the term *civil society* in a

Hegelian sense,[1] as synonymous with the peculiar pattern of socialization through which both inner differences in society and the necessity for the state's mediation are recognized and legitimized. Only such a society can put into practice the representative, not the mass, pattern of democracy. The fundamentalist or nationalist articulation is unavoidable at this stage of transformation, but it is highly dysfunctional for both gradual change and emerging "politics."

The second dilemma for democracy in Eastern Europe is rooted in the character of the transformation itself and could be deduced long before the whole process started.[2] The ontology of the real socialist societies leads to the situation in which *change has to be conducted from above* in the name of "theoretical interests." This is particularly characteristic of the privatization process that is essential for the whole transformation. People with "real" and not only "theoretical" (based on knowledge that this is economically rational, not on their own material motives) interests in such change are absent; such interests have to be created by the state. The crucial point of the breakthrough is exactly the change in the web of interests, with an increase in the number of people interested in privatization as it continues. In other words, during the first stage of transformation the new political elite (composed of reform-oriented ex-party apparatus and ex-oppositional leaders) projects on society its vision, rather than representing the interests of concrete social groups. The legitimizing argument here is the interest of society as a whole in abandoning real socialism and not the expansion of interests of a particular, well-defined constituency. New relationships, actors, and interests are created. Such state activity, rather than representing existing interests, is essential for the whole process of transition. The above situation, unavoidable as it is, creates, however, a danger of making (to some extent) a sort of facade of newly created democratic institutions. These institutions can also be manipulated by the new vanguard (often in the name of pure politics and power struggle). The lack of well-articulated interests in a society that is in transition gives the new elite the illusory feeling of "free hands." What is more, it happens at a time when the interests of the empire are well defined and guarded.[3]

It is worth reminding ourselves that "most of the leading perspectives on social change assumed that the origins of social transformation are to be found in processes internal to society. Change is presumed to occur via mechanisms 'built into the very structure of a given society.'"[4] Analyzing revolutions from above in Eastern Europe calls for a more elaborated paradigm that would take into account not only systemic contradictions and social forces mobilized by them but also the active role of the state, as well as chance phenomena.

What is more, even in the advanced capitalist societies, the idea of the public interest cannot be fully rejected and politics cannot be reduced to legislative activity only (or to defending a "free competition structure" against special-interest groups). Some interests (such as environmental problems) have to be defined from above as "quasi-objective goods" without waiting for the spontaneous contracts decided on in the marketplace. In the case of Eastern Europe, which is now in transition, it is clearly not possible to ground this process on the competition of individual interests only. First of all, such a competitive structure has to be created from above. What is more, some interests do not exist, due to the legacy of real socialism with its statist economy. In such a situation the idea of "general interest" cannot be reduced (as liberals would wish) to the "interest in reaching an agreement." Some alternatives have to be defined by the state itself as being clearly in no one's particular interest. The state has also to create actors who would treat those alternatives as being in their own best interest (or somehow to imitate them as the party to a contract). But the consequence of this is not only an eventual fallacy of representation but also the danger of abuse by the state of its power of defining what is the public interest during the period of transition.

The issue of privatization is especially instructive here. It is the key issue of transformation and strong arguments are formulated to depoliticize it as much as possible (with the "minimal state" claim as an "anti-politics" attitude.) But even in the case in which privatization would be conducted through commercial agencies selling stocks, the role of the state would be a crucial one and not substantially reduced. Remember that it is the state that is shaping the economic conditions of "becoming an owner" during the privatization procedure. The state not only defines which capital is legitimized and which is not (with recent attacks on capital accumulated by ex-*nomenklatura* through a political capitalism mode); it also makes decisions about the future distribution of property rights (in the Polish case, it is decided through administrative limits on stock sold to employees, which are kept on the level of 20 percent of the privatized enterprise's fixed capital) and creates the legal and institutional framework (for instance, credit facilities) that is decisive from the point of view of the speed and mode of future privatization.

Political debate in Eastern Europe now focuses on how to control and check this unavoidable role of the state during transition. One proposal (from neo-conservative groups) is to create such a system of checking standards on the base of "prefigurative communities" (such as, "the social teaching of the Catholic Church"). But here we come again to the first dilemma for democracy in Eastern Europe: is "neo-traditionalization" the only possible way to get safely out of real socialism when civil society does not yet exist?

Both the dilemmas for democracy described above are rooted in a specific attitude that is somewhat reminiscent of *postmodernist culture*. In the case of the elite who are proceeding toward privatization from above, this is a peculiar *politics of pastische*, with its half mocking and self-doubting imitation of some forms of nineteenth-century capitalism ("pure" market; personal ownership). Such an imitation of capitalist prehistory is seen as the necessary step to enter the modern capitalist world. This is based on the assumption (signaled by Fukoyama) that stylistic innovations are no longer possible. On the level of popular consciousness such a postmodernist attitude can be observed in society's efforts to overcome its own atomization and to form itself into a political entity. This is done with help of action on the one hand (rebel as politics of identity), and on the other hand, with the peculiar *neo-traditionalization*. Both features are characteristic of postmodernist culture.

Paradoxically enough, such postmodernist attitudes are treated by the elite and society as instruments to enter modernity (two steps forward in order to actually make one step).

Is such postmodernist culture rational, in the instrumental sense of the word, from the point of view of the East European current problems, or is it a refusal to engage the present and to think historically?

The third dilemma for democracy in Eastern Europe is linked to the fact that, from my point of view, the recent transformations should be interpreted not as the dissolution of the empire, but as the empire's effort to adjust better to the world system. This is followed by an evolution from formal to informal empire, based on the logic of a division of labor and the "natural" gravitation of markets, instead of on coercion only.[5] This new form of colonial state, however, limits and distorts to some extent the power structures that have recently emerged in Eastern Europe.[6] We observe here a clash of two processes. On one hand, it is an effort on the side of emancipating Eastern European societies (and their political elite) to create a "national power container"[7] with the crystallization of structural properties as well as "authoritative and allocative resources" into a form of nation-state, ruled by constitutional government. On the other hand, this is a process through which *a new form of colonial state* emerges. The latter is based mostly on extraconstitutional arrangements (for instance, the Committee for National Defence in Poland or extraordinary "commissions"). What is more, economic and political dependency always works as a segmenting force that excludes some fields and resources from the control of the local and national government and destroys to some extent the "systemness" of the nation-state. This creates serious limits on the democratically elected bodies.

The fourth dilemma for democracy is rooted in a peculiar ambiguity of the legal relationship between the institutions of state. The stabilizing and balancing role of the later Communist party is now taken by the institution of the presidency, which is nearly as unclearly formalized as the "leading role of the party" was before. This is linked to the political function of that office, which is treated as a guarantee for the evolutionary character of change by both Moscow and the West. This adds, however, to the characteristic *ambiguity of the formal structure of the emerging state.*

The fifth dilemma for democracy is connected with the fact that the freedom of maneuver of the Eastern European governments (formed with the participation of ex-oppositional leaders) is very limited. The reason is the severe indebtedness as well as COMECON obligations and a deep economic crisis. As a result, the new elite often conducts the very same economic policies that the old elite would have liked to introduce but could not due to social resistance and a lack of legitimacy. This, together with the strong impact of the new elite on the evolutionary character of change,[8] followed by the very good adjustment of the old party *nomenklatura*, created a peculiar type of *new cynicism* (both among the "well-informed public" and the people of the new elite themselves). It also increases the *passivity* of society, leading to all the paradoxes of representative democracy in the apathetic society. This is especially true where the "majority" is not absolute but relative. This was sometimes the case during the May 1990 election in Poland (in which only 42 percent of the population voted) and, as a result of growing passivity, is now the rule. With growing social apathy, it is appropriate to ask with what right the will of the greatest number is substituted for the will of the majority. This is especially valid when choices are made not between well-elaborated alternatives but between symbols, loyalties, and "ethoses" (and the latter is often the case in Eastern Europe). It is worth adding here that the aura of cynicism, delicate as it is, corresponds well to the peculiar cynicism of Western politicians and professionals dealing with Eastern Europe. Those who know the rules are impatient with those who break them (as in Lithuania).[9] Those who are responsible for the monitoring of Eastern European transformations are tired of the unpredictability of the whole process. The cumulation of nearly unsolvable economic problems decreases the credit worthiness of Eastern Europe. Such attitudes in the West have been the source of a self-fulfilling prophecy. The lack of Western capital involvement that follows these perceptions held by Western politicans stops the transformation in the middle of the process (especially when the capital necessary for privatization is absent). This increases the dilemmas for democracy indicated above and leads to a peculiar "Argentinization" of that region.

All these dilemmas can lead to the "electoral fallacy,"[10] the illusion that the new electoral rules are enough to guarantee democracy.

Here I will deal only with the first of these dilemmas. I will also try to present the pattern of state that is now replacing the old party-state. At this first stage of transformation the category of Standesstaat[11] is very useful, as is the concept of "exclusionary corporatism."

The first stage of the transformation in Eastern Europe should be labeled as the "politics of identity" and is connected with the shift from desocialized society to society as an actor of change. In other words, from a society that is atomized and systematized by the state (even in the actions of previous rebels which were to some extent mere rituals of change,[12] directed from above)[13] to a society acting on its own as a political entity. The functional imperative that would make such change possible is a shift in the collective imagination of society and its new perception of itself.

This shift is connected with the search for the concepts that would define terms of society's independence from the state, as well as for values that would justify such independence. Highly bureaucratized social relations (due to the type of property rights, with the state as the necessary binding mechanism) make such a shift especially difficult. This shift reminds us to some extent of the *bricollage* pattern of reasoning.[14] The new existential experience (Solidarity, "unegoistic" strikes of 1980) activated dormant (latent) values and promoted them to the role of cognitive categories.[15] The latter made possible the "politics of identity" when the axis of society's conflict with the state was defined and the value base for society's independent status as well as the borders for the penetration by the state were articulated. Values inherent in political fundamentalism and in rapidly accelerating nationalism can play such roles. They are alternative patterns of the initial mass mobilization that later on (as a generalized threat) is one of the main reasons for the ensuing revolution from above.

But both patterns of mass articulation have to be demobilized when such revolutions from above take place. What is more, such demobilization is administered from above at a stage when an ontological base for a genuine civil society is not yet created and eventual reform of property rights is on the level of discussions. This leads (as in Poland today) to a peculiar social vacuum and passivity (when fundamentalist political articulation is gone and the new form of the political entity has not yet emerged on a mass scale). The other reaction is one observed in Romania and the Soviet Union in the form of violent clashes between society's vision of how to fulfill the newly created space for autonomous activity (nationalistic fights with minorities) and the vision of "politics" formulated from above.

In all Eastern European societies the base for the pattern of socialization typical of civil society would emerge only after the dissolution of state ownership. The presence of political space is clearly not enough. The state-owned economy (even when it is deregulated and decentralized) continuously leads to the atomization and segmentation of society and the economy, due to the lack of universalized market rules as well as concepts, such as "capital," which would make possible a perception of economic activity as a process. The etatized economy is also one of the causes of the "natural" anarchism so characteristic of Eastern Europe, where the state is treated as a particularistic body acting in the name of its own interests (rationality of control). The popular answer concerning the prerogative philosophy of power (treating law as the mere instrument of politics) entails a substantive—not a formal—vision of justice. The legitimacy of the new elite, built on trust, has reduced that attitude but has not created the new pattern of socialization that could eventually substitute private property rights as the base for socialization leading to a civil society. I do not believe that such an alternative base is possible at all. An absence of such a base is responsible for the fact that the initial form of society's self-articulation as a political entity, separate from the state, has to be either *nationalism* or *fundamentalism* (as in Poland in 1980). Nationalism can take the variant of claiming full sovereignty (as in the Baltic republics) or, as in the southern Soviet republics, a variant of aggression against both Russians and local minorities due to unsolvable territorial claims.[16]

The other patterns of political articulation now observed in the Eastern bloc and *emerging only in a situation when society is relatively passive* and only when the elite is mobilized are:

• the soft national orientation (without strong nationalistic accents directed against minorities or without claims of immediate independence) combined with a strong orientation toward institutional reform. Such articulation has appeared recently in some Soviet republics (for instance, in the "Ruch" formula in the

Ukraine) as well as in Czechoslovakia and Hungary. However, such an orientation can very easily shift toward the first type of orientation;

• the drive toward technocratic autonomy that, through decentralization, would make it possible to solve at least some local problems. Such orientation is often seen among the Russian elite in the Soviet Far East;[17]

• DDR party politics in East Germany that awakened the old political facade and was reinforced by the West German party machines and the new issue of reunification. The surprisingly good electoral results of the reformed Communist party[18] can be explained only by the voters' rejection of the fundamentalist attitude. The latter would eliminate the Communist party, on moral grounds, as during the Polish election in June 1989 when the names of both party reformers and hard-liners were crossed out. With voting based on merit, the Communist party in the DDR gained some chances due to its present position on unification which is shared by some East Germans (these same people would reject communists when voting on the past record or moral grounds). Such party politics in the DDR took place in the initial (the Popular Front) articulation that combined elements of political fundamentalism with strong accents of revisionist orientation, reminding one of the politics of the Polish revisionists inside the Communist party in October 1956.

Some forms of corporatist orientation that developed in the late 1970s emerged only among the professional elite that formulated the "theoretical proposals for reforms": in other words, proposals that were based on professional standards and knowledge, not on the interests of their own social group. In the 1980s such forms of the separate articulation of society were rejected consciously as leading to local concessions only and isolating the intelligentsia from the rest of society. However, such rejection of corporatist bodies as political channels only reinforced the tendency to operate in the paradigm of the "general will" and mass democracy.

Two of these patterns—nationalism and fundamentalism in its religious as well as secularized form—must now be demobilized from above. Techniques of such demobilization oscillate between "exclusionary corporatism" and the threat (or even actualization) of state violence (as in Lithuania or the southern Soviet republics).

The technique of "exclusionary corporatism" is connected with the elaborated web of selective mobilization of electoral support and the demobilization of articulation of social conflicts. The former takes the form of a supraparty bloc that is based on trust and loyalty rather than on an elaborated political program.

Three remaining patterns of articulation can be to some extent combined with the representative democracy model. But remember that these forms are possible only in a relatively passive society lacking its initial mobilization. So this is democracy without the broad will to participate, with only an elite that is active. In other words, when the revolution is from above from its first step, not from below, the atomization of society does not cease to exist and its new identity vis-à-vis the state is not created. The mutiny of society is, however, now not due to the lack of legal possibilities to organize or to the threat of repressions. Instead it is rooted in the fact that the new elite (in order to demobilize fundamentalist articulation, or any articulation that is seen as harmful for the gradual character of change) reinforces, with its whole authority, structures of articulation that, to a great extent, are irrelevant from the point of view of the real axis of conflicts and the matrix of social interests.[19] At the same time, political parties that emerged from below are too weak (and without access to the mass media)[20] to compete effectively with a supraparty bloc such as the one in Poland that captured Solidarity symbols. The lack of an economic base for a genuine civil society increases the remote and abstract character of the party-type articulation. These parties do not even know who forms their constituency.

So, paradoxically, in those Eastern European countries where people do not care enough to enter politics and only the elite is mobilized, we can expect democracy in more lasting forms than one-time electoral activity. Yet when society is mobilized (as it was in Poland in 1980 and 1981) or is demobilized from above by the new elite, it has at its disposal institutional networks created from above, which are to some extent irrelevant from the point of view of the contradictions of the transitional period or of new conflicts between society and state.[21]

What type of state will now emerge in Eastern Europe? I have already mentioned one striking feature of it: it has to operate in a pattern of "exclusionary corporatism" in order to demobilize a society that formed itself into a political entity in a fundamentalistic (or nationalistic) way. The wave of such techniques of rule is visible from Poland to Romania and the Soviet Union. In each case the techniques are different, however. Other elements are already visible as well: new forms of the colonial state (following the new pattern of segmentation of both economy and state), the ambiguity of presidential office, and a clash between efforts to create a legal state and, at the same time, a necessity (due to previous political agreements with communists as well as to imperial rule) to keep some extraconstitutional arrangements.

It is worth adding here that the motives behind recent transformations in Eastern Europe[22] are strikingly similar to those that led to the development of absolutist states in the past.[23] According to A. Giddens, three factors are important here:

- intellectual revolution linked to the "reflexive monitoring of the international system of states"; in the case of Eastern Europe it is the rapid shift in the cognitive paradigm of the ruling elites toward the world-system perspective that changed both their perception of crisis and necessary reforms;[24]

- change in war technologies rather than in production; in Eastern Europe it is the impact of computer chips and nuclear power. Both changed drastically the base of military strength and made economic innovativeness (absent in real socialism) one of the key elements. What is more, they made an evolution from formal to informal empire less painful;

- the necessity for a new mode of financing military organization; in the case of Eastern Europe there is financial crisis in both the state-owned economy (losing its power of capital formation) and the state treasury. These crises made necessary an evolution toward more efficient relations of production and introduced an imperative of privatization.

Afterword

In the introductory chapter of this book, completed in Spring 1990, I wrote that analysis of the contradictions of socialism allows us only to understand the moment at which this system has wholly exhausted all its possibilities. That is to say, the moment at which the resolution of crisis or even the reduction of tensions ceases to be possible within the existing formational framework. Material and symbolic reserves have run out, and there is no more institutional freedom of maneuver. But—as I added in the paragraph that followed—the acceleration of changes witnessed during 1989 is not simply the result of these contradictions becoming even sharper: it is also a consequence of a series of chance events. I added also that the new dilemmas—dilemmas of transition itself—are more and more visible.

Now, nearly one year after completing the writing of this book, it is clear that the Eastern European societies are not yet finished with the transition stage of transformation and that the consolidation of the new order has just started. In spite of deep political changes (free election, multiparty system) the economic structure of property rights has remained intact. The stabilization policy imposed by the IMF moved the economy from the shortage to the supply situation. But it is only a relative shift, accomplished through a deep recession, with only slight improvement in the sturcture of production or efficiency. And the micro-level rationality on the State-owned enterprise level did not change. Further, the maneuver of the "opening," based on an assumption of relatively easy integration with Western Europe, seems to be unsuccessful or even reversed by the recent pressures (coming from the West) for a new regionalization in Eastern Europe which, to some extent, would play the same role as COMECON in the past.

This leads us to the conclusion that in order to understand the first stage of the Eastern European transformation (1989–1990) one has to look deeper into the dilemmas of the transition itself—dilemmas that are now even more obvious than one year ago.

In this afterword, I will deal with these new dilemmas in a very simplified way, mostly on a conceptual level. But this is necessary if we want to grasp the complexity and the dramatic dimension of the transformation in Eastern Europe. First of all, I will look more carefully into the four dilemmas characteristic of this stage of transformation, namely, the dilemma for democracy, for capitalism, the cultural dilemmas, and the dilemma of "opening."

Second, I will describe the ideological leitmotifs of the Eastern European "revolution from above."

Third, I will try to answer a question: are processes and mechanisms observed today in the Eastern bloc unique or do they have some universal quality—were they present in the other, known cases of socioeconomic change on the macro-level?

Dilemmas of Transformation

Dilemmas for Democracy

The first stage of transition in Eastern Europe can be labeled as the stage when "politics" (as a peculiar type of social action and institutional structure) emerges. The socialist pattern of domination can be described as "power without politics."[1] This pattern is now gone but the new institutional framework is not yet consolidated. What is more, we have to remember that society in Poland (and in all these cases when the transformation started with the popular mobilization) formed itself into the peculiar type of antipolitical political entity. Such a pattern of articulation was based on nationalistic and fundamentalist rhetoric due to the lack of an economic base for a genuine civil society in the Hegelian sense.[2] One of the features of such type of political articulation is its rejection of "politics" as a type of social activity. "Politics" is seen as a compromise with the "alien"—or "evil"—forces. In such a situation the first condition for building the working political system, aiming toward procedural-type democracy, is to demobilize the aforementioned type of articulation. It is not so easy. As the November–December 1990 presidential election in Poland shows, nearly one-third of the voters (mainly the less skilled workers from small towns—described in this book as "postmodernist workers"—but also local, small ex-*nomenklatura*) supported the candidacy of Mr. Tyminski. It was not only the sign of the growing distrust of Solidarity leaders in their new political roles but also the rejection of the "politics" as such. The main asset of Mr. Tyminski was his "outsider" status on the Polish political arena. He presented himself as an anti-political, self-made, small entrepreneur, underlining at the same time (somehow surprisingly for his "capitalist" status) that the "labor force" (the only asset his constituency possessed) is the most valuable factor of production.

The second dilemma for emerging politics is rooted in the fact that—at this initial stage—the reforms have to be conducted from above because of the initial lack of social actors with strong motivation in transition (e.g. in privatization of the State-owned industry). In other words, during this stage of transition the new political elites are projecting onto society their vision rather than representing the interests of the concrete social groups. The legitimizing argument is the interest of society as a whole to get out of the socialist-type economy and domination, and not the expansion of interests of a particular, well-defined constituency. However, in opposition to this, one of the main objectives of the new regime during this initial, painful stage of stabilization policy is to keep society demobilized, somehow mute and unable to overload the fragile system with its claims. Such policy of demobilization began in Poland right after the "round table" and was conducted by institutional as well as political means. An example of the former was a conscious (and agreed upon by Walesa) demobilization of Solidarity as an active labor union. An example of the latter was an artificial unity (and a voting discipline) kept in the Solidarity Parliamentary club, when conflicts were presented as illegitimate and dangerous from the point of view of the new order. At the same time a peculiar rhetoric of political discourse was imposed which was based on Solidarity ethos less and less relevant to the real choices made by the Solidarity government.

The mounting tensions, rooted in the gap between such a priori imposed "consensus" (based on trust and Solidarity symbols) and new conflicts (that cannot be expressed in the official discourse), culminated in the presidential competition between Mazowiecki and Walesa. This gap added also to the popular distrust of "politics" and the Seym. The latter was stripped of its essential nature of "representation" (and responsibility) because of its claims of unity. The deepening apathy, frustration, and distrust can be labeled as the "Weimar syndrome"[3] with its wild strikes[4] and the popular feeling that "nothing changed."

A paradoxical situation occurs here: the rebellion of 1980–1981 (with its symbolic politics and newly acquired identity of society via-à-vis State, but without deep institutional changes) is perceived as a "real" breakthrough, whereas the revolution from above of 1989–1990 is seen as "unreal" (in spite of the fact that the latter is transforming the whole institutional and legal fabric).

At the same time when apathy on the mass level grows, the new socioeconomic elites (that emerged during the first two years of transition) became more active in politics as well. They started to ask for representation and demanded to limit the contingency of the revolution from above. They agreed, however, with the "round table" elite that the "masses" have to be kept demobilized during this initial, painful stage of reform. But at the same time, these new elites demanded that the policy formation (and consensus building) would occur on a slightly lower level: not only in the Seym but also through agreements between corporatist elites (union leaders, new businesses). In other words, they wanted to shift policy formation from the political, intelligentsia-type, ex-oppositionist elites to the new middle class. This would change not only the content but also the style of politics. The new elite (that dominated the Polish political scene when Walesa was elected president) is more professional, more pragmatic, and less oriented toward symbolic politics, but at the same time—more provincial. In spite of this, the new elite is somehow "more modern"—the new politicians know whom they represent and to whom they are responsible. This new generation of politicians rejected the rhetoric of Solidarity as irrelevant to the new choices facing society and the government. The ongoing politics of demobilization, seen as a functional imperative of transition, is now conducted not through distorted discourse or inactive labor unions but by the distortion of political channels (with shift of power from the Seym to the executive bodies)[5] and with the help of Walesa's populist rhetoric that delegitimizes the "particularistic" class interests.

The next political dilemma of this stage is rooted in the inner contradictions of the "legal revolution." One of the main objectives of the new government in Eastern Europe is to build the system of rule based on law. This is often interpreted by the frustrated society that is looking for "revenge" as too much continuity.[6] The visible clash between the formal and substantive ("revolutionary") justice increases the popular distrust to the newly elected leaders. This (together with the visible gap between the abstract rationality of the IMF stabilization policy[7] and the micro-level approach to economic crisis adds to frustration and apathy.

The political changes that occurred at this stage of transformation can be summed up as follows: the total exclusion, characteristic of the totalitarian stage (and followed by the manipulative co-optation of the 1970s) was contested in 1980–1981 with Solidarity's myth of total inclusion. This myth was built on the assumption that the unity of State and society is possible— without mediation of "politics"—if both would follow the same value-orientation. When the dream became real and the opposition took power in Poland (and in other Eastern European countries), this myth was refuted and the painful path of the following patterns of selective inclusions and exclusions took place.

Dilemmas for capitalism

The change of ownership pattern is one of the few policies treated as crucial for successful transformation in Eastern Europe. The privatization scheme has to meet four objectives:

- to promote the development of the capitalist pattern of growth; during the first stage of transformation it has to be the mechanism that would make possible a redeployment of capital from the "traditional" (State-owned) to the "modern" (private) sector of economy;
- to create the capital market;
- to make both use and allocation of production factors more rational;

• to accelerate (by the greater coincidence of the private and social gains/costs) the economically rational adjustment on the enterprise level to the macro-level policy of stabilization.

The first dilemma for capitalism is caused by the fact that not all schemes for privatization meet these objectives to the same extent. For instance the redeployment of capital from the State-owned to the private sector is best served by the political capitalism that is described in this book.[8] However, the political and eithical arguments (justice) make such arrangements very unpopular.[9] A capital market can be created with the help of the various privatization schemes (from "citizens' ownership" to employees' or institutional ownership), but each of these forms has different implications for the efficient use of production factors. For example, employees' ownership can halt the necessary restructuring of the economy.

These various implications make the choice of privatization schemes both ambiguous and highly politicized.

Capital formation is the other key factor for capitalist development. It can be obtained in Eastern Europe with the help of the aforementioned intersectoral links at the production level (as "political capitalism") but also:

• by the shift of surplus from agriculture to industry;

• by the redeployment of capital from the State to private sector via selective use of interest rates and taxes (both higher in the State-owned branch of the economy) with the State budget as a redistributive mechanism;

• by forced savings.

The second dilemma for capitalism in Eastern Europe is that the new governments seem to be unable to reinforce and execute any of these capital formation patterns necessary to start capitalist growth. It is not only for economic reasons (deep recession, poor society, inefficient agriculture) but also for political reasons (well-organized farmers and workers in the State sector, strong egalitarian attitudes).

The third dilemma of transition to capitalism is caused by the contradictory role the State has to play in the economy. One of the paradoxes of the Eastern European transition to capitalist, "not constructivist," order (using Hayekian terminology) is that such a shift has to be completed with the help of revolution from above.

In other words, with the help of anti-Hayekian, constructivist methodology. This is so because of the systemic lack of the key economic interests, actors, and institutions that have to be created by the State.

The form and extent of the State's involvement in the economy is not the only dimension of this third dilemma. The problem is that the State has to conduct five contradictory policies at once. It has, first of all, to stabilize the economy. This means not only tight fiscal and monetary measures but also the making up for the absent interests in capital formation with the help of tight administrative control and tax policy.[10] The second objective of the State is to fight recession and to start an industrial policy that would meet new challenges. This again implies a very active State. The third objective is privatization. But, as I argued before, the choice of the privatization scheme seems to be more political than economic. The fourth aim is to promote capital formation. As the Polish case shows, it is also the pure political decision on reinforcement and legitimization of some forms when rejecting the legitimacy of other forms.[11] The last objective of the State at this stage of transition is to create conditions for export-led development. But, with the wide technological/efficiency gap the only comparative advantage the Eastern European economies have are low wages (imposed by the strong authoritarian State) or the lower prices of exported goods (subsidized by the State). Both mean the deep involvement of the State in economic affairs.

As we can see, at this stage of transition the State has to be active and—at the same time—willing to withdraw from the economy when it is possible. But it is very difficult to imagine such self-limiting bureaucracy. What is more, the State has to be very elastic and able to conduct contradictory policies (e.g., fighting recession when stabilizing the economy, introducing universal market rules and industrial policy, based on a selective use of economic instruments). The State has to create basic economic institutions (commercial banks, a stock exchange, an insurance system), but at the same time it should avoid the temptation to use these new institutions as political instruments. Unavoidable as it may be, such a contradictory situation creates a lot of ambiguity and tensions in the State apparatuses themselves. What is more, the necessary elasticity has to be combined with the rule of law. The judge-made law seems to be more useful here as well as the relative independence of the State's agencies and an avoidance of the clear-cut blueprints. And last but not least: strong local government on the community level would make it easier to absorb ambiguity and to balance inner contradictions of economic transformation.

Finally, it is worth mentioning the free rider dilemma. As we observed in Poland in 1990, the tight monetary and fiscal measures imposed on the economy led to the deep recession in the State-owned sector. At the same time the massive adjustment in terms of factors, shift did not occur. The chain of events described by North[12] as the prerequisite of capitalist growth based on innovations and capital formation was not induced at this stage of transition. Despite property rights in the State economy now being slightly better defined,[13] the production factors' markets did not improve and new specializations as well as the new division of labor did not occur on a massive scale. Paradoxically enough, with recentralization of property rights in the State sector (as the initial step to privatization conducted by the State as an owner), the managerial decisions were decentralized and the liberalization of prices was introduced. But, as North rightly underlined in his book, such steps cannot work because they do not reduce the gap between the individual and social returns. Only exclusive and alienable property rights and the dissolution of State ownership can begin the capitalist pattern of growth. In such a situation the individual gains that occurred in Eastern Europe during the initial stage of transition were made mostly by the "free riders." They exploited the State economy's inefficiency, as well as the aforementioned lack of systemic adjustment, and made fortunes—for example, by importing cheaper goods from the West or Far East. This only added to the recession in the mainstream economy. "Political capitalists" also exploited the free rider phenomenon, using their social access as well as their unique location between the State and private economy.

In such a situation the new value orientation that would reinforce the capitalist contract-oriented mentality did not occur as well. And the free rider fortunes added only to the growing resentments and reinforced the populist reaction that would make transition to capitalism even more difficult.

Dilemma of Opening

One of the basic targets of the transformation in Eastern Europe was to restructure the dependency situation in the region.

The dependency pattern in the Eastern bloc was characterized by bi-level dependency:[14] first, the whole bloc's dependency on the World capitalist system, and second, the politically imposed, interregional dependency inside COMECON. The latter was treated as an instrument for an adjustment to the first-level dependency. Two political viewpoints for restructuring the dependency pattern emerged:

• First was the idea of "selective opening"[15] which began in the mid-1980s. The mixture of "political capitalism" (treated as a channel for the controlled influx of foreign capital) and rationalization of COMECON (with more links on the production level) were the main elements of that policy.

• The next viewpoint called for full integration with the European Economic Community, based on massive privatization in Eastern Europe and the dissolution of COMECON because of its isolating impact. Such a view, expressed by the phrase "coming back to Europe," become popular after the 1989 democratization.

In Eastern Europe now, however we can observe the corrosion of the myth of easy integration. What is more, the West itself seems to be much more skeptical about the possibility of integrating Eastern Europe into the European Community.

There are two reasons for such a shift in the Western position:

• First, the West received a shock after the unification of Germany exposed the dramatic situation of the East German economy (which was perceived as the best in the Eastern bloc). The Western conclusion is that without massive investments[16] which have not been forthcoming Eastern Europe would be not competitive enough to be integrated into the European Economic Community;

• Second, the Soviet crisis (with its peculiar feedback between the collapse of the State's hierarchy and collapse of the economy)[17] has deepened, reinforcing Western expectations that Eastern Europe will play the role of shock absorber in the region.

Both arguments led recently to the formulation of a vision of the new regionalization in Eastern Europe (including the Soviet Union).[18] Proposals are at this stage somewhat ambiguous: from a monetary union (that would absorb part of the Soviet inflation) to strengthening the trade and production links in the region (that were recently broken) to keeping migration from the Soviet Union within the borders of Eastern Europe.[19] The West decided to combine its credit policy (beginning in 1991) with the development of such new regionalization, seeing it as a muct more realistic option than the full integration of Eastern Europe with the EEC. As it is now, all Eastern European countries hope that they will be able to enter the EEC on individual terms: of course, such a situation leads to growing competition for Western credits as well as to deeper regional disintegration.[20]

The rapid shift of Western policy vis-à-vis the Eastern bloc will add to frustrations in this region. What is more, the emergency State situation that appeared as of this writing (January 1991) in the Soviet Union would make such new regionalization even more difficult. Not only are the real centers of power and control even less clear than before and the legal framework even more distorted, but it would be very difficult to develop new economic links with Moscow and at the same time to keep the value orientation that is so important for transition in Eastern Europe. However, such new regionalization should not be viewed only as a threat; rather, if Eastern Europeans would take the lead, it could be a chance to find for the region the new role between West and East.

The Cultural Dilemmas of Transition

It is very difficult to express cultural dilemmas in political terms; and one is helpless when trying to use ideological labels known from the Western context. The best way to present these dilemmas is to look on the problem as a triangle of three competing cultural orientations: neotraditionalization; modernism; postmodernism.

Paradoxically enough, the neotraditionalization of Eastern Europe was a precondition of its transition to modernity. The politicization of ethics, the new wave of nationalism, the deprivatization of religion and political activization of the Church created the initial network for the political awakening of society. This network was a substitute for the genuine civil society that cannot develop in an State-owned economy.

The initial stage of transition (in all these cases when it started with genuine mobilization from below) can be labeled as rebellion. It was a moment when individuals, brought up in the totalitarian situation (characterized by a gap between common-sense morality and rules imposed in the name of "objective reason"), were able to overcome their own moral indifference to society and to themselves.[21] The moral experience of Solidarity strikes was also a peculiar cognitive experience. People discovered that they were ready to risk in the name of values and that others would act in similar way: the initial atomization (a legacy of totalitarianism) was broken. At the same time the new political taxonomy was articulated, dividing social space into the domain of "good" fighting "evil." This made easier the expression of the complex map of conflicts in the State-owned society.

The rebellion in Eastern Europe was followed by a deprivatization of religion, due to efforts to rebuild the elements of the social fabric inside the Catholic Church. Neither the politicization of ethics nor the popular use of the Church as the shelter for reemerging society were neutral. Rather these situations added to strong antisecularization and anti-individualistic emotions, so characteristic of every mass mobilization. And with the 1989 democratization the highly politicized Catholic Church demanded its toll.[22] This added to the further distortion of the border line between the public and private spheres.

Two different reactions occurred in such a situation. The one was "modernist," invoking the European tradition of moderation, tolerance, and individualism.[23] The other was "postmodernist" with its vision of a new type of social order, built on a neotraditional foundation.[24]

The clarity of this division was distorted by two factors: the dynamics of political life itself and the inner split within the Catholic Church.

To illustrate the dynamics of political life, let us examine the presidential election in Poland. During the election both camps had to strengthen their ties with the Catholic Church. The "European" side (being at that time in government) tried—in a preemptive way—to meet the claims of the "postmodernist" side's constituency. For instance, religion was introduced to schools without obeying constitutional procedure, using the argument of "natural law" (which was presented as more important than formal law).[25] Paradoxically enough, this policy was attacked by "neotraditionalists" for taking political advantage of the religion issue.

As for the inner split within the Catholic Church, the Polish Catholic Church seems to be somehow the pre-soborian church. The impact of John XXIII's ecumenical teaching in Poland is very weak indeed. At the same time the social teaching of the Church which developed under John Paul II (with its focus on the dignity of labor and strong anticapitalist undertones characteristic of the moral vision of economy) became very popular.

Both added to cultural dilemmas of transition to "Europe" and capitalism. What is more, both divided the Church hierarchy. These new divisions compound those described earlier, the complex relationship between Eastern European ideas of neotraditionalization, modernity, and post-modernism.

Perception of History as an Ideology

A popular cliche of "coming back to history" circulating now in Eastern Europe takes for granted that the history to come back to is European history. This is not so obvious: one can say for instance that the Japanese pattern (both with its nineteenth-century *zaibatsu* "political capitalists" and the contemporary "developmental" strategy based on an active State and contractual agreements) is more suitable for the Eastern European dilemmas and challenges.

But when "coming back to history" is seen as synonymous with European history, "deconstruction" of the latter plays an important ideological role.

Four features of this deconstruction of European history (that occur on both the elite and the mass consciousness level) seem to be the most characteristic:

- First is the silent assumption that the unilinear model of development was the prevailing model in European history and that is was only a political "accident," a unique outcome of World War II that things in Eastern Europe "went wrong." Eastern Europeans seem to forget that their region was always at the periphery of Europe and always had its own specific pattern of development.

What is more, the existence in Eastern Europe of the very same oppressive socioeconomic institutions that were already rejected by the West was often functional from the point of view of World capitalism's logic. For instance the development of the new serfdom east of the Elbe was connected to the growth of international trade and capitalist development in Western Europe. By analogy, the aforementioned "new regionalization" (so frustrating for Eastern Europeans) can be seen as rational from the Western stability point of view. People in Eastern Europe do not understand that to be integrated into the Western economy does not mean to live at the same level as developed societies. Eastern Europeans look on capitalism as a peculiar thing rather than as a set of relationships that can vary according to local conditions of production, realization, and accumulation;

• Second, the interpretation of European history is usually based on textbook cases (England). Most of these cases, however, are not so useful for Eastern Europe as, for instance, the less known, unique cases of Austria or Italy;

• Third, the role of the "nation-state" unit in Western Europe as the necessary step in its evolution to capitalism is overestimated in Eastern Europe[26] where the recent patterns of integration in Western Europe as well as the Western debate on political economy of separatist movements are virtually unknown;

• Finally, the vision of capitalism in Eastern Europe is a mixture of Marxism (with its proprietary or corporate capitalism) and the Hayekian tradition of an unregulated market. The latter is mistakenly seen as synonymous with liberalization of prices and not as a competition based on private ownership. Also, the concept of capital formation is rooted in Eastern Europe in a Marxist labor theory of value: the repression of wages is seen as the main source for accumulation.

The second feature of the ideological aura in Eastern Europe is linked to the peculiar mentalities of the new political elites. They are, in most cases, antirevolutionaries at heart who have to conduct the revolution from above, due to a lack of socioeconomic base for evolutionary type processes of for a revolution from below, which would be more than the mere rebellion. Some of these new politicians for many years believed in "revolution" (in their socialist youth) and in later years began to disagree with the artificiality and desubstantialization of socialism that was rooted in the revolutionary origin of this formation. The younger generation (that started its activity in the 1970s) held from the beginning strong newconservative beliefs, rejecting revolution as a type of social action.

The new Eastern European elites, caught in the dilemma of anti-revolutionaries put into a revolutionary role, are trying to adjust using the policy of a passive State (liberalization of prices, end of subsidies, rejection of industrial policy and planning, marketization of culture and social services).

At this point, it would be wise to make the very useful distinction between "radicals" and "liberals." As Nisbet wrote of revolutionary France:

It is possible to separate liberals from radicals in the French eighteenth century in terms of the amount of action that was held to be necessary to achieve the natural order.[27]

The first generation of the new politicians in Eastern Europe (with its fear of both a revolution and an active State) seems to be not very "radical" from the point of view of the above definition. They did believe (as did most of the population) that the natural, "normal" economic order and the market logic will come, in an evolutionary way, out of socialist reality when government withdraws from the economy. The amount of constructivist activity that is necessary before the economic tissue is ready for the market economy has been underestimated. As a result, the creation of new economic institutions is much slower than political reforms. This will change now, with the new, second generation political elites who came into power after Walesa was elected president. They are younger, more pragmatic, and have less of an ideological vision of both the State and themselves. What is more, they do not have the "revolutionary" past of the 1940s and 1950s and are much less afraid of the active State.

The third ideological leitmotif in Eastern Europe is a concept of "normalcy." As we all know, socialism was created from above, following an ideological blueprint. As I put it elsewhere,[28] using the Hegelian concept *Der Schein*, the socialist system was in a way the "illusory being." It was unable to become what it had posited about itself but at the same time possesed a real content it was unable to grasp in its own ideological language. However—ironically—the rejection of this language would destroy the system's identity and expose its absurdity. Thus, the real "immediacy" of socialism, different from the posited, ideological interpretation of reality could not be articulated and communicated in the official language that was used inside the Party-State web. This made reforms even more difficult and added to popular feelings of artificiality of social life.

At the same time the lack of key economic interests in the State-controlled society led to the situation where the only way to overcome the initial atomization was a momentary, sometimes hysterical, integration around symbols. Such symbolic politics of identity[29] was unavoidable but not neutral. When emotion was gone, the feeling of mutiny (due to the irrelevance of symbolic semantics to the real life problems) came back. As we can see, the artificiality of social life was not reduced even during the relatively "free speech" situation.

The idea of "returning to normalcy" expresses longings to get out of such an artificial social life. It is not so easy: transformation itself brought a new dimension of artificiality—for instance, the gap between macro- and microeconomic rationality.

What is more, the concept of "normalcy" is highly ideologized. The new political elite decides itself what is the "normal" social price for the move toward the market economy, or what does "normal" social structure mean.[30] For people living all their lives in the redistributive economy, it is very difficult to judge for themselves what is "normal" in the market-type economy. This increases the danger that the category of "normalcy" would be overexploited in order to cover the government's mistakes and inefficiency.

Finally, Eastern European societies that are entering what is for them an unknown world of politics not only have to revise their own vision of themselves (and accept internal conflicts as normal) but also have to adjust to a much higher level of ambiguity, so characteristic of democratic order. As evolution from the moral (rebellion) order to the new, procedural "political" order is as painful as the end of the socialist welfare state itself.

The last ideological leitmotif characteristic of contemporary political life in Eastern Europe is an existence of two ideological syndromes: social-democratic liberalism[31] and corporatist liberalism.[32] These syndromes remind us to some extent of the ideological divisions that existed in Eastern Europe before World War II. This is not accidental: the challenges are similar, namely, to escape the status of the periphery and to accelerate capitalist development while redefining the dependency situation. Each of these syndromes invoke the notion of "liberalism" but each in a different meaning. The social-democratic-liberal syndrome is closer to J. S. Mill's liberalism with its vision of administrative involvement in the economy, cooperatives of producers, and the "industrial partnership." The corporatist-liberal syndrome reminds us of Nozick's and Rawl's contractualism, underlining however not only the notion of "fairness" but also a peculiar presumptivism, promoting interests of developmental elites. As we can see, both syndromes are critical of the dogmatic laissez-faire market approach and demand some brackets and regulations: the former looks mostly for administrative regulations whereas the latter prefers agreements and contracts between the key economic actors.

In summation, the slow development of the ideological content of social life in Eastern Europe (with mentalities playing ideological roles) is not only the result of a socialist legacy (that reinforced the suspicious approach to all ideologies). It also supports our general knowledge that the rapid change on an institutional level (especially when it is conducted from above) is not necessarily parallel to much slower changes on the social consciousness level.

A relative stability at this stage of transition in Eastern Europe is not due to an absence of conflicts or a result of an efficient ideological justification of the new order. It is rather a consequence of the subtle techniques of demobilization used by the new elites: from the notion of "normalcy" (that justifies some social costs as unavoidable) and the skillful use of populist rhetoric (making it more diffiult to express specific interests) to the use of irrelevant political rhetoric or the direct distortion of political channels.

The additional factor, adding to stability, is a free rider mechanism: it is relatively easier to find and individual way of adjustment than to look for a collective solution for the new dilemmas. This is so not only due to the lack of an alternative collective vision that would differ from returning to socialism but also due to popular knowledge that most of Eastern Europe's problems are outside the control of the elites.

Unique or Universal?

The transformation in Eastern Europe follows some paths already known in the past. Three such analogies can be mentioned here, perhaps in a very schematic way.

First of all, this is a transition from feudalism to capitalism. Besides the repetition in contemporary Eastern Europe of some political forms existing in the past (e.g., the Standestaat), some motives behind the recent transformation are strikingly similar to those that led to the development of the early modern State in Western Europe. Three factors were important in the latter case, namely:

• An intellectual revolution, linked to the "reflexive monitoring of the international system of States";[33] in the case of Eastern Europe, it was the rapid shift of the cognitive paradigm of the reform-minded communist elites toward the World-system perspective that changed their perception both of the crisis and of necessary reforms;

• the change in war technology rather than in production forces; both the deepening of the economic crisis (that decreased military capabilities as well) and the new vision of global security made the reform-minded communist elites more eager to enter the risky path of reforms from above;

• in both cases (Western Europe in the past and Eastern Europe today) the modernization of the State started with the improvement of tax-collecting capacities. The financial crisis of the State was—in both cases—one of the main motives behind a tendency to reinforce the new, more efficient structure of property rights.

The other similarities of the "emerging politics" stage in Eastern Europe and the beginning of the early modern State in Western Europe are:

• the dynamics of the legitimacy crisis—a collapse of the so-called "revolutionary legitimacy" of the Communist party (when confronted by the workers' fundamentalist rejection based on moral grounds) is reminiscent of the impact of the religious wars on the dissolution of traditional legitimacy in Western Europe;

• the early stage of the modern State with its Court politics (e.g., the similar "balancing patronage" system,[34] with fiscal policy as a vehicle to modern bureaucracy and with similar tensions between the judicial power (and the judge-made law) and the legislative body (parliament).

The second area of comparison is the French Revolution. There, too, some similarities are striking.

First, on a methodological level, in both cases (Eastern Europe and revolutionary France) the continuity in change is a key problem. As K. Baker[35] underlines, "the Revolution must be seen not simply as the repudiation of the Old Regime but as its creation." In both cases, the revolution (in the Polish case I prefer the term "rebellion" when dealing with the 1980–1981 events) was a cognitive experience when the "Old Regime" was reconstructed, articulated on the popular consciousness level in order to be rejected. And in both cases the Old Regime's impact was felt during transition. In the case of Eastern Europe, it was a stigma of systemic lack of the key economic interests that made "revolution from above" unavoidable. What is more, the "transformation through transactions" (with the "round table" technique) would be impossible if not for the peculiar political culture that developed in Poland in the 1970s and 1980s. Even the stage of martial law added to transition: the web of Party-State was dissolved (with the army taking the role of the Communist party) and the State apparatus was professionalized. This added to dynamics of revolution from above in which the inner tension in the power structure was a necessary element. General Jaruzelski can be labeled—in the same way that Lousi XVI was—as the Hamlet of the revolution.

The other similarity of the Eastern European transformation and the French Revolution is that in both cases the "rebellion" (with its mass mobilization and symbolic politics) was perceived as "real," when the deep institutional changes were seen not as a rupture but as a continuity. In other words, in both cases the "revolution" (as historical phenomenon) had to be reconstructed as an ex post facto category.

Also the three stages of the French Revolution are present as well in the Eastern European transition (at least in the Polish case), namely:

- the stage of enlightened absolutism that started the revolutionary dynamics when the Old Regime tried to reform itself;
- the lame liberal constitutionalism that—in both cases—introduced the parliament but without its essence of representation (and responsibility) due to the claim for unanimity;

- the republican stage that (in the Polish case, after Walesa was elected) took not jacobinic form but a Rousseauean, contractual one. In both cases the similar distrust of political machines as well as elements of plebiscitarian democracy are visible. And in both cases, this third stage is less cosmopolitan, urban.

In the case of the French Revolution, a fourth stage occurred: the technocratic regime of Napoleon I. Is this the future of Eastern Europe?

There are a few other similarities. In both cases the logic of the revolution at the central and the local level was different. The local revolutions were more pragmatic and creative and—like France—left alone with their problems. In both cases the tensions between "localism" and "universalism" were visible.[36]

Further, similar to both cases was a theme of the "regeneration" of the people: in Eastern Europe this was reinforced by the politicization of the Catholic Church. In addition, a similar dilemma of "representation" in a political vacuum existed in both cases. It was the revolution that started "politics" (as a type of social activity) and started—not concluded—the political organization of society.

Also, in both cases, the dynamics of political and social revolution were not synonymous. In Eastern Europe the political preceded the social. And in both cases the new institutional political order had in itself some ambiguity from the point of view of social transformation. In the case of Eastern Europe this ambiguity occurred in workers (against emerging capitalism) and in the new middle class (against reminders of socialism).

In both cases the liberals had a very ambiguous position when confronted by the revolutionary situation. On the one hand they were against revolutionary social action, but on the other hand they perceived revolution as the only way to start normal political life. So they supported revolution but wanted it to be as short as possible.[37]

And, finally, both revolutions have difficulties with supplying modern political culture. The ambiguous relations between the public and private sphere, as well as the aforementioned neotraditionalization in the Eastern European case added to these difficulties. Also postrevolutionary development in Western Europe, rooted in the tensions of early capitalism, could emerge in Eastern Europe as well. I am reminded here of the peculiar brand of Christianity with a left orientation which emerged in Western

Europe in the first half of the nineteenth century. We can expect similar development in Eastern Europe in the near future, with growing hostility toward economic liberalism on the one hand and the populist image of Christ on the other. This can shift the reform movement from an objective of "liberty" to "equality/fraternity" themes.

The third area for comparative analysis is the process of democratization in Spain and Latin America. Both striking similarities and differences are visible here.

The technical side of transition followed the same methodology in Eastern Europe and in Spain and Latin America. The professionalization of the power apparatuses and the army as well as the inner conflicts in the ruling elite were as important for starting the "democratization" from above as was the relative demobilization of society (making the process of reform more safe from the point of view of reformers). In both cases the stage of "liberalization" (which included granting society greater autonomy but not participation in power) preceded a "democratization" stage. The atmosphere of early 1970s Spain was strikingly similar to that of Poland after martial law (mid 1980s) with the elite's efforts to improve the system but without deep political changes and with their faith that the new economic opportunities (as well as the free rider phenomenon) would add to stability. In both cases this tactic was unsuccessful, leaving the oposition undivided.

The "ruptura pactada" in Spain that started in 1976—with its inner contradictions and tensions—is reminiscent of the "legal revolution" that started in Eastern Europe in 1989. In the case of Poland even the role of the Church was very similar. In both cases we observed the dissolution of the new center after parliamentary elections when the initial agreement seemed to be too tight to meet the growing political aspirations of society. What is more, the initial euphoria in both cases was followed by the decline of the popular support, apathy, and the de-alignment of society.

However, despite these similarities, the differences are even more crucial. Two such differences should be mentioned here:

First, the economic and social context of democratization differed. In the Spanish case economic reforms (with a painful stabilization policy) took place under the Old (Franco) regime and did not overload the consolidation phase of the new, democratic order, as occurred in the Eastern European case. What is more, Spain was an underdeveloped but capitalist society and from the start political reforms (as well as an "opening" to Europe) have had a strong base in economic interests. The growing industrial sector wanted to terminate the fascist state in order to expand its economic contacts with the World. In Eastern Europe such economic actors do not exist and an economic opening plus privatization and political reforms are conducted because of a strong value commitment and not because of economic interests of well-defined social groups. This adds to the greater ambiguity of the Eastern European transformation.

The second difference is rooted in the dissimilarity of the World-system context of both cases of transition. In the case of Spain the U.S. (and other Western countries) were strongly interested in an accelerated and smooth incorporation of Spain into Europe: one of the motives was to disarm the growing Euro-communist opposition. In the case of Eastern Europe, the reverse is true. The strategy of neoregionalization in Eastern Europe indicates the West is interested in keeping the problems of Eastern Europe inside the former communist bloc, therefore isolating Eastern Europe from the European Community.

In the case of Latin America, the similarities are also intertwined with important differences. Once more, as in the case of Spain, the technology of transition is somewhat similar, but the deep structural processes seem to be different.

First of all, in the case of Latin America and Eastern Europe, one of the main objectives of transformation is a change of the dependency pattern. In Latin America, this means an intensification of the export-led growth (with wider opening of the economy); renegotiation of the role of the multinational companies; the redefinition of the role of the State in the economy and promotion of the domestic capital's interests. However, in Eastern Europe the shift in the dependency pattern and an "opening" toward the West has to be preceded by the difficult maneuver of an "ontological opening" (privatization) as well as the creation of the domestic capitalist sector. This makes the whole process much more fragile and ambiguous than Latin America's case.

Another dierence is that although in both regions the painful stabilization policy imposed by the IMF is a must, in Eastern

Europe it seems to be relatively easier to implement such a policy than in Latin America. This may be due to the initially higher social and political integration in Eastern Europe, rooted in a common fight with the communist regime on the one hand and in the higher egalitarianism of social structure—a legacy of socialism—on the other.

There is one striking similarity: in both cases the politics of populism was used first as a popular mobilization technique (with the myth of total inclusion) and later on as an instrument of demobilization which makes it more difficult to articulate and express specific group and class interests.

In summary, then, the transformation in Eastern Europe brings with itself new dilemmas and conflicts, some of them known from other historical cases of macro-social change. These new problems led to the corrosion of three myths characteristic of the first stage of transformation: the political myth of the unity of State and society; the myth of "coming back of Europe," and the myth of a relatively easy, non-constructivist road to capitalism.

The dilemmas described in this book lead us to the conclusion that the two-level approach is necessary if we want to analyze transition in Eastern Europe.

The new political and economic elites that are the main actors of the "revolution from above" can be analyzed with the help of the "rational choice" theory due to their relatively clear-cut objectives and their means–end type of reasoning. At the same time such an approach would not work on the level of mass society. The "politics of identity" (with a painful shift from moral to political order) and the ambiguity of both the matrix of interests and patterns of articulation are the most characteristic of this level at the present stage of transition.

The above gap is not only important from the methodological point of view but also adds to the new tensions in Eastern Europe. Not only are the perceptions and patterns of learning different on both levels but characteristic misunderstanding occurs as well. The new elites overestimate the role of "politics" as a type of social action, when societies not only feel alienated from both "revolution from above" and transition to capitalism, but also represent strong antipolitical resentments.

Los Angeles, January 1991

Notes

Chapter 1

1. See F. Braudel, *Capitalism and Material Life* (New York: Harper, 1973); J. A. Hall, *Powers and Liberties* (Oxford: Blackwell, 1985); A. Inkeles and D. H. Smith, *Becoming Modern: Individual Changes in Six Developing Countries* (Cambridge: Harvard University Press, 1974).

2. On "regulation through crisis," see Jadwiga Staniszkis, *Poland: Self-limiting Revolution* (Princeton, N.J.: Princeton University Press, 1986).

3. S. Gomulka, *Technological Equilibrium Gap* (London School of Economics, 1987, manuscript).

4. S. Gomulka and J. Rostowski, *On Material Intensity of Production in East Europe* (London School of Economics, 1987, manuscript).

5. In the Lenin Steel Works (Nowa Huta, April 1988) the strikers discussed the right of the state to taxes by virtue of owner's rent.

6. D. C. North and R. F. Thomas, *The Rise of the Western World* (Cambridge: Cambridge University Press, 1975).

7. This procedure has the aim of forcing enterprises to release part of their reserves and invest them where the broader interest of economic equilibrium requires (given a shortage of state funds). The method is the following: the government announces a list of enterprises scheduled for liquidation (these are cooperating parties—monopolists—whose production is indispensable for the operation of a number of enterprises). The alternative is to have the cooperating parties buy out the company threatened with bankruptcy and transform it into a joint-stock company belonging to a few state enterprises.

8. Recent proposals of the Peoples' Fronts of Lithuania, Latvia, and Estonia. See *The Economist*, 15–21 October 1988, p. 61.

9. In eighty large enterprises in Poland, joint-stock companies created by management use machines and equipment on their own (when the state is unable to make use of these assets) or to provide services (operations) for the enterprise which the latter cannot provide on account of the stringent regulations. The number eighty is for 1987; in February 1990 nearly 42,000 private firms linked somehow to state enterprise (forms of such symbiotic relations are described in chapter 2) existed in Poland.

10. On the distinction between theoretical and real interests see G. Lukacs, *Introduction to the Ontology of Social Being* (in Polish, Warsaw: Panstwowe Wydawmictwo Naukowe, 1978).

11. See Susan Strange, *States and Markets* (New York: Blackwell, 1986), chap. 2.

12. Studies among those in the executive power apparatus show that the main reason for resistance to the reforms is not ideological but concern about their future and occupational careers. See J. Staniszkis, "Patterns of Change in Eastern Europe," *East European Politics and Society*, January 1990.

13. See Michael Mann, "European Miracle" in: J. Baechler, J. A. Hall, and M. Mann eds., *Europe and the Rise of Capitalism* (Oxford: Blackwell, 1989); M. Mann, *The Sources of Social Power* (Oxford: Blackwell, 1986).

14. Timothy Garton Ash, *Miemieckość NRD* (Polish edition) (Warsaw: Puls, 1989).

15. See Staniszkis, "Patterns of Change."

16. In an interview the present head editor of *Pravda*, N. Frolov, shows how this group (headed by A. Rumiantsev) criticized the Brezhnev regime (*La Reppublica*, 19 April 1989).

17. See J. Staniszkis, "The Dynamics of Breakthrough in Eastern Europe," *Soviet Studies*, October 1989.

18. See the analysis of the rhetoric of the Ninth Congress of the Communist party in: J. Staniszkis, "Form of Reasoning as Ideology," *Telos*, Winter 1986.

19. See K. Jowitt, "Gorbachev: Bolshevik or Menshevik?" Working paper, University of California (Berkeley), October 1989.

20. Expression from Jowitt, "Gorbachev."

21. Pronouncements at the June 1989 Plenum of the Communist Party of the Soviet Union, FBIS-SOV-89-139, pp. 52–79. 21 July 1989. Also the interview with Vorotnikov, FBIS-SOV-89-174, September 1989, p. 64.

22. In both of these countries Communist party cells in the army and civic militia are being eliminated and other parties are forbidden to engage in political activity there.

23. Voting at the founding Congress of the Social Democratic Party of the Polish Republic, 28 January 1990 (see *Trybuna Kongresowa*, 29 January 1990; also *Gazeta Wyborcza*, 29 January 1990).

24. An example is the refusal of some ambassadors (General Baryla in Syria) to return from their posts, in spite of being called to do so by the Minister of Foreign Affairs of the Solidarity government, or the sudden change of position on the stationing of Soviet troops in Czechoslovakia after Gorbachev's letter to president Havel (February 1990).

25. Among others, the ambassador of the U.S.S.R. in Poland, V. Brovikov, who attacked Gorbachev at the February 1990 Plenum and during a visit to Wałęsa honored the latter as president (January 1990).

26. An organizational expression of this tendency is the establishment in Czechoslovakia of the Party for Moderate Progress (February 1990).

27. See J. Staniszkis, *Ontologia socjalizmu* [The ontology of socialism] (Warsaw: Biblioteka Krytyka, 1989; also Oxford: Oxford University Press, in preparation).

28. The lack of political will in the social-democratic faction dominant in the Citizens' Parliamentary Club in the Polish Seym; the pressure by President Jaruzelski for long consultations before sending to the Seym the antimonopoly bill on cooperatives. As a result, the bill, which was published in *Rzeczpospolita* on 17 October 1989, did not reach the Seym until 11 January 1990, which gave the cooperative hierarchy time to change into companies formed on commercial bases and to appropriate cooperative property.

29. In January 1990 inflation was 75 percent (planned: 45 percent); the fall of real wages was 40 percent (planned: 25 percent). From the report of the Chief Central Statistical Office (GUS), Warsaw, February 1990.

30. The number of registered small craftsmen's shops shrank in January by 20 percent (in some regions by more; e.g., in Lodz 860 of 1200 cancelled their registration). Information from "Interpolations," Polish TV First program, 2 February 1990.

31. A resolution of the Economic Committee of the Council of Ministers (December 1989) called for prosecuting monopoly practicies in private companies and also forbade managing directors of state enterprises to establish companies to compete with their parent enterprises. In his speech in the Seym (21 December 1989) Prime Minister Mazowiecki sharpened this position when he spoke about taking legal action against *nomenklatura* companies.

32. Taking advantage of its foreign trade surplus in rubles, Hungary has reduced the supply of the most energy-consumptive goods to the COMECON countries. The Czechs are attempting to revise the agree-

ments on specialization in COMECON of 1986. The Hungarians are also making structural cuts from above, while in Poland work in this direction has only begun by establishing a Commission at the Council of Ministers (February 1990).

33. In Hungary more than fifty enterprises have closed (or will be closed in the near future).

34. During the supplementary elections to fill the vacant senatorial seat in the province of Opole (February 1990) the candidate with the populist program won in nine out of twenty-two communes. In several large industrial regions (Łódź, Wrocław, Szczecin) candidates of the Working Group (see chap. 3 of this book) won in the elections in Solidarity. Also the position of the Economic Council at the Council of Ministers (a body parallel to the Economic Committee—KERM), taken in February 1990 on privatization, is typically populistic (employee stock ownership as the main path of privatization; political–parliamentary control). *Rzeczpospolita*, 17–18 February 1990.

35. Only 14 percent voted in supplementary elections in Opole (first round).

36. In response to the exclusionary election law of the "majority" type (Senate proposal), the political parties excluded from the Citizens' Committees began to organize themselves in blocs: from the anarchistic PPS-RD through the Christian-National Party to the ultra-liberal Union of Real Politics. They have in common a critical (for various reasons) attitude toward the stabilization program. The first two parties will permit a more active role of the state in the economy.

37. Enterprises which in the past exported to the U.S.S.R. (with prices set below costs) and benefited from state subsidies are threatened with bankruptcy. Today these subsidies are being abolished, and left to themselves, these enterprises are unable to negotiate better prices with the U.S.S.R. This often touches the most modern enterprises of the machine industry (e.g., the Factory of Textile Machinery in Bielsk). The second mechanism of bankruptcy is connected with the elasticity of demand: here also good operations (textile industry; crafts) that worked efficiently in the past and achieved relative equilibrium in their areas, are faced with bankruptcy. Their products are most often noncompetitive in the West, and in the exports to the U.S.S.R. Poland already has a surplus, for which she cannot buy goods she needs (e.g., oil).

38. See the discussion on special powers for the government (Seym, December 1989) or temptations to use retroactive tax laws or to expropriate bureaucratic cooperatives on a base of substantive—not formal—legality (see the first version of the law on the cooperatives, *Rzeczpospolita*, 17 October 1989).

39. A wave of occupying buildings of the former Communist party—from Gdańsk to Kraków—occurred from autumn 1989 through winter 1990.

40. As in the brutal breaking up of the student demonstration during the founding Congress of the Social-Democratic Party. This party was organized by officials of the dissolved Communist party, Warsaw, 27–28 January 1990.

41. The most frequently used form is dismissing managing directors (with the help of workers' councils).

42. The new configuration of influences (today based on economic and not political power) paradoxically uses the rules of the game introduced by the new government. Thus in a situation of "demand barriers"; in relations between enterprises, the managing directors from the old *nomenklatura* send orders to their "buddies" (from the old network) thereby helping their enterprises to survive. Organizational property (belonging to political and social organizations) is legally leased out to private persons (from the old *nomenklatura*). In this situation they turn out to be de facto owners of property formerly regarded as public goods (cultural centers, clubs). The political mechanisms are unable to touch this new elite (people of the old elite who changed the social base of their privileged position). Breaking up these arrangements would require violation of market rules and legal property rights (though it is common knowledge that in the past these organizations acquired such rights by abuse of the monopoly of power). Too radical a fight with this phenomenon, however, might also strike at the parties in the political coalition with Solidarity (the Democratic party; the Peasant Movement). However, the passivity of the government concerning new methods of the accumulation of money and influence on the local level gives rise to tensions and frustrations.

43. See Adam Michnik's pronouncement on the need for an evolutionary strategy (*Gazeta Wyborcza*, 9 February, 1990).

44. See the discussion in the Seym, 24–26 January 1990.

45. With the majority election formula (when the winning party is talking all mandates on the spot) that is exploiting the "ethos of Solidarity" in behalf of the Citizens' Committees, tensions are increasing among national minorities. What is decisive here is their absence in the Committees, which are most often gathered around the Catholic Church. These minorities include Byelorussians, Ukrainians, and Germans. A proportional election law would tone down this phenomenon and give a chance in elections to these minorities.

46. See Staniszkis, *Ontologia*, chap. 5.

47. Its result is a peculiar politicization of professional associations

from the Sociological Association in Poland and Hungary to the political role of the Stone Company in China during the June 1989 uprising. (Stone Company is the computer company created at the Academy of Science with some links to the party apparatus.)

Introduction to Part I

1. An analysis of the genesis of real socialism in categories of opening the "ontological blockade" is contained in J. Staniszkis, *Ontologia socjalizmu* [The ontology of socialism], (Warsaw: Biblioteka Krytyki, 1989; also Oxford: Oxford University Press, in preparation).

2. See the economic debate of the 1920s in the U.S.S.R., especially the polemic of Nikolay Bukharin. The most complete analysis is in M. Lewin: *Political Undercurrents in Soviet Economic Debate*, (Princeton, N.J.: Princeton University Press, 1974).

3. See Arif Dirlik, "Socialism and Capitalism in Chinese Socialist Thinking: The Origin," *Studies in Comparative Communism*, vol. 21, no. 2, September 1988.

4. See Staniszkis, *Ontologia*, chap. 2.

5. Involved here are such elements as the way of articulating protest and the level of social mobilization, the severity of the economic crisis, the depth and nature of factional divisions in the power elite; see J. Staniszkis, "Patterns of Change in Eastern Europe," *East European Politics and Society*, January 1990.

6. See Staniszkis, *Ontologia*, chap. 3, especially the analysis of new forces of integration that were formed in the 1980s and their management.

7. See Tamas Bauer, "Perspektiven der wirtschaftlichen integration," a paper read at a conference in the Konrad Adenauer Stiftung, Bonn, 29–31 May 1989, "Ost-Mittel Europa, Die Herausforderung der Reformen."

8. Staniszkis, *Ontologia*, chap. 2.

9. See the rhetoric justifying the use of force in China in the June 1989 series of articles in the *New York Times*.

Chapter 2

1. See H. Hankiss, "Reforms and the Conversion of Power," paper read at a conference in the Konrad Adenauer Stiftung, Bonn, 29–31 May 1989, "Ost-Mittel Europa, Die Herausforderung der Reformen."

2. Used for the first time as a political slogan in the resolution of the working group of Solidarity (December 1988) in *Poza Ukladem*, no. 1, Gdańsk, 1989.

3. In 1989 in Katowice alone about 2,000 companies of various types were formed within the state sector (*Gazeta Związkowa*, June 1989).

4. This legally unregulated trade (often associated with dirty business and dismissals of higher officials, e.g., the governor of Lublin in 1988) includes trade in kind and the more developed forms, with selling to each other on credit (in Poland with the help of cooperative banks). In 1988 in only three provinces there were 120 companies engaged in the frontier trade in food. These companies are formally set up by farmers' associations (peasants' organizations formed to service agriculture), but in fact they work for the association apparatus, for the most part at the provincial level, "sharing" with local activists.

5. An example is the Polish-English company that sells wood and wood products (Majnówka), whose co-owner is the former representative of the foreign trade office of Paged in London.

6. One of the activities of the cooperative Promotor, which is owned by the head office of the All-Polish Agreement of Trade Unions, is the computerization of institutions in the Ukraine.

7. Until recently (February 1989) an additional tax of 25 percent of the value of each transaction with the private sector was paid into the Treasury. So it was worthwhile to pay, let's say, 15 percent to a cooperative (regarded as social ownership) in exchange for its status as a brokerage, thought most often that status was fictional.

8. Ever more often the managers of state enterprises are charged with "mismanagement" and corruption for raising prices in transactions with the private sector and then splitting the profits with it.

9. An example is the wholesale abandonment by farmers' associations of agricultural services in favor of setting up transportation-trading companies to engage in frontier trade with the U.S.S.R. In three eastern provinces of Poland alone there are about 120 such companies that are the de facto group property of the full-time employees of farmers' associations (whose original purpose was to be social peasant organizations to provide self-help and not profit).

10. An example is a company whose owner is the managing director of the Port of Gdańsk. This company exploits unused space in cargo holds to make shipments whose profits go into private pockets. It has gradually transformed itself into an independent foreign trade enterprise that, among other things, imports used cars from the West.

11. An expression contained in the so-called consolidation plan proposed by the Rakowski government and passed by the Seym in March 1989.

12. An example of the private profits gained from separating functions previously performed by a department of a state enterprise (and of the costs that have to be covered by the Treasury) is the private company

Modernizacja, which was set up in place of the Department of Modernization and Construction of the Central Water System in Warsaw and provides services connected with the cleaning of filters and water treatment. Charges to the municipal budget rose nearly 70 percent in spite of only a 1.1 percent increase in the amount of drinkable water supplied to Warsaw. (Source: A. Leszczyński, "Fortuny Pośredników" [Fortunes of middlemen], *Trybuna Ludu*, 19 July 1989). For merely organizing the job, companies that use the equipment and the crew of a state enterprise take 15 to 30 percent of the profit for themselves, and besides this they tack on the expenses of "brokerage" to the cost estimate of the job.

13. A survey made by the author in the province of Gdańsk in 1989 indicates that about 30 percent of the computer services performed for state enterprises and the administration by private computer companies is accountancy that is not used in decision making and often is in excess of what the law requires.

14. See Hankiss, "Reforms."

15. In the Warynski factory in Warsaw seventeen companies of this type lease elements of their assets. More than a dozen such companies are in the Naval Shipyard in Gdynia, and in the wire factory in Gliwice the department working for export has been separated from the enterprise and formed into a private company.

16. An example of bankruptcy by fiscal methods (additional taxes ruining an enterprise that in the past had earned a 40 percent profit) and the compulsory transformation into a private company (whose shareholders are private persons and state enterprises cooperating with the "bankrupt") is Stolbud (a monopolist in prefabricated wooden houses). An example of bankruptcy by political means (and transformation into private companies) is the Gdańsk Shipyard.

17. The managing director of the company Igloopol is the deputy minister of agriculture responsible for environmental protection. This company is popularly believed to be damaging the natural environment in the Bieszczady region.

18. These companies receive tax breaks and also more favorable terms for the compulsory sale to the state of foreign currency than other state and private enterprises operating in foreign markets: the favored companies must sell 15 percent of foreign currency to the state at the official exchange rate; the others must sell 50 to 80 percent. The favored companies sometimes begin to speculate—with the help of foreign partners—on the free-market sale of foreign currencies (engaging in arbitrage). As their "contribution" local partners sometimes give a segment of the market in which they had operated before as a state enterprise (e.g., in the fruit business; see: P. Tarnowski, "W malinach" [In the raspberry bushes], *Polityka*, 14 July 1989.

19. In 1987 the Communist party had productive assets worth tens of billions of złotys (shares in the publishing cooperative Prasa-Książka-Ruch valued at 20 billion; in Hortex, the first enterprise in Poland that is modernizing itself with credits from the World Bank; and in industrial and service enterprises). Similar activity, though on a smaller scale, is conducted by the United Peasants' party and the Democratic party. Source: M. Dąbrowski, W. Anyszkiewicz, and W. Radomski, *Działalność gospodarcza organizacji społecznych* [The economic activity of social organizations] (Warsaw: Wydawnictwo Związkowe, 1988), pp. 40–60. Material production constitutes 46.5 percent of the economic activity of social and political organizations; services, the remaining 53.5 percent (ibid., p. 61). Here it is worth mentioning that the productive activity of firms belonging to these organizations makes up one-sixth of the output of the traditional private sector. Services make up a bigger share and are rapidly increasing.

20. Productive and service enterprises operate both at the central level (examples are the aforementioned Promotor, publishing enterprises, the Multibranch Cooperative) and in individual branch trade unions. For example, the Trade Union of Workers of Light Industry and the Trade Union of Sailors and Fishermen are currently setting up companies with export ambitions, and trade unions in particular enterprises often encourage the formation of worker teams that lease part of the assets (function) from the enterprise.

21. Good examples here are youth organizations and social associations of lay Catholics. The Association of Polish Students has an extensive network of travel offices, publishing houses, the multibranch enterprise MFB, and service cooperatives with branches in more than twenty provinces. The Union of Rural Youth and the Union of Socialist Youth, in addition to activities similar to those of the ASP, run housing cooperatives and construction enterprises (Dąbrowski, *Działalność*, pp. 42–43).

22. Cooperatives and enterprises belonging to social organizations provide (chiefly for their own members) about 10 percent of all of the construction and travel services in the country (ibid., p. 65).

23. The commercial code of 27 July 1934 with amendments introduced by the Civil Code in 1964 (*Dziennik Ustaw*, no. 13, item 94) is the legal foundation for the activities of commercial trading companies. Cooperatives belonging to organizations operate on the basis of the law on cooperatives of 1982 (*Dziennik Ustaw*, no. 30, item 210). The operations of so-called separated works (which operate like enterprises, but without their own legal status) are based on the decree of the Council of Ministers of 22 October 1985 (par. 3, passage 3). Finally, mixed enterprises operate on the basis of the law of 10 July 1985 (*Dziennik Ustaw*, no. 32, item 142). With the exception of a few areas (where permission of

the Ministry of Domestic Trade is necessary), so-called nonseparate economic activity by an organization does not require any administrative approval. In 1985 such nonseparate activity brought political organizations 3.5 billion złotys in profit; trade unions, 2.5 billion; social organizations, 35 billion (Dąbrowski, *Economic Activity*, p. 75).

24. Hankiss ("Reforms," p. 15) describes activity in this area by the League of Communist Youth (KISZ), which buys up for symbolic sums tourist equipment and centers (that it had been using up to that time) and begins to run them for profit (a sort of private company of the apparatus of the organization).

25. In Poland, organizations and associations of lay Catholics such as PAX (with about 5 billion złotys in profit from economic activity in 1985; Dąbrowski, *Działalność*, p. 50) or the Polkat works (belonging to the Society of Polish Catholics) with 1.4 billion in profit.

26. Two studies of the economic policy of Minister S. Witte are examples of analysis of the beginnings of political capitalism in czarist Russia: T. van Laue, "The Witte System in Russia," *The Journal of Economic History*, 1953; and A. Kahan, *S. Witte and the Industrialization of Russia* (New York: Columbia University Press, 1967).

27. The discussion on the future of companies in the Gdańsk Shipyard gives an indication of the lack of any guarantee of permanence and the climate around the new owners from the *nomenklatura*. The *Polityka* journalist (no. 24/1989) H. Jezierski writes: "There should be no problem in canceling leases to managers' companies operating on the premises of the Shipyard."

28. See the discussion of Liski's idea in: J. Barsony, "Tibor Liski pomysł przedsiębiorczośći socjalistycznej" [Tibor Liski's notion of socialist initiative], *Acta Oeconomika* 1982, vol. 28, no. 3–4; reprinted in: *Socjalizm ludzi zamożnych* [Socialism of the affluent], A. Pawłowski (ed.) (Warsaw: *Sigma publications*, 1988).

29. See the argument in "Forms of Privatization in the Socioeconomic Context," this chapter.

30. Term from a paper read by A. Łukaszewicz at the Third Ideological Conference of the Communist party, Warsaw, February 1989.

31. See the interview with Rakowski, a supporter of this line, in *Polityka*, 8 July 1989.

32. See the special issue of *Review of the Fernand Braudel Center*, vol. 11, Spring 1988, on the transformation of the Ottoman Empire.

33. Such mediation and two types of private sector developing under the influence of Westernization in the Ottoman Empire are analyzed by R. Kasaba, *The Ottoman Empire and the World Economy, the Nineteenth Century* (Albany, N.Y.: State University of New York Press, 1988).

34. P. Evans, *Dependent Development: the Alliance of Multinational, State and Local Capital in Brazil* (Princeton, N.J.: Princeton University Press, 1979).

35. An example is the export of food to the U.S.S.R., where the state foreign trade authorities negotiated especially unfavorable financial conditions for Poland (Tarnowski, "W malinach"). This trade is gradually being taken over by private companies, which operate more efficiently and increase the volume of export (to the satisfaction of the Soviet side) and profits (though sometimes this has an inflationary effect on the domestic market).

36. The law on the finances of state enterprises of 31 January 1989 (*Rzeczpospolita*, 13 February 1989).

37. The law on the state enterprise of 1982.

38. Company Law (Statute, 1988, no. 6) Budapest.

39. The law on economic activity with the participation of foreign capital, 23 December 1988.

40. See L. Loos, "Przedsiębiorstwa zmieniają włascicieli" [Enterprises are changing owners], *Trybuna Ludu*, 26 June 1989.

41. For example, the Lang Works of the machine industry, the Ikarus bus factory, the Taurus enterprise of the rubber industry, and forty-nine other large plants (ibid).

42. Ibid.

43. Tomas Beck, Hungarian minister of trade (cited from Loos, "Przedsiębiorstwa").

44. This reservation was made by M. Dąbrowski in the paper "Własnosc grupowa" [Group ownership] read at a conference in the Main School of Planning and Statistics (17–18 November 1988) and in his article "Rozdać czy wyprzedać" [To give away or sell], *Konfrontacje*, June 1989.

45. S. Kawalec in: "Wiązka praw—jaka własność i czyja?" [A cluster of laws—what kind of ownership and whose?], *Zmiany* 1989, no. 8.

46. See the interview with P. Mayo, an English conservative, who is engaged in transforming enterprises into employees' companies (*Zmiany* 1989, no. 8).

47. Dąbrowski, "Własnosc grupowa."

48. In the opinion of Kawalec (paper "Zarys programu prywatyzacji gospodarki polskiej" [Outline of a program of privatization of the Polish economy] read at a conference in the Main School of Planning and Statistics, 17–18 November 1988), all of the resources in the hands of the population would suffice to buy up 11 percent of the fixed assets in the hands of the state. (See also Z. Fedorowicz, "Objektywne uwarunkowania czy chiejstwo?" [Objective determinants or greed?], *Życie Gospo-*

darcze 1988, no. 19. After adding foreign currency reserves and the possibility of taking out mortgages on private property, the potential for buying up state property increases. Kawalec believes that after twenty-five years two-thirds of state property would pass into private hands.

49. Dąbrowski, "Własnosc grupowa."

50. This is the proposal of J. Lewandowski and J. Szomberg from the University of Gdańsk (paper at the conference in the Main School of Planning and Statistics, 17–18 November 1988, and the interview in *Konfrontacje*, June 1989).

51. Dąbrowski, "Własnosc grupowa."

52. In Poland about 500 such groups are permanently active; in Hungary, 17,337 (C. Kadas, *The Hungarian Enterprise, Issue of Size and Ownership*, Ph.D. thesis, University of Washington, Seattle, Wash., 1989.

53. M. Swięcicki, "Reforma własnośćiowa" [The ownership reform], paper at the conference in the Main School of Planning and Statistics, 17–18 November 1988.

54. See "Forms of Privatization in the Socioeconomic Context" in this chapter.

55. See M. Misiak, "W obliczu depresji" [In the face of depression], *Życie Gospodarcze*, 25 June 1989.

56. Ibid. From May 1988 to May 1989 production in the petroleum industry fell 25 percent, and the supplies of gas imported from the U.S.S.R. also declined.

57. An average decline of output of 0.9 percent, depending on the industry: 5 percent in the electronics industry, 2.2 percent in light industry, 0.3 percent in the chemical industry (ibid.), with a simultaneous increase in wages.

58. Employment in state industry in May 1989 was 3.5 percent lower than in May of the previous year.

59. An example is enterprises of light industry, which lack the funds to purchase at auctions foreign currency required for cooperative import (Misiak, "Depresji").

60. W. Niskanen, *Bureaucracy and Representative Government* (Chicago: University of Chicago Press, 1971), and W. D. Nordhaus, "The Political Business Cycle," *Review of Economic Studies*, 1975, 62:2.

61. Purchase prices rose an average of 35 percent and in some cases exceeded market equilibrium prices (at bazaars). See the statement of M. Swięcicki in the editorial discussion in *Życie Gospodarcze*, 9 July 1989 ("Zaczęły się schody" [The descent has begun]).

62. About 30 percent of the Polish population lives in the countryside, and labor productivity is the lowest in Europe.

63. In May 1989 the budget deficit soared to 3.5 trillion złotys (with a planned deficit at the end of the year of 998 billion). In addition to the outflow of money connected with raising purchase prices and wages in departments financed from the budget, other reasons for the budget deficit are the decline of income tax revenues due to tax breaks negotiated through bargaining (chiefly in export areas) and lower than expected revenues from the so-called dividend (moneys owned to the state for its ownership rights)—payments were suspended in special production, the power engineering industry, and the Gdańsk Shipyard (a total of 80 billion złotys). At the same time, the private sector paid more than anticipated into the Treasury, but these revenues are only a small part of the budget (867 billion from the private sector in planned revenues of 17 trillion). In the first quarter of 1989 124 billion (397 billion planned for the year) flowed into the state budget from private activity in production, trade, and services. This is due to the creation of about 126,000 new economic units (only 1,000 of which are in the state sector). Data: "Budżet na minusie" [The budget in the red], *Życie Gospodarcze*, 25 June 1989.

64. During the period between the "round table" and the elections, wages rose 35 percent faster than prices.

65. Slowdowns in payments without paying interest; tax breaks (raised by law to 80 percent).

66. The expression of G. Kłodko in: *Crisis, Adjustment and Development in Socialist Economics: The Case of Poland*, mimeographed, University of Warsaw, 1988, p. 106.

67. Ibid., pp. 106–107.

68. In the budget law of 1989 in Poland, revenues of 40 billion are expected from the sale of bonds.

69. The export of food, services, building materials, machines, energy, etc.

70. In Poland the necessity of investing in the power industry (an increase of 42 percent in 1986 through 1990) and metallurgy (an increase of 89 percent)—with an increase of only 13 percent in agriculture to 1990—is connected with specialization in the COMECON and production obligations to the U.S.S.R. signed in 1986). Data on investments: Kłodko, *Crisis*, p. 132.

71. See also the opinion of R. Bugaj in the editorial discussion in *Życie Gospodarcze*, 9 July 1989.

72. Report from the deliberations of the Seym Committee on Indexation, July 1989.

73. Program declaration of the so-called Working Group of Solidarity, passed on 18 December 1988 in Gdańsk and published in *Poza Układem*, no. 1.

74. The fullest account is in: M. Rakowski, "Wspólne rozmowy" [Common talks], published by Kolegium Studiów Społeczno-Gospodarczych "Polska Przebudowa," February 1989.

75. See the opinion of G. Kłodko in the editorial discussion in *Życie Gospodarcze*, 9 July 1989.

76. Ibid. See also the statement of W. Baka, Political Bureau of the Central Committee of the Communist party, (television news, "Program 1," 27 June 1989).

77. Proposals to transform ownership relations in the opinion of workers and managers of enterprises (research report), Bulletin of CBOS, Warsaw, 131: 8, 1989; also: the suggested model of management of the enterprise, in the opinion of managing directors and the managerial staff (research report), Bulletin of CBOS, Warsaw, 149: 9, 1989, Center for the Study of Public Opinion.

78. "Co to znaczy sprawiedliwie?: omówienie badan," [What does "just" mean?: Discussion of a research project], *Życie Gospodarcze*, 25 June 1989.

79. "Postulowany model," p. 8.

80. Ibid., p. 3.

81. Resolution of the Second National Forum of Workers' Councils, Wrocław, February 1989 (*Trybuna Ludu*, 13 February 1989).

82. Morawski and Cichomski, Życie Gospodarcze, 25 June 1989.

83. The paper of A. Łukasziewicz at the Third National Theoretical Conference of the Communist party and the discussion related in *Trybuna Ludu*, 13 February 1989 (A. Leszczyński, "Własność" [Ownership]).

84. See the statement of J. Hausner (secretary of the provincial committee of the Communist party in Kraków) in the editorial discussion in *Życie Gospodarcze*, 9 July 1989.

85. Paper at the Tenth Plenum of the Central Committee of the Communist party (December–January 1989); also the statement in the Political Bureau on 27 June 1989 (television news, 27 June) suggesting a ban on combining positions in the state sector with shares in the private sector.

86. A postrevisionist mentality, with economic views influenced by O. Lange and W. Brus in his earlier period (decentralization, not ownership changes).

87. See the statement of J. Hausner in the discussion in *Życie Gospodarcze*, 9 July 1989.

88. *Polityka*, 8 July 1989.

89. NIK report for the Commission of Economic Policy (Seym library, December 1989). Also: D. Frey "Spółki pod specjalnym nadzorem" [Co-ops under special control], Rzeczpospolita, 28 February 1990.

90. Ibid.

91. This expression comes from J. Poldys, *Poszukiwania* [Explorations] (Warsaw: Sigma Publ. 1988).

92. See J. Staniszkis, *Ontologia socjalizmu* [The ontology of socialism] (Warsaw: Biblioteka Krytyka, 1989; also Oxford: Oxford University Press, in preparation).

93. A hypothesis put forward in an article in *Moskovskoye Novosti* by M. Pavlowska-Silvanskeya.

94. T. Bauer, "Economic Reforms and Bloc-Integration," paper read at a conference in the Konrad Adenauer Stiftung, Bonn, June 1989.

95. See Staniszkis, *Ontologia*, chap. 3.

96. Bauer, "Bloc-Integration," p. 3.

97. See M. Rakowski, *Szacunek korzyśći i strat z obrotow miedzy Polska a ZSSR* [An estimate of gains and losses from trade between Poland and the U.S.S.R.], manuscript, p. 6, Warsaw, 1989. In the case of Poland this is specialization in the export of energy-consuming and/or subsidized products (metallurgy, mining, food).

98. Ferenc Kozma, a Hungarian expert, estimates about one million unemployed in Hungary if the COMECON is abolished. I cite this from Bauer, who argues against this prognosis (Bauer, "Bloc-Integration," p. 5).

Part II Introduction

1. See Jadwiga Staniszkis, *Ontologia socializmu* [The ontology of socialism] (Warsaw: Biblioteka Krytyka, 1989; also Oxford: Oxford University Press, in preparation).

2. An example is indexation, which was agreed upon at the "round table" in a fuller version than was later ratified by the Seym (with the participation of Citizens' Parliamentary Club deputies who—in their new role—took the budget deficit into consideration). Grażyna Staniszewska (a deputy and participant in the "round table" talks) spoke about tensions in the trade union Solidarity on this issue ("Na górę źle, a na dole?" [Bad at the top, and at the bottom?], *Gazeta Wyborcza*, 25 July 1989).

3. An example is meetings of the so-called Interventionary Team, headed jointly by J. Kuroń and A. Gdula (former deputy minister of the Ministry of Internal Affairs, at this time head of the organizational department of the Central Committee of the Communist party and also secretary of the Committee for Understanding (a permanent, though extraconsititutional, body that in Wilanów and Magdalenka continued the consultations begun before the "round table" in January 1989).

4. The candidates of Lech Wałęsa's Citizens' Committee competed with so-called independent candidates, who often were selected by local Citizens' Committees, for a limited number of mandates (a decision of the "round table").

5. For example, the president has the right to declare a state of emergency, veto decisions of the Seym, and dissolve the latter.

6. See Staniszkis, *Ontologia*, chap. 4.

7. Since martial law, the center of this Committee has shifted from the army to the Ministry of Internal Affairs and the party apparatus afflliated with the latter. This center seems to be subordinated to a similar Committee in the U.S.S.R. headed by A Lukyanov which watches over legislation (including special laws) that will ensure stability during the period of reforms and deals with the operative administration of crisis situations ("putting out fires").

8. The Committee for Understanding includes, among others, an interventionary team and a team for economic matters.

9. See the appendix to chap. 3.

10. A. Celinski (Citizens' Parliamentary Club senator) spoke of farmers (and not workers) as the social base of the Citizens' Club in an interview ("Pułapki dwoistości" [The pitfalls of duality], *Gazeta Wyborcza*, 11 July 1989).

11. "Sacrifice of the economy on the altar of politics" is the expression of J. Osiatyński at a meeting of the Citizens' Parliamentary Club (*Gazeta Wyborcza*, 2 August 1989).

12. An example is the backing out from participation in preparing elections to the Seym on the part of representatives of neo-conservative circles (A. Hall and M. Król) who had taken part in the "round table" talks. The dispute concerned the manner of selecting candidates for deputies by the Citizens' Committee. Subsequent divisions (i.e., the resignation of J. Grzelak, head of the Election Committee of Solidarity) were linked with the protest against the arbitrary decision to lower the percentage of required votes for party candidates in the second round of the elections. The election law was changed in a narrow circle at a session of the Committee for Understanding. See J. Lindenberg, "Bardzo lubię, gdy inni decydują w moim imieniu" [I like it very much when others decide in my name], *Tygodnik Solidarność*, 23 June 1989.

13. One of the contributing factors was the poll taken by the Center for the Study of Public Opinion after the "round table" which showed the increasing popularity of the "authorities" (in connection with the agreement reached with the opposition). In this situation it was assumed that persons associated with the authorities—and placed on a national list—would have the best chances of being elected. The wholesale rejec-

tion of the authorities in the elections (including the reformers responsible for the "round table") combined with the dramatic economic situation and the election tactics of the opposition (and the Church) dashed these hopes.

14. See the speech of J. Reykowski at the Thirteenth Plenum of the Central Committee of Communist party (*Trybuna Ludu*, 29–30 July 1989).

15. Speech of Communist party deputy K. Komornicki at the Thirteenth Plenum (broadcast "live" on Polish Radio, 28 July 1989; in the *Trybuna Ludu* version there were no figures).

16. Ibid.

17. Statement of M. Król, Communist party deputy and newly elected Secretary of the Central Committee, Thirteenth Plenum, 29 July 1989.

18. "Wasz Prezydent, nasz Premier" [Your president-our prime minister] is the title of Adam Michnik's article in *Gazeta Wyborcza*, 4 July 1989.

19. See Wałęsa's statement after the meeting with President Jaruzelski, TV news, "Program 1."

20. Interview with the Secretary of the Democratic party, J. R. Nowak, in Przegląd Tygodniowy, July 1989.

21. Some of the deputies of the coalition voted against the candidacy of Jaruzelski. He was elected by one vote thanks to several invalid votes from Citizens' Parliamentary Club deputies (put into the ballet intentionally in order to elect Jaruzelski).

22. The June 1989 events in China (massacre of students, politicization of the army) increased the pressure from the Red Army in the U.S.S.R. to expand the role of the military in the process of government on account of spreading strikes and nationalist protests. In such a situation a military man as president in Poland (even one as loyal as Jaruzelski) is troublesome for Moscow, especially since Jaruzelski was used by the Soviet Army as an example of the positive role of the military in politics. It was only after additional consultations in Bucharest (meeting of the Political Committee of the Warsaw Pact States after the visit of President Bush in Poland) that Gorbachev seems to have changed his opinion on this matter.

23. The discussion in the Senate on local self-government on 29 July 1989, especially the statement of the chairman of the Committee on Local Self-Government, J. Regulski (broadcast on Polish Radio and TV; also the editorial "Przyspieszyc wybory" [Speed up the elections], *Gazeta Wyborcza*, 31 July 1989).

24. In August 1980 people from the region of Gdańsk turned to the Interplant Strike Committee for help in solving practical problems (e.g.,

provisions) and treated it as a sort of local administration.

25. The opinion of Senator A. Wielowiejski during the session on local self-government (broadcast on Polish Radio, 29 July 1989).

26. For example, making the crucial decision on "introducing market mechanisms" in agriculture (and taking the lid off prices) outside the Seym.

27. Agreements on specialization in trade with the U.S.S.R. to the end of the decade signed in 1986 or the recent turn in the import policy of the U.S.S.R. (reducing supplies to Poland by 15 percent, including a 25 percent reduction in the supplies of gas, coupled with pressure to speed up the payment of Poland's debt to the U.S.S.R. (See D. Rossati, "Z kraju" [News from home], *Polityka*, 5 August 1989.)

28. The appeal of B. Gieremek, president of the Citizens' Parliamentary Club, to vote for the first (inflationary) version of the law on indexation (*Gazeta Wyborcza*, 2 August 1989).

29. This cleavage was evident during the debate on a "government of the opposition." The opponents of this idea (T. Mazowiecki, K. Modzelewski, and R. Bugaj) were aware that such a government would be in an extreme (crisis) situation—e.g., forced to put an end to strikes or temporarily suspend Solidarity (in order to suspend the All-Polish Agreement of Trade Unions). This could bring about a dramatic rift in the opposition.

30. Report on a meeting in Warsaw of some political groups not represented in Wałęsa's Citizens' Committee, at which district Citizens' Committees reached a horizontal agreement (*Gazeta Wyborcza*, "Struktury poziomowe" [Horizontal structures], 25 July 1989).

31. The opinions of W. Baka and Z. Michalek at the Thirteenth Plenum (27–28 July 1989) as broadcast on Polish Radio and TV; also in *Trybuna Ludu*.

32. Speech in the Seym after the voting for the president (*Trybuna Ludu* 3 August 1989).

33. The statement of Wałęsa after a meeting with President Jaruzelski, or rather, visual signals of victory in transmission.

34. See Staniszkis, *Ontologia*, Chap. 4.

35. This slogan was visible on the election posters of Lukasiewicz (candidate from Warsaw) and other candidates supported by Communist party members.

36. Phrase is from the speech of M. Orzechowski at the Thirteenth Plenum (*Trybuna Ludu*, 29–30 July 1989).

37. Differences between factions; chap. 4 of this book.

38. The meeting of Rakowski with the Club of Deputies of the Communist party on 31 July 1989 (*Trybuna Ludu*, 1 August 1989).

39. The meeting of L. Miller, Secretary of the Central Committee, with the provincial secretaries of the Communist party, 31 July 1989.

40. The convergence of the average incomes of peasant and worker families.

41. The appeal of Z. Martyniuk (vice president of All-Polish Agreement of Trade Unions) to Solidarity (TV news, 27 July 1989) caused a radicalization of the latter and a resolution of the Solidarity's National Committee demanding 100 percent indexation (*Gazeta Wyborcza*, 31 July 1989).

42. The notion of "effective strategies of survival" as the basis of control was formulated by J. Migdal in *Strong Societies and Weak States* (Princeton, N.J.: Princeton University Press, 1988).

43. Compare the speech of Yeltsin in the Council of Deputies of the U.S.S.R. (Polish TV, 24 July 1989).

Chapter 3

1. Daniel Bell's expression, from *New Perspective Quarterly*, 1987 (Symposium on Liberalism).

2. Pronouncement of Prime Minister Rakowski at the Tenth Plenum of the Central Committee of the Communist party (*Trybuna Ludu*, 18 January 1989).

3. See chap. 5 on 1956 as a "ritual drama" in J. Staniszkis, *Poland: The Self-Limiting Revolution* (Princeton, N. J.: Princeton University Press, 1986).

4. Resulting from knowledge and not material interest.

5. François Furet, *Interpreting the French Revolution* (Cambridge: Cambridge University Press, 1986).

6. Resolution, "The position of the Central Committee on political pluralism and trade union pluralism," *Trybuna Ludu*, 20 January 1989.

7. Statement of the National Executive Committee of Solidarity of 22 January 1989 (*Trybuna Ludu*, 23 January 1989).

8. Corporation solutions and more seats in the Seym, but not a legalized multiparty system as in Hungary.

9. Interviews of M. Rakowski, among others, during his stay in Austria (reprinted in *The Independent*, London, 25 November 1988: "Democracy Can Develop without 'Solidarity'").

10. Speech of W. Baka at the Tenth Plenum (*Trybuna Ludu*, 21 December 1988); position of the workers' self-management forum against the law on enterprises as the property of the state treasury (the first step in the separation of ownership) in *Trybuna Ludu*, 14 January 1989.

11. The position of A. Miodowicz at the International Labor Organization session (Geneva, October 1988) in response to the Tenth Plenum, in *Trybuna Ludu*, 21–22 January 1989.

12. See Theses at the Tenth Plenum, published by *Trybuna Ludu*, December 1988.

13. The consolidation plan presented in the Seym on 30 January 1989.

14. See the position of the Gdynia group expressed by A. Gwiazda in *Poza Układem*, no. 1, 1989 (journal outside the censorship).

15. All-Polish Association of Trade Unions, part of the party apparatus, and the group from the Academy of Social Sciences. At the Central Committee of the Communist party (around Professor P. Wojcik). The Wrocław journal *Sprawy i Ludzie*.

16. The Working Group of the National Committee of Solidarity that was established in Gdynia on 18 December 1988. The declarations were reprinted in *Polityka*, January 1989.

17. Changes in the election law and setting up councils of deputies from which the Councils of the Republics will be picked. The procedure of selecting candidates reduces the relative share of the dominant national group in a given republic. This will change the composition of Republican Councils and thus also their attitude toward the expression of national aspirations by the mass media (November 1988).

18. The report *Five Years after August* (prepared by Solidarity experts); also the pronouncement of the Citizens' Committee (18 December 1988).

19. The position of Bugaj-Wielowiejski (manuscript, 1988).

20. The position of the Working Group in *Poza Układem*, no. 1, 1989.

21. Gwiazda (see n. 14) is employed in a cooperative that paints chimneys. A member of this cooperative is the managing director of a factory producing scarce paints, who receives a high salary from the cooperative for putting it on the distribution index. Thus power over goods in short supply generates capital.

22. See S. M. Lipset and E. Raab, *The politics of Unreason* (New York: Basic Books 1970), pp. 484–515.

23. P. Georgica, *Postawy sekretarzy szczebla wojewodzkiego PZPR* [Attitudes of provincial secretaries of the Communist party], Academy of Social Sciences at the Central Committee of the Comunist party, manuscript, 1988.

24. K. Field, *The End of Serfdom* (Cambridge, Mass.: Harvard University Press, 1976).

25. Law on Associations, March 1906 (see G. L. Freeze, *From Supplication to Revolution* (Oxford: Oxford University Press, 1988), pp. 197ff.

26. Owing to the educational policy of the 1970s and the low level of technology in the backward structure of Polish industry, only about 60 percent of elementary school graduates each year manage to finish factory-run vocational schools.

27. B. Cichomski, *Sprawiedliwość spoleczna w przemyśle (opinie pracowników, grudzień 1988)* [Social justice in industry (opinions of workers, December 1988)], Institute of Sociology, Warsaw University, manuscript.

28. Association of Workers' Self-Management Activists; the chairman is in L. Wałęsa's Citizens' Committee.

29. Staniszkis, *Poland*, chap. 1.

30. Strongly accented are ties with the Polish Socialist Party (the old one, before the merger with the Polish Workers' Party) and with the new, unlegalized one; also with the liberal establishment, such as former members of the Council is State against martial law and the Polish ambassador to the United Nations.

31. These people include a few former Catholic deputies; Gierek's adviser, who resigned after a few years; a member of the Central Committee of the Communist party after 1980 (removed).

32. See J. Strzelecki, *Kontynuacje III* (Warsaw: Wola Publishers, 1986), pp. 5–9.

33. September 1946, see *Krytyka* 1979, no. 4.

34. The confession of Silony, in: J. Strzelecki, *Kontynuacje*, p. 24.

35. See the pronouncement at the session of the Polish Sociological Association devoted to S. Ossowski.

36. The pronouncement of Z. Reiff at the organizational session of Wałęsa's Citizens' Committee, in which he emphasized the necessity for separating "civil matters" from "trade-union matters" (*Tygodnik Mazowsze*, no. 276, 4 January 1989).

37. In a lecture at Warsaw University, 19 December 1988.

38. Resolution of the Ninth Congress of the Communist party, July 1981, materials issued by Książka i Wiedza Publishers.

39. Discussion at the session on Stalinism organized in the Institute of Prophylaxis and Resocialization at Warsaw University by J. Kurczewski (November 1988).

40. Ibid. Paper read by M. Król.

41. See the texts in *Kontynuacje*: "U źródeł spotkania" [At the sources of the meeting], pp. 67–72; "Wokół Laborem Exercens" [Con-

cerning laborem exercens], pp. 73–86; "Pojęcie wartości ludzkiej w nauce spolecznej Kościoła" [The notion of human value in the social teaching of the Church], pp. 87–97.

42. Cited from an opinion in a discussion in a meeting of the J. Strzelecki Club on 19 January 1989.

43. *Młodzież w świetle badań socjologicznych* [Young people in the light of sociological research], Warsaw 1987. Materials from the conference in Zaborów, September 1986, pp. 341ff.

44. See the report of studies on the opposition (P. Szwejcer, Polish Sociological Association, 1988, with the participation of J. Kuroń, who pointed out the double standard used by the opposition: it praises itself "for acting" [regardless of the effects], but holds the authorities accountable for the effects of their actions).

45. Considerations based on an analysis of publications that appeared during the May and August strikes of 1988, talks with young workers, and also a report of studies on the new generation of protesting workers conducted by the team of J. Wertenstein-Żuławski, P. Szwejcer, et al.

46. On postmodernism as an attitude see S. Morawski (ed.), *Zmierzch estetyki* [The twilight of aesthetics] (Warsaw: 1987).

47. On fundamentalism see the introduction to Staniszkis, *Poland*.

48. A dramatic example: the leader of the strike in the Wisła Shipyard (November 1988, after the decision to close the Lenin Shipyard) suffered a nervous collapse (and was in the hospital); Wałęsa (in spite of earlier decisions) came after a few hours to end the strike. Yet in its report of this event, Radio Free Europe mentioned only Wałęsa.

49. Report of the Żuławski team.

50. For example, a news sheet written by workers in the Gdańsk Shipyard, May 1988.

51. The fairy-tale about stupid Johnny is in *Poza Układem*, Gdańsk, January 1989.

52. About 80 percent of the young striking workers live in workers' hotels.

53. According to the studies of L. Beskid and Z. Sufin (Institude of Philosophy and Sociology of the Polish Academy of Sciences, 1986), nominal wages make up about 50 percent of average family income. The rest comes from supplementary income, such as from participation in the second economy.

54. A journal supporting the Working Group (*Poza Układem*) is issued jointly with the editorial board of the journal of young workers from the Gdańsk Shipyard (*Trzecia Brama*).

55. A conflict appeared in many plants, e.g., in Ursus and the Gdańsk

Shipyard. Regional authorities associated with Wałęsa pressured for the choice of old activists, many of whom no longer worked in the plant (politicians), whereas the young members of the crews wanted people from the plants (autumn 1988).

56. See Lipset and Raab, *Unreason*, p. 433: democratic constraint.

57. Street clashes with the constabulary; brutality in arrests. According to studies of the Academy of Social Sciences entitled *Położenie klasy robotniczej* [Position of the working class], every other worker at one time in life was arrested or in jail.

58. The expression of J. Orzeł in *Podmioty przełomowej reformy* [Subjects of the crucial reform], unpublished manuscript, Institute of Philosophy and Sociology, Polish Academy of Sciences, Warsaw, 1988.

59. This was the motivation for the attitude toward the law on the state treasury. See Resolution of the Workers' Self-Management Forum, Wrocław, 12 January 1989.

60. See J. Jedlicki, *Jakiej cywilizacji Polacy potrzebuja?* [What kind of a civilization do Poles need?] (Warsaw: Panstwowe Wydawmictwo Naukowe, 1988).

61. Based on the analysis by A. Florczyk, T. Zukowski, and J. Najdowski: "Nowa geografia polityczna Polski" [The new political geography of Poland], *Tygodnik Solidarnośći*, no. 6, 6 July 1989.

62. Poll of the Center for the Study of Public Opinion (August 1989) on a national sample of the adult population: 1498 persons. Symbol BS/185/14/89.

63. See the points in chap. 4 in "The Opposition: Crisis of Identity after Legalization."

Chapter 4

1. "Coexistence of Capitalism with Socialism in Poland" (responses to the seventh questionnaire of the Center for the Study of Public Opinion (CBOS), May 1989, mimeographed, symbol ZT/163/1.89). These are long passages of the statements of seventy-three persons, among them employees of the party apparatus and coalition parties, members of the horizontal structures of the Communist party in 1980 and 1981, intellectuals of circles identified with the left, and also a few persons from opposition circles with an orientation close to the new center. Selections from their statements were compiled for the politburo of the Central Committee of the Communist party, with Jaruzelski as first secretary.

2. See M. Gorbachev, *Perestroika: New Thinking for Our Country and the World* (Warsaw: Ksiajikna i Wiedza, 1987; also Gorbachev's Report to the 27th CPSU Congress, 25 February 1986, *Pravda*, Mos-

cow; also J. Afanasyev, "Vospitanie istinoy," *Komsomolskaya pravda*, 1 September 1987.

3. See J. Staniszkis, *Dynamics of Dependency*, The Wilson Center Papers, Washington, D.C., 1987.

4. V. Bunce, "Decline of a Regional Hegemony," Eastern European Politics and Society, vol. 3, no. 2, Spring 1989.

5. K. Jowitt, "The Moscow Center," *Eastern European Politics and Society*, vol. 1, no. 3.

6. The Soviet Union triangle can be presented in symbolic terms as a competition between Yakovlev, Yeltsin, and Ligachev, with Gorbachev moving among them and shifting his position according to the actual relationship of forces (in Poland Jaruzelski is shifting in the same way). There has been a recent (autumn/winter 1988) weakening of the Moscow globalists (signaled during the Reagan and Kohl visits in Moscow as well as in Gorbachev's UN speech in December 1988, when he used the typical phrase of the populists underlining the "freedom of choice," i.e., the right of the state to pick the type of regime that meets its needs, not "universal human rights," the globalists' phrase). An echo of the above shift came to Poland during the "round table," but it was not strong enough to stop the four trade-offs described in this chapter.

7. See my analysis of the 1970s in Poland in *Poland: The Self-limiting Revolution* (Princeton, N.J.: Princeton University Press, 1986).

8. This dyarchy can assume either a radical form (continuation of the extraconsititutional Committee for Understanding, which gathers the leading activists of the opposition and the present center of the prerogative state and makes the real decisions behind the parliamentary facade) or a more moderate one (e.g., the Senate–Seym Committee, which coordinates economic decisions with the government before they are made, thereby infringing the division of powers into legislative and executive).

9. Statement of the Soviet Ministry of Foreign Affairs after the letter of Wałęsa on forming a coalition government without the Communist party, which stresses the destabilizing influence—on a European scale—of the government crisis in Poland (Polish Radio, "Program 1," 14 August 1989).

10. Meeting of Rakowski, First Secretary of the Central Committee of the Communist party, with the active party members of the Ministry of Internal Affairs (August 1989).

11. Regional Committees of Law and Order of the Ministry of Internal Affairs set up in the U.S.S.R. in August 1989 (similar in their functions to the regional military Defense Committees organized in Poland before the imposition of martial law in 1981).

12. July 1989.

13. The radical globalist view was presented in a paper by Z. Cackowski ("Theoretical–Political Problems of Socialist Renewal"), the moderate globalist view by A. Bodnar ("Reforms in the Party"), and the populist view by S. Wiatr and others ("Structures and Mechanisms of Action in the Party in Conditions of Socialist Renewal"). Nearly all the speakers were social scientists in minor political positions (Z. Cackowski, for instance, is a member of the Central Committee), but they represent the point of view of more powerful actors (the moderate globalists: Kiszczak. Jaruzelski, St. Ciosek; the radical globalists: Orzechowski; the populists: the Warsaw Party Committee, the main core of the domestic security forces, and part of the army).

14. S. Gabrielski, "Gwarancje socjalistycznej dominacji" [Guarantees of socialist domination], *Trybuna Ludu*, 16 January 1989; also A. Czyz, "W kierunku społeczenstwo obywatelskiego" [Toward a civil society], *Trybuna Ludu*, 2 February 1989.

15. Theses of the politburo at the Tenth Plenum of the Central Committee of the Communist party, "Reforma partii—warunkiem odnowy" [Reform of the party—a condition of renewal], *Trybuna Ludu*, 17–18 December 1988.

16. Ibid., p. 15.

17. Wiatr, "Structures," pp. 11, 17.

18. Cackowski, "Socialist Renewal," p. 8.

19. Theses, "Reforma," p. 26 (also p. 7).

20. Wiatr, "Structures," p. 19.

21. W. Malinowski, "Socjaldemokratyzacja, realność czy złudzenie" [Socialdemocratization, reality or illusion?], *Trybuna Ludu*, 2 March 1989; also Theses, "Reforma," p. 14.

22. Staniszkis, *Poland.*

23. J. Bartkowski, "Modele kariery w lokalnej strukturze władzy" [Career models in the local power structure], Ph.D. work, Institute of Sociology, Warsaw University, 1988, based on an empirical survey in two districts.

24. Ibid., p. 240. For instance, every fourth employee of the "justice/order" sector was a member of the city council; every fifth was a chairman of a local branch of a professional association, every fourth was a PRON activist (PRON, the Polish Council for National Salvation, was created in 1983; its members supported General Jaruzelski and usually were local apparatchiks).

25. Ibid., p. 214.

26. Ibid., concluding chapter. Also J. Wasilewski, *Kariery społeczno-zawodowe dyrektorów* [The Socio-occupational careers of managing directors] (Warsaw, 1981).

27. Bartkowski, "Modele kariery," p. 262.

28. Ibid., pp. 240–255.

29. P. Georgica, *Party Apparatus and Reforms*, Social Academy of the Central Committee of the Communist party, Warsaw, 1988 (mimeographed).

30. Otto Kuusinen, Secretary of the Comintern Presidium, wrote in *The Communist Solar System* (London, September 1933), edited by the British Labour Party: "We must create a whole solar system of smaller organizations . . . working actually under the influence of the Party, but not under mechanical leadership."

31. F. Burlacki, leading *glasnost* figure (see his "Uchitsia demokratii," *Pravda*, 18 July 1987) in the 1960s was a member of the Kuusinen circle in Moscow and was accused of revisionist ideas.

32. See M. Levin, *Political Undercurrents in Soviet Economic Debates* (Princeton, N.J.: Princeton University Press, 1974), p. 38.

33. *Współistnienie* (see n. 1), p. 61. A contemporary use of the moral argument against introducing elements of capitalism that recalls the narodnik arguments of Tkachov in nineteenth-century Russia. See A. Walicki, *Od oświecenia do Marksizmu* [From the Enlightenment to Marxism] (Warsaw: PWN, 1978). Here is a contemporary quote showing onological reosoning taken from *Współistnienie*, p. 23 (published by CBOS—see n. 1): "The social order for which we paid with blood and tears, which in its values is more human than capitalism, which in the bargain is the direction in which the world is going, must have a chance to survive. We have the moral obligation and [this sounds vulgar] the historical profitability to give it [ourselves?] this chance. For it might turn out that the rich West, for whose appearances many of us pine today, will imperceptibly and automatically [hence in an evolutionary way] reach the thresholds of socialism. Maybe it is already reaching them. In this same time should we be experiencing a return of ruthless nineteenth-century capitalism, with its tremendous injustices, a system introduced by another swindle and manipulation? I believe that *we have to withdraw a little*. I write this with hesitation and vexation. . . . To retreat *in order that the category might be fulfilled* [to build socialism once again—completion of the author's thought – J. S.]."

34. Levin, Undercurrents, p. xvi: "The same questions—coming back—as the genuine discovery, a reaction to present realities."

35. The government alliance (Rakowski's) with the United Peasants' party decided on parity (and not costs) as the threshold of purchase prices; in turn the Citizens' Parliamentary Club of Deputies (CPC) agreed to indexation that would cover farmers (in spite of hikes in purchase prices) in order to build a coalition with the Club of Deputies of the UPP (debate in the Seym, July 1989).

36. A statement by Trotsky quoted in Levin, *Undercurrents*, pp. 68–69.

37. *Współistnienie*.

38. Ibid., pp. 76–77. The notion of "agrosocialism" has a favorable climate on account of the peasant origin of a considerable part of the present elite (via the channel of the Association of Polish Students, in which the active members are most often students from the countryside residing in dormatories).

39. *Współistnienie*. . . , p. 34.

40. Ibid., p. 35.

41. Ibid., p. 36.

42. Ibid., p. 36.

43. Ibid., p. 38.

44. Ibid., p. 36.

45. Ibid., p. 68.

46. Ibid., p. 68.

47. Ibid., p. 68.

48. Ibid., p. 68.

49. Ibid., p. 38.

50. Ibid., p. 42.

51. Ibid., p. 39.

52. Ibid., p. 39.

53. Ibid., p. 40.

54. Ibid., p. 40.

55. Ibid., p. 42.

56. Ibid., p. 56.

57. Ibid., p. 44.

58. Ibid., p. 44.

59. Ibid., p. 46.

60. Ibid., p. 46.

61. Ibid., p. 45.

62. Ibid., p. 47.

63. Ibid., p. 48.

64. Ibid., p. 48.

65. Ibid., p. 58.

66. Ibid., p. 58; also M. Gulczynski, *Nowe Drogi* [New ways], no. 12, 1988.

67. *Współistnienie*, pp. 59–60.

68. See appendix to chap. 3.

69. Even the decision to appoint T. Mazowiecki as prime minister did not stop the wave of strikes in the coal mines: on 21 August 1989 six mines were on strike or on strike alert (*Gazeta Wyborcza*, 22 August 1989).

70. The expression "governments go, problems remain" was used by Prime Minister Messner when he handed over power to Rakowski and then by the departing Deputy Prime Minister I. Sekula (in a TV interview, 22 August 1989).

71. Resolution of the National Committee (NC) of Solidarity on regional and local Citizens' Committees of 17 June 1989 (*Tygodnik Solidarność*, 23 June 1989).

72. Members of the Committee for Understanding from the opposition are Wałęsa, Gieremek, Mazowiecki, Michnik, Kuroń, M. Gil, W. Frasyniuk, Z. Bujak, J. Ślisz, W. Trzeciakowski, Wielowiejski, and A. Stelmachowski. Also present were observers from the Polish Episcopate (i.e., Bishop B. Dąbrowski) and the legal adviser of the Episcopate—J. Ambroziak—as secretary. Members from the authorities are, among others, Kiszczak, Gdula, Ciosek, and Cypryniak.

73. The manner of making decisions in the legalized opposition gave rise to a protest on the part of representatives of Farmers' Solidarity in the Seym. They were not consulted about either the dissolution of the Citizens' Committees, in whose existence they were vitally interested, or the manner of entering into a coalition with the United Peasants' party (and with its party—not parliamentary—center, vide Wałęsa's meeting with Malinowski). As the head of Solidarity of Private Farmers stated, "This authenticates the old, decayed structures." He announced the formation of a section of deputies—farmers ("for the time being within the CPC"- *Gazeta Wyborcza*, 22 August 1989).

74. See Staniszkis, *Poland*, chap. 5.

75. See the reports from Zamość, for example, in L. Wolyńska, "Solidarność—stan na dzis" [Solidarity—condition today], *Gazeta Wyborcza*, 5 July 1989.

76. Solidarity has not yet reached one-third of its size before martial law. See Wolynska, "Solidarność."

77. The expression of M. Boni in *Tygodnik Solidarność*, 20 August 1989.

78. The statement of Marek Król, Secretary of the Central Committee of the Communist party, on TV (20 August 1989), commenting on letters sent to *Trybuna Ludu* and published 19 August 1989, which spoke about "treachery of members of the coalition" and "threats to socialism."

79. J. Malczyński in a political commentary, Polish Radio, "Program 1," 20 August 1989.

80. T. Mazowiecki on TV news, 19 August 1989.

81. Statements of plant secretaries of the Communist party in the Central Committee, *Trybuna Ludu*, 19 August 1989.

82. A declaration about the economic situation signed by opposition

deputies and senators—"W obliczu hiperinflacji" [In the face of hyper-inflation]—anticipates the sale (privatization) of about 1 to 2 percent of the total value of the property of the state sector; formation of new companies in the state sector is banned (*Gazeta Wyborcza*, 28–30 July 1989). Earlier, as a remedy, it was suggested that a national economic council be set up and that privatization of the state sector be based on the individual decisions of a newly formed institution: Fund for National Property (deliberations of the economic team of the "round table").

83. An example of the disrespectful attitude toward the law and of sacrificing it in the name of immediate political goals was the acceptance by representatives of the opposition in the Committee for Understanding of the notion of changing the election law during the course of the elections by a decree of the Council of State, while a legal way was possible (changing the law by the newly elected Seym and supplementary elections). Another example is the manner of changing the deputies' oath and the number of deputy marshals of the Seym and also the existence of extraconstitutional institutions such as the Committee for Understanding (brought up by Wałęsa during a meeting with President Jaruzelski after the opposition already had entered the Seym). Finally, there was the unrealized (but considered even before the opportunity arose for Solidarity to form a government) plan of setting up a Senate-Seym Committee, with which the government would have to coordinate important economic decisions before they were made (a plan that would have erased the division between the legislative and executive powers).

84. Change of the election law in the Committee for Understanding (and not by the Seym) creates a situation in which most of the deputies of the Communist party find themselves in the Seym by the grace of the opposition.

85. Letters to *Trybuna Ludu*, 19 August 1989.

86. In its declaration the Club of Deputies of the Communist party (headed by Orzechowski) received the initiative of creating a government by Solidarity "with satisfaction that the opposition wishes to assume the burden of joint responsibility" (*Trybuna Ludu*, 18 August 1989), while the First Secretary of the Central Committee of the Communist party said: "We have entered the period of the open fight for power. . ." (*Trybuna Ludu*, 17 August 1989).

87. Z. Romaszewski, for example, initiated the declaration of the Senate condemning the dispersing of the illegal demonstration of the Confederation for an Independent Poland before the Seym building (against the election of General Jaruzelski as president). An earlier example was the fight for a moratorium for the illegal press (F. H. Luczywo at the "round table").

88. The statement of J. Onyszkiewicz during the "round table"; also, from Senator A. Wielowieyski: "Czym sa dzisiaj lewica i prawica" [What are the left and the right today?], *Tygodnik Solidarność*, no. 11/89.

89. Horizontal agreements initiated by the Citizens' Committees; initiative of Club 88, the Political Group Wola, and other political groupings (some of them called the nonparliamentary opposition). See *Gazeta Wyborcza*, 18 June 1989.

90. Wałęsa about Jan Rulewski (member of the Working Group): "When I needed help, when I was weak, he did not help me. He betrayed me." (*Gazeta Wyborcza*, 23 June 1989, about the meeting in Bydgoszcz of 20 June 1989).

91. The Citizens' Committees began to use the name Solidarity on posters during the election campaign; before this they had been an offshoot of Lech Wałésa's Committee.

92. See the interview with H. Wujec (member of the Election Staff) in *Gazeta Wyborcza*, 10 May 1989, "Gra z dołem się zejdzie" [The game with the grass roots will pass]; also, the statement of K. Modzelewski at a meeting of Lech Wałęsa's Citizens' Committee on 22 June (*Tygodnik Solidarność*, 6 July 1989).

93. One committee was closer to KOR (Kuron-Michnik), the other to the catholic political opposition, ROBCIO (Ruch Obrony Praw Człowieka i Obywatele).

94. For example, the liberal current (Gdańsk, Kraków, and Lublin circles) and the national current (Confederation for an Independent Poland, circle of *Przegląd Katolicki*) were rejected.

95. Among others, A. Hall and M. Król.

96. Wujec, "Gra z dołem."

97. The Citizens' Committee in Piotrków Trybunalski succeeded in putting its own candidate on the Solidarity list (Professor A. Zawiślak), who was not supported by Wałęsa's Citizens' Committee. This move was resisted, and the Election Staff tried to dissolve the Committee.

98. The conflict in Radom, where the local election committee and the Church did not want to support the candidate from the national Solidarity list, J. J. Lipski. He did not pass until the second round of the elections, after a TV broadcast (with the participation of Gieremek, who sailed into this Citizens' Committee).

99. It was calculated that the trade-union organization of Solidarity existed in only thirteen provinces and could win the election only in these areas—the "new political geography" was overlooked.

100. Wujec, "Gra z dołem."

101. Ibid.

102. See the appendix to chap. 3.

103. A meeting of heads of Citizens' Committees of the provincial level in Warsaw, 12 June 1989 (M. Radziwiłł, "Związek i Komitety Obywatelskie" [The union and Citizens' Committees], *Tygodnik Solidarność*, 6 June 1989).

104. The statement of W. Frasyniuk, *Gazeta Wyborcza*, 22 June 1989.

105. Resolution of Solidarity's NC of 17 June, *Tygodnik Solidarność*, 23 June 1989.

106. Meeting of Wałęsa's Citizens' Committee, Warsaw, 22 June 1989. See: "Burza w Audytorium Maximum" [A storm in the auditorium maximum], *Tygodnik Solidarność*, 2 July 1989.

107. In some regions (Mazowsze, Wrocław) the provincial Citizens' Committees were disbanded and municipal ones immediately set up (which does not collide with the decision of Solidarity's NC). See: B. Majewska, "Chodzi o samorząd terytorialny" [The issue is regional self-government], *Tygodnik Solidarność*, 11 August 1989.

108. K. Modzelewski at a meeting of the Citizens' Committee of 22 June ("Burza"). Also: J. Kaczyński (Senator, Secretary of the NC) in: "Lepszy slalom niż zjazd" [Better a slalom than a downhill course], *Gazeta Wyborcza*, 26 June 1989.

109. W. Arkuszewski, "Przez K. O." [Through the Citizens' Committee], *Tygodnik Solidarność*, 6 July 1989.

110. Kaczyński, "Slalom."

111. M. Zalewski (connected with the political Wola group): "Od czego zaczac?" [What should we start from?], *Tygodnik Solidarność*, 6 July 1989.

112. A. Hall at a meeting of the Citizens' Committee ("Burza").

113. Arkuszewski, "Przez K. O."

114. Frasyniuk (see n. 72); Bujak, *Gazeta Wyborcza*, 22 June 1989.

115. Kaczyński, "Slalom"; Modzelewski, "Burza." The Club 88 declared itself in favor of the vision of the Citizens' Committee as an institution integrating the nonparliamentary opposition (J. Orzeł, *Podmioty przełomowej reformy* [Subjects of the crucial reform], unpublished manuscript, Institute of Philosophy and Sociology, Polish Academy of Sciences, Warsaw, 1988).

116. Kaczyński, "Slalom."

117. Frasyniuk (see n. 72).

118. Kaczyński, "Slalom."

119. Z. Kuratowska (deputy marshal of the Seym): "Spor o Komitety" [The dispute over the Committees], *Gazeta Wyborcza*, 22 June 1989.

120. Baehr, "Spor."

121. Radziwiłł, "Związek."

122. Opinions at a meeting of the Citizens' Committee ("Burza").

123. P. Wojciechowski, "O Komitetach Obywatelskich uwagi niepolityczne" [Some nonpolitical comments on the Citizens' Committees], *Tygodnik Solidarność*, 6 June 1989.

124. Ibid.

125. Radziwiłł, "Związek"; J. Regulski, "Ruch samorządnośći obywatelskiej" [The movement of citizens' self-government], *Gazeta Wyborcza*, 3 July 1989.

126. Radziwiłł, "Związek."

127. The Warsaw Citizens' Committee, with about 400 members, already has met several times. It undertakes initiatives of various kinds, from improving the school system in the city and district to matters of trade, health, and social aid. Standing committees have been formed and efforts undertaken to gather independent funds (see: Majewska, "Samorząd terytorialny").

128. "Mazowsze propomuje sejnik krajowy" [Mazowsze proposes a national council], *Tygodnik Solidarność*, 11 August 1989.

129. Ślisz, meeting of the Citizens' Committee; see "Burza," n. 106.

130. Arkuszewski, "Przez K. O."

131. See J. Kwaśniewski, "Gdzie się podział entuzjazm" [What happened to enthusiasm], *Gazeta Wyborcza*, 24 July 1989.

132. J. Jankowiak, "Wielkie materii pomieszanie" [A matter of great confusion], *Gazeta Wyborcza*, 22 August 1989.

133. A Soviet scholar on the Finlandization of the socialist countries (report on the statement of A. Migranian from the Institute of World Economy in Moscow), *Trybuna Ludu* 20 August 1989. Also in the same issue: the statement of Y. Gremitsky of the U.S.S.R.

134. M. Boni, "Potrzebny sukces związkowy" [The union needs a success], *Gazeta Wyborcza*, 5 July 1989.

135. J. Jankowiak, "Koło naprawde ruszyło" [The wheel really has started turning], *Gazeta Wyborcza*, 11 August, 1989.

136. Boni, "Sukces."

137. For example, the unsuccessful attempt to set up a joint committee in Łódź in order to prepare elections in the union (see: "W regionach: szukaja zgody" [In the regions: the search for agreement], *Tygodnik Solidarność*, 3 June 1989.

138. Interview with M. Jurczyk from the Committee for Understanding on behalf of democratic elections in Solidarity on Polish Radio, "Program 1," 22 August 1989.

139. At a meeting of Solidarity's NC (with the participation of the Presidium of the CPC) on 19 August 1989, Wałęsa said: "I singly played this hand and took care of the prime minister for you on my own. . . .

And since you have entered the parliament on my and his back, you ought to help him." To the charges that the decision was made outside the NC and CPC he replied: "I made the choice for you because you were not able to do so. . . . I alone succeeded in doing what two hundred and sixty of you were unable to do" (*Gazeta Wyborcza*, 22 August 1989).

140. In "Rulewski nie przeszkadzaj" [Rulewski, don't interfere], *Gazeta Wyborcza*, 23 May 1989.

141. At the above meeting Wałęsa said: "I will go this way with those people whom I recommend to you and against others—perhaps equally meritorious—but acting on their own, as partisans, and not part of a team."

142. Wolyńska, "Solidarność."

143. Declaration of L. Wałęsa of 7 August 1989 and also the joint declaration after the meetings with Malinowski and Jóżwiak on 17 August in Warsaw (*Trybuna Ludu*, 18 August 1989).

144. Gieremek (interview after Wałęsa's statement, Polish Radio, 8 August 1989): "I found out from foreign correspondents"; earlier, the discussion in the Citizens' Club of Deputies on where political decisions are made (*Gazeta Wyborcza*, 27 July 1989), which was continued in the same tone after Wałęsa's statement (*Gazeta Wyborcza*, 10 August 1989).

145. Information on Polish Radio, "Program 1," 30 August 1989; also on TV news.

146. The protest of Farmers' Solidarity (interview with J. Ślisz in *Gazeta Wyborcza* of 22 August 1989).

147. J. Kaczyński, secretary of the NC (and senator), was the brains behind forming the new coalition and shifting the center of power in the legalized opposition to Wałęsa.

148. The casting of invalid votes by CPC deputies (and the absence of some of them) contributed to Jaruzelski's election as president, in a situation when some deputies from the coalition around the Communist party voted against him.

149. Such signals (especially from the Democratic party) had already appeared in the autumn of 1988 (see chap. 1).

150. The declaration of the Sixteenth Plenum of the Central Committee of the Communist party (*Trybuna Ludu*, 21 August 1989).

151. When M. Rakowski became First Secretary at the Thirteeth Plenum, Ciosek and Orzechowski, among others, left the top leadership, and Miller and Wiatr entered it.

152. Statements in the Club of Deputies of the Communist party on 16 and 17 August (report from deliberations of the Club on Polish Radio); also the statement of a Communist deputy: "Dlaczego głosowalismy za" [Why we voted yes] (*Trybuna Ludu*, 25 August 1989).

153. Meeting of secretaries of the Communist party from large plants in the Central Committee of the party, *Trybuna Ludu*, 18 August 1989; also Rakowski's speech in the Club of Deputies of the Communist party, using such expressions as "we are threatened with breaking the agreements reached at the 'round table'" (*Trybuna Ludu*, 17 August 1989) and his statement at a meeting of the active party members of the Department of Internal Affairs on 9 August in Warsaw (*Trybuna Ludu*, 11 August 1989).

154. At the Thirteenth Plenum L. Miller attacked the Club of Deputies of the Communist party for excessive autonomy and promised to "discipline it"—at the same Plenum Communist deputy Komornicki criticized this stance (radio report).

155. In the assumptions of the "market operation" (and in working out compensation to wage earners), it was expected that the prices of meat would rise to 80 percent of bazaar prices before the operation, while the real increase exceeded 200 percent. At the same time the anticipated increase in supply and purchase of agricultural products did not take place.

156. J. Sachs of Harvard University suggested rapid privatization, abolishing government subsidies to industry and control of prices, a moratorium on the payment of foreign debts, and complete exchangeability of the złoty (*Gazeta Wyborcza*, 24 July 1989).

157. V. Zagladin: "Every government will be a partner for us" (press conference in Paris, 3 July 1989, reprinted in *Gazeta Wyborcza*).

158. *Pravda* correspondents wrote from Warsaw (excerpts in *Trybuna Ludu* of 17 August 1989): "All of this does not contribute to relieving political tension in Poland, whose increase might have an unfavorable impact on all-European processes." The significance of the latter declaration was weakened by a pronouncement by P. Rodionov, reprinted in the same issue of *Trybuna Ludu*: "We ought not solve the problems of another country by force" (article in the monthly *Znamya*).

159. The spokesman of the Soviet Ministry of Foreign Affairs, Y. Gremitsky, recognized as "sensible" the declaration in Wałęsa's pronouncement that Poland belongs to the Warsaw Pact (*Trybuna Ludu*, 18 August 1989).

160. The commentary of M. Pavlova-Silvanska in *Moskovskoye Novosti* of 16 August 1989 (excerpts in *Trybuna Ludu*, 18 August 1989). She wrote that only one thing ought to be important for Soviet foreign policy: that the "clearly expressed will of the citizens of a given country gives those who won the elections a completely legal and unshakable status, in the face of which all other arguments should become secondary."

161. The pronouncement of A. Migranian in "Epitaph for the Brezhnev doctrine" in *Moskovskoye Novosti* (excerpts in *Trybuna Ludu*, 19–20 August 1989).

162. J. Gromnitsky (first deputy director of the Department of Information, Ministry of Foreign Affairs) at a press conference in Moscow. Also: "All political forces ought to behave constructively," in *Trybuna Ludu*, 22 August 1989).

163. Sixteenth Plenum of the Central Committee of the Communist party, 19–20 August 1989, Materialy [Materials], in *Trybuna Ludu*, 21 August 1989.

164. Statement of L. Miller at meetings with Communist party activists, *Trybuna Ludu*, 1 September 1989.

165. The most friendly statements concerning the Polish changes (Pavlova's and Migranian's) come from the Institute of World Economy of the Socialist Countries in Moscow, headed by I. Bogomolov, where, it seems, a staff of experts evaluating changes in Eastern Europe is located.

166. *Gazeta Wyborcza*, 4 July 1989.

167. A polemic with the position of Michnik: Senators J. Żiółkowski and Stelmachowski (*Gazeta Wyborcza*, 6 July 1989); Deputy J. Onyszkiewicz (*Gazeta Wyborcza*, 5 July 1989).

168. TV program on Solidarity, 8 July 1989.

169. Response in a poll of *Gazeta Wyborcza* (5 August 1989); also, paper in the CPC on 4 July 1989.

170. Staff headed by J. Kaczyński, senator and secretary of Solidarity's NC.

171. Statement for *Gazeta Wyborcza*, 5 July 1989.

172. K. Modzelewski, "Nie róbmy rządu, nie idźmy stąd" [Let's not form a government, let's not move from here], *Gazeta Wyborcza*, 6 July 1989.

173. J. Kuroń, "Rząd—kiedy—jaki—czyj" [The government—when—what kind—whose], *Polityka*, 20 July 1989.

174. Gieremek (in the name of the CPC): "We shall remain in opposition" (*Gazeta Wyborcza*, 27 July 1989).

175. The attempt by the CPC to form a coalition (with United Peasants' party deputies) to block the election of General Kiszczak as prime minister failed: one of the reasons was a sharp attack by one of the CPC deputies on the deputy prime minister from the UPP, A. Oleśiak.

176. "W stronę gabinetu cieni" [Toward a shadow cabinet], *Gazeta Wyborcza*, 27 July 1989.

177. Ibid.

178. J. Rokita, "Nowa umowa?" [A new agreement?], *Gazeta Wyborcza*, 10 July 1989.

179. The visit of Wałęsa, Malinowski, and Jóźwiak paid on President Jaruzelski, 18 August 1989.

180. Interview with Rakowski, *Trybuna Ludu*, 2 September 1989.

181. Statement of J. Bisztyga, press spokesman of the Central Committee of Communist party, Polish Radio, 2 September 1989. In sharp contrast with this is the pacificatory tone of the interview with the chairman of the party's Club of Deputies, Orzechowski: "Tylko zgodnie i wspolnie" [Only in agreement and together], *Trybuna Ludu*, 31 August 1989.

182. L. Miller on solidarity in the party (*Trybuna Ludu*, 1 September 1989).

183. Information from Budapest, from deliberations of the trilateral "round table," August 1989.

184. An example is the strike of the railwaymen in Łódź (August 1989), which was organized without the participation of the legal trade-union head offices (APATT, Solidarity), but on the initiative of activists from the Union of Socialist Polish Youth, who probably were under the influence of the local party apparatus.

185. See J. Staniszkis, *Ontologia socjalizmu* [The ontology of socialism], Warsaw: Biblioteka Krytyka, 1989; also Oxford: Oxford University Press, in preparation, chap. 2.

186. See the statement of Senator J. Ciesielski during the budget debate in the Senate (11 July 1989). Budget revenues of 1.5 trillion złotys are anticipated from fines (for comparison, the annual budgetary expenditures for science are 89 billion złotys).

187. An example is the supply of fuels from the U.S.S.R. In spite of earlier agreements, in June 1989 the Russian side announced that over the next five years it could supply only 40.7 billion cubic meters of gas (of the 45.7 billion planned). The plan covers only the present customers of gas—without investments in industry and housing construction. See "Podwójna zapaść" [A double collapse], *Życie Warszawy*, 24 August 1989.

188. During the "round table" talks, the desire to eliminate quickly the seeds of social conflict led to a considerable rise of wages in the socialized economy: in February, 27 percent; in March, 34 percent (see: J. Baczyński, "Wszyscy maja racje" [Everyone is right], *Polityka*, 26 August 1989).

189. See chap. 2. Today in Poland the ratio of the purchase price of meat to the price of grain (relation kg - kg) is 1 to 10, whereas in the EEC the ratio is 1 to 6.5. This difference results from the principle of parity (with an overpopulated countryside) and the inefficiency of animal breeding (longer cycles than in the EEC).

190. The notion of exacting obedience (that is, control in the hierarchical order) by having superiors contribute elements to the survival strategy of subordinates comes from J. Migdal, *Strong Societies and Weak States*, (Princeton, N.J.: Princeton University Press, 1988).

191. The meeting of Communist party secretaries in Poznań with the participation of M. Król, Secretary of the Central Committee (report on Polish Radio, "Program 1," 25 July 1989; also the meeting of L. Miller with members of the PUWP in the Kalisz WSK (machine factory) and the meeting of the active Communist party members with ministers of central offices; both reports in Trybuna Ludu, 28 July 1989).

192. Exposé of Prime Minister Mazowiecki delivered in the Seym (text in *Trybuna Ludu*, 25 July 1989).

193. Some managing directors of state enterprises, who came to these posts from the *nomenklatura*, are quitting the Communist party. This was announced at a meeting of Basal Party Secretaries of the party from 208 of the largest plants in the Central Committee; see *Trybuna Ludu*, 19 August 1989.

194. "Wolny obszar Malaszewicze-Terespol" [The Malaszewicze-Terespol Duty-free Zone], *Trybuna Ludu*, 19 August 1989.

195. Communique of the Ministry for Economic Cooperation with Foreign Countries, *Trybuna Ludu*, 23 August 1989. One of the purposes of this decree was to prevent the export of food from Poland in frontier trade, since—even after the last round of price hikes—the production of food is still subsidized and shortages in the domestic market are contributing to the inflationary spiral.

196. W. Staskiewicz, Local administration in the mid-80s, fragments of Ph.D. thesis (Warsaw University, Law School, 1988).

197. J. Jabłoński, mimeographed (Warsaw University, Law School, 1988).

198. Decree of the Minister of Finances of 30 September 1988 on meeting tax obligations.

199. An example is the question of so-called complete indexation (also for those who won wage increases in the second quarter of 1989 by going on strike). Only four members of the CPC supported this form of indexation in the discussion, but all members voted for it because they did not want to oppose the National Committee of Solidarity. The latter, in turn, pushed for this form of indexation, which is ruinous to the economy, prodded by the APATT and the competition with this organization for trade-union members.

200. The theatricalization of political life (as in the live broadcasts from the parliament) causes a revival of the rhetoric of black-white symbols and spectacular attacks of the previous government. The executive

power apparatus fears that, in spite of the assurances of Prime Minister Mazowiecki, this might touch off a wave of "settling scores" in enterprises. Already some things have taken place that recall the climate of autumn 1981, e.g., wheeling the managing director out in a barrow (a case described in *Gazeta Wyborcza*, 26 July 1989, which reported on the conflict in the Szczecin branch of Hortex).

201. For example, Prime Minister Rakowski invited Professor Trzeciakowski to join his government, and in trying to form his government General Kiszczak invited Professor Kuratowska.

202. Exposé of Prime Minister Mazowiecki, *Seym*, 24 August 1989.

203. In the first phase this was the Committee for Understanding (the composition of which was described earlier in this chapter); today, in addition to this committee, there is the extraconstitutional tandem of Jaruzelski–Wałęsa (as the "people's president"), who only as a pair are capable of playing a stabilizing role and regulating conflicts.

204. That is, a pattern of democracy based on extraconstitutional agreements among elites which are renewed from time to time.

205. For a historical analysis of this form of state, see G. Poggi, *The Development of the Modern State* (Stanford, Calif.: Stanford University Press, 1978); for an earlier analysis, see the histroical writings of Otto von Gierke. See also Otto Hinze, *Feudalismus—Kapitalismus* (Gottingen: Nap. 1970).

206. Poggi, *Modern State*, p. 37.

207. An example is the social base of the CPC, which is made up of wage earners of the state sector and private farmers, groups that are clearly entering into a conflict of interests.

208. See chap. 1; also chap. 5.

Chapter 5

1. Law on associations, Moscow, March 1906.

2. Memorial of Nicolas II, 17 October 1905.

3. An example is the program of the Artisan party of 8 January 1906, which called for legislative powers for the Duma, its superiority over the executive branch, and the right to set the budget of the state (from Gregory L. Freeze, *From Supplication to Revolution* (Oxford: Oxford University Press, 1988), p. 263. An opposite position, stating that the law on the Duma is inconsistent with the constitutional principle of autocracy, was formulated by the Congress of Noble Circles on 22–25 April, 1906.

4. An expression used by G. Freeze, *From Supplication*, p. 198.

5. After 1905 the trade unions in Russia used typically Western forms

of activity, such as participation in industrial arbitration, insurance activity, running cooperatives of producers and consumers (see Victoria E. Bonnell, *Roots of Rebellion* [Berkeley, Los Angeles, London: University of California Press, 1988], chap. 7).

6. The memorial of the Ministry of Internal Affairs of March 1906, which stated that the delegalization of trade unions in Russia is "inconceivable" for several reasons: the government by itself cannot satisfy all the aspirations of the society; employers themselves believe that trade unions help to mitigate conflicts; the time has come to recognize workers' rights. In 1907 it was added that "it is easier for the police to penetrate legal trade unions" and that the chief concern ought to be to isolate radical intellectuals (from Bonnell, *Roots*, p. 277).

7. 3 June 1907.

8. See Bonnell, *Roots*, chaps. 7 and 8.

9. From an interview with Senator A. Celinski in *Życie Warszawy* (9–10 September 1989): "Many of the blockades to the changes necessary for raising the country from ruin have their roots in people themselves." Later he mentions the absence of a middle class, which would support the reforms, and blockades to the reforms in the trade-union movement.

10. An uprising on the Lena (Siberia) on 4 April 1912, where many workers were killed and which touched off a wave of strikes in the European part of Russia.

11. Barrington Moore, Jr., *Injustice: The Social Bases of Obedience and Revolt* (New York: Basic Books, 1978).

12. Attacks on political capitalism in the Resolution of the National Committee (NC) of Solidarity (August 1989).

13. An example is opposition of the workers' self-management movement in enterprises to the formation of private companies and the position of the NC (*Tygodnik Solidarność*, no. 14, 1989).

14. Max Weber, *Economy and Society*, ed. Guenther Roth and Claus Wittich (Berkeley, Los Angeles, London 1979) pp. 871, 1209.

15. R. Kosseleck, *The Origin of the Modern State* (Boston: MIT Press, 1988).

16. An observation of K. Jowitt during a lecture in the Jackson School of International Studies, University of Washington, May 1989.

17. See R. Kasaba, "A Time and Place for the Non-State," lecture, mimeographed, University of Washington, June 1989, p. 1.

18. Celinski, 9–10 September 1989 interview (n. 9).

19. See J. Staniszkis, "Political Articulation of Property Rights," in: I. Białecki, J. Koralewicz, M. Watson (eds.), *Crisis and Transformation* (London: Matrix, 1988).

20. T. Syryjczyk, Seym, 8 September 1989 (*Życie Warszawy*, 9–10 September 1989).

21. For an interesting analysis of the links of *perestroika* with nationalist upheavals, see A. Motyl, "Nationalist Behavior," in: S. Bialer, *Inside Gorbachev's Russia* (New York: 1988). Motyl shows that the movements in behalf of national autonomy are often based on economic and not national interests (autonomy is profitable for the elite associated with new rules of the economic game).

22. A. Blok, *Diary* (in Polish) (Warsaw: Polski Instytut Wydawmiry, 1978).

23. At the end of August and beginning of September celebrations were held: Days of Prayers for Peace (in which representatives of the Jewish community refused to participate), the anniversary of the outbreak of the war, the dedication of monuments to these events, celebrations of the anniversary of the agreements signed with the authorities in 1980.

24. An anecdotal example of blackmail with the charge of anti-Semitism: A. Michnik was criticized by a Solidarity member of the National Election Committee (June 1989) for having agreed (during backstage negotiations with the Kiszczak-Gdula group) to change in the election law by decree without deliberations in the Seym. The latter said to him: "Adam, you have put yourself above the nation!" Michnik responded: "So you're saying that I am not a part of the nation?" The fear of the label of anti-Semitism shut the mouth of the critic.

25. A fascinating example of the way in which Russian liberals perceive the situation in Poland is the recent (February 1990) meeting of members of Interregional Parliamentary Club with Wałęsa. One of the Soviet parliamentarists said to Wałęsa, "You are like Sancho Panza. We in the Soviet Union do not need Sancho Panza." Wałęsa (not knowing who Sancho Panza is) answered with some ambiguity, "Let's see." But the most interesting question is who—from the point of view of Soviet reformers from above—is Don Quixote? Gorbachev? Russian intelligentsia who do not need folk heroes? In the above context the important difference between the Soviet and Polish situations was visible: Soviet intelligentsia do not have and do not look for relationships with the "people": they do things for the people but not—as it was in Poland in 1980 and 1981—with them.

26. Kosseleck, *Origin*, chap. 2.

27. Of the 2 million members of the Communist party, 900,000 hold managerial positions. The rest of the managerial posts (around 300,000) are left for the 23 million adults who are not Communist party members.

28. See the discussion in the Seym on the law of election to local

government (the majority formula contra the proportional formula: the bloc based on the "Solidarity ethos" contra the parties), TV First Program, 25–27 January 1990.

29. Bulletin of the Center for the Study of Public Opinion (CBOS), Warsaw, November 1989.

30. Solidarity's membership, as revealed in the December 1989 elections for union leadership, was about one-fifth of what it was in 1981. In Warsaw about 180,000 people belong to Solidarity (1 million in 1981); in Szczecin, about one-seventh of its 1981 numbers. According to the figures of Minister A. Hall (see Interpelations, TV First Program, 25 January 1990) about forty parties and political clubs are active in Poland; twenty of them maintain regular contacts with his office. The largest one (Confederation for an Independent Poland) numbers about 350,000 members.

31. The Senate determined that Clubs of Deputies must number no fewer than twenty deputies; this is to prevent the appearance of political differences within the Citizens' Parliamentary Club (CPC). Discussion in the Seym, 25 January 1990.

32. The formula of such a plebiscitary democracy dominated the elections to the Seym and Senate of 4 June 1989 and is supposed to be applied in elections to local offices (April 1990). See the discussion in the Seym: 25–27 January 1990.

33. See the report of the Catholic *Tygodnik Powszechny* of 17 September 1989, entitled "Falszerstwo Reutera" [Falsification of Reuter]. I quote: "And Reuter now comments on its own about the agreement of 1987, stating that Cardinal Macharski believes it is invalid today, but omitting one detail—that this agreement is synonymous with the so-called 'Geneva Declaration' to which the Commission of the Polish Episcopate (with Cardinal Macharski as its chairman) refers positively twice (which Reuter, as we have seen, carefully omitted). As the result of Reuter's falsification, the French press—we have not yet read any other—reported completely misleading information." It is worthwhile to add that this happened before the planned visit in Warsaw of R. Dumas, the French minister of foreign affairs (with France as temporary leader of the EEC), who was supposed to sign—in the name of the EEC—an agreement on favorable trade conditions and help for Poland.

Conclusion

1. See G. Hegel, *Philosophy of Right*, trans. T. M. Knox (New York: Oxford University Press, 1942).

2. See J. Staniszkis, *Ontologia socjalizmu* [Ontology of socialism] (Warsaw: Biblioteka Krytyka, 1989; also Oxford: Oxford University Press, in preparation).

3. An example is the unsuccessful efforts of Eastern European countries to change their obligations in COMECON during the January 1990 session of that organization at Sofia.

4. D. Held and J. B. Thomas, eds., in introduction to *Social Theory of Modern Societies: Anthony Giddens and His Critics* (Cambridge: Cambridge University Press, 1989), p. 14.

5. See J. Staniszkis, "The Dynamics of Breakthrough in Eastern Europe," *Soviet Studies*, October 1989; also J. Staniszkis, "Patterns of Change in Eastern Europe," *Eastern European Politics and Society*, January 1990.

6. The description of the old form of colonial states in Eastern Europe as well as the emerging new form is in J. Staniszkis, "Dynamics of Dependency," The Wilson Center papers, Washington, D.C., 1987; also Staniszkis, *Ontologia*, chap. 3.

7. Nomination of A. Giddens, *The Nation-State and Violence* (Cambridge: Cambridge Polity Press, 1985), p. 47.

8. See, for instance, A. Michnik's position on the need for an evolutionary strategy of transition (*Gazeta Wyborcza*, 9 February 1990).

9. The Lithuanians' decision for secession from the Soviet Union (March 1990) voiced a similar reaction from the Western powers during the nineteenth-century crisis of the Ottoman Empire from the point of view of Great Britain.

10. J. Buchanan's remark during his lecture "European Constitutional Opportunity," Australian National University, Canberra, 29 March 1990.

11. See G. Poggi's analysis of the German tradition of political thought in *The Development of the Modern State* (Stanford, Calif.: Stanford University Press, 1978).

12. An analysis of rituals of change appears in V. Turner, *The Ritual Process* (Ithaca, N.Y.: Cornell University Press, 1966).

13. See J. Staniszkis' analysis of October 1956 in Poland as a "ritual drama" in *Poland: Self-limiting Revolution* (Princeton, N.J.: Princeton University Press, 1986).

14. C. Levi-Strauss' concept, *La Pensée Savage* (Paris: PLON, 1962).

15. See J. Staniszkis "Form of Reasoning as Ideology," *Telos*, Spring, 1986.

16. A peculiar twist of nationalism and religious fundamentalism is possible as well. An example is the current conflict between the Orthodox Church and the Uniate Church in the Ukraine. The latter was found-

ed in 1596 as a combination of Catholicism and the Greek Orthodox religion, delegalized by Soviet authorities in 1946; Gorbachev's government rejected its present claims for relegalization. The Uniate Church is treated by the emerging Ukrainian intelligentsia not only as a religion but as the symbol of Ukrainians belonging to Central Europe; its past ability to combine elements of Western and Eastern culture is seen today as a prospect for its future role. The politicized vision of Unified Church is based on many historical distortions but, at the same time, is a necessary element of the emerging national identity.

17. See for instance, A. Mannanikov's electoral platform (before the 4 March 1990 election) in the *Press Bulletin* of the Independent Siberian Information Agency, no. 36, 1989, quoted in *Sibirskaja Gazeta*, 15 January 1990. According to V. Tolz, "Informal Political Groups Prepare for Elections in the Russian Federal Republic" (in *Radio Liberty Bulletin*, 23 February 1990) the Khabarovsk Popular Front asked for the proclamation of the Far Eastern Republic, demanding at the same time higher wages for specialists working in Siberia as well as private cooperatives to build garages for private cars.

18. Sixteen percent of votes were gained by the reformed Communist party (CDU: 40 percent, SPD: around 21 percent).

19. An instructive example here is the supraparty bloc created in Poland from the network of so-called Citizens' Committees: during preparation for the May 1990 elections to the local government, the position of Committees (that use the Solidarity ethos as their trademark) was to reject the right to enter their electoral lists for all with any (not only communist) party affiliation.

20. See letters discussing access to mass media, *Tygodnik Solidarność*, no. 12, 1990. Also in the same issue is M. Zaleski's article on the conflict between efforts to build a party system "from above" (out of the Solidarity Parliamentary Club) and grass-roots activists.

21. See Staniszkis, "Breakthrough."

22. See Staniszkis, "Breakthrough"; also Staniszkis, "Patterns."

23. See North and Thomas, "The Rise of the Western World" (Cambridge: Cambridge University Press, 1974); also, A. Giddens "Nation-State and Violence" (Cambridge: Cambridge Polity Press, 1985).

24. See the description of such an intellectual shift in the "globalist" faction standing behind Gorbachev in Staniszkis, "Patterns."

Afterword

1. Jadwiga Staniszkis, *Ontology of Socialism* (New York: Oxford University Press, forthcoming), chap. 4.

2. Ibid., chap. 6.

3. Peter Gay, *Weimar Culture: The Outsider as Insider* (New York: Oxford University Press, 1968).

4. December 1990 was marked in Poland with massive wild strikes (miners, railway workers).

5. Walesa, when elected president (December 1990) invited the leaders of all political parties (those in support of him and those in opposition) to his Political Council. This added to the ambiguity of the political identities: none of these leaders is now sure if he is in power or in opposition. Such a situation may distort as well the forthcoming parliamentary elections in Poland.

6. The former Communist party property rights and personal policies are the main issue here.

7. The IMF program was based on a strategy to fight inflation with correctional inflation that added recession (with deep realization problems in the economy when prices are kept as a barrier to consumer demand).

8. See chapter 2 of this book.

9. New elites (after 1989) already started to use their access to information and an intimate knowledge of the new rules to capitalize and create business opportunities.

10. An example of making up for nonexisting interest in capital formation is a tax on wage increases at the enterprise level which has the objective of imitating the absent interest of the owner.

11. An example is the legislation on "unjust profits" which was introduced by the Polish parliament in Spring, 1990 and was aimed at "political capitalism"—which was legal due to rules introduced by the communist regime in 1987.

12. Douglass C. North, *Structure and Change in Economic History* (New York: Norton, 1981).

13. Before the scheme for privatization was decided the parliament made a decision regarding who has the right to privatize (and issue the bonds). Ambiguity of ownership in a socialist economy was one of the reasons for legalizing the possibilities of introducing the "political capitalism" scheme that was decided on at the enterprise level. To prevent such a situation, the first step—before privatization began—was to centralize property right in a State-owned economy and to put the rights to alienate property rights and issue bonds into the hands of the newly created Ministry for Privatization.

14. See J. Staniskis, *Ontology of Socialism*, chap. 3.

15. See J. Staniszkis, "The Dynamics of Breakthrough in Eastern Europe," *Soviet Studies*, October 1989, see also J. Staniszkis, "Patterns

of Change in Eastern Europe," *East European Politics and Society*, January 1990.

16. J. Attali, the president of the new European Bank for Restructuration and Development evaluates that capital needs of Eastern Europe are around $1.37 trillion U.S., whereas the total foreign investment in Eastern Europe greatly exceeds $2 billion U.S., which is about 0.5 percent of all foreign investment worldwide. See G. Meritt, "The European Community Can't Afford To Let Eastern Europe Founder," *The International Herald Tribune*, 8 December 1990.

17. The present stage of the Soviet crisis can be described as follows: collapse of the State hierarchy due to lack of transmission; dual (until recently) power on the top level and full ambiguity of the power structure after the crackdown in the Baltic States; irrelevant duality one the lower level where the local party committees are blocking reforms (in order to survive) and where the new social organizations are somehow irrelevant from the point of view of reforms (looking for autonomy and playing politics of identity). The state of emergency, introduced before the army was modernized, can slow down centrifugal tendencies but would not solve the anarchy problem of the State, which adds to economic crises (the State is the main actor in the State-owned economy).

18. Such suggestions came from the European Economic Community when it was directed by Italy: the most outspoken proposal was formulated by Mr. Rugierro, the Italian Minister of Foreign Trade, and was supported by the Germans (and to a lesser extent, by the French government).

19. For intance, in the scheme for absorption by Eastern Europe, the new wave of migration from the Soviet Union was discussed.

20. The best example is Czechoslovakian policy vis-à-vis Poland, with its unwillingness to open the borders between both countries due to the fear that it would make it more difficult to integrate into the European Economic Community when Soviet migrants (already in Poland) spread out.

21. See an analysis of rebellion in Hegel's *Phenomenology of Spirit*, trans. A. V. Miller (New York: Oxford University Press, 1977) as well as in A. Camus, *Rebel* (New York: Vintage Books, 1963).

22. This included among other things: the Church's broadcasting on Radio and TV, the antiabortion law, the Church's influence on personal policy on all levels of the State administration, and introduction of religion to schools.

23. These are declarations of the ROAD (Mazowiecki's party).

24. This is Porozumienie Centrum (the electoral bloc supporting Walesa and including the main center-right parties).

25. An argument used by E. Majcher (secretary of the Church Commission for contacts with the Ministry of Education); see "Spor o racje" (Conflict over Rights), *Zycie Warszawa* (Warsaw Daily), 21 September 1990.

26. See, for example, the rapid shift of A. Jakovlev's position on the national question in the Soviet Union when he become convinced (among ather things, by E. Gellner's books!) that the "nation-state" stage is necessary if one wants to move toward capitalism; see Jakovlev's Kiszyniew speech, April 1990.

27. Robert Nisbet, *Social Change and History* (New York: Oxford University Press, 1969), p. 142.

28. See J. Staniszkis, *Ontology of Socialism*, chap. 1.

29. See J. Staniszkis, *Poland: Self-limiting Revolution* (Princeton: Princeton University Press, 1986); see also J. Staniszkis, "Political Articulation of the Collective Property Rights" in I. Bialecki, J. Koralwicz, M. Watson, *Conflict and Transformation* (London, 1988) and J. Staniszkis, *Ontology of Socialism*, chaps. 5 and 6.

30. See the argument, "Poverty is Normal," used during the debate on the social costs of the stabilization plan (*Voice of America*, in Polish, June 1990).

31. ROAD, Unia Demokratyczna.

32. Porozumienie Centrum, Kongres Liberalow.

33. See A. Giddens, *Nation State and Violence* (Cambridge: Cambridge Polity Press, 1985). See also, D. North and R. Thomas, *The Rise of the Western World* (Cambridge: Cambridge University Press, 1974).

34. When none of the Court officials was granted the exclusive right to conduct personal policy in the name of the King. See M. A. R. Graves and R. H. Silcock, *Revolution, Reaction and the Triumph of Conservatism: English History 1558–1700* (London: Longman Paul, 1984).

35. See the introduction to Colin Lucas, ed., *The French Revolution and the Creation of Modern Political Culture* (London: Pergamon Press, 1988).

36. It was visible both on the identity level (when local officials ask themselves do we represent local interests or transmit the central policy?) and on the fiscal level (conflict over taxes).

37. P. Bouretz, "Charles de Remusaf: Witness to the Dilemma of Liberal Reason," in *Legacy of the French Revolution*, ed. F. Fouret and M. Ozouf (Paris: PUF, 1989). In the case of Poland this dilemma is well illustrated by inner debate inside the neoconservative circle (e.g., in the monthly journals, *Polityka Polska* and *Respublika*).

Index

Absolutist states, development of, 225
Ademiec, 85
Afanasyev, J., 14
Agency for Ownership Transformations, 67
Agricultural cooperatives, 22
Agriculture, 19
"Agrosocialism," 132–133, 275 n. 38
All-Polish Association of Trade Unions (OPZZ), 97, 98, 153, 154, 172, 178; establishment of, 92, 178
Ambiguity, of formal structure of state, 219
Anarchy, 2, 3, 4, 75, 88; attitude toward law and, 167–168; conscious introduction of, 163; contradictions as cause of, 4; democratization from above and, 169; economic conditions in COMECON and, 164; economic reform and, 168–169; inflation and, 58, 164; reasons for, 4, 163–169, 212; recession and, 57; in Soviet Union, 15; uncertainty about power apparatus and, 164–165
Andropov, Yuri V., 13, 15
Apathy, social, 20, 143, 181, 185, 230; exclusionary corporatism and, 20; increase in, 220. See also Passivity of society
Attitudes, social, 220; on new center, 98–99; on privatization of state sector, 64–69
Auctioning, of state enterprises, 54, 55
"Authoritarianism with authority," 202, 203–205
Avant-garde, myth of, 2, 89, 105, 170, 189; rejection of, 170

Avant-garde of the new establishment, 16, 22, 90, 94; defined, 22; formation of, 16; identity crisis of, 22–23

Baka, Wladystav, 63, 65
Balcerowicz, Leszek, 67
Balcerowicz Plan, 46, 63, 191
Bank of the National Economy, 209
Bankruptcy, 256 n. 16
Blok, Alexander, 185
Breakthrough in socialist system: characteristics of, 8–10; first phase of, 6, 8–9, 90–110, 173, 176, 180, 211–214; role of society in, 179–185; second stage of, 116–175. See also Transition from socialism to capitalism
Brezhnev, Leonid, 13
Brokerage, private: aim of, 40–41; forms of, 39–40
Budget deficit, 261 n. 63
Buffer zone, 40, 52
Bukharin, Nikolay, 131
Bulgaria, 182–183

Capital: formation of, 68, 206, 207, 232, 233; legitimization of, 217–218; and power, in production, 42–42; privatization and, 68–69
Capitalism: dangers of introducing into socialism, 136–137; dependence of socialism upon, 3, 31–32, 120, 189, 235; dilemmas for, 231–234; East European vision of, 239; global, 69–72; introduction into socialism, 134–135, 136–137; and local socialism, 69–72; "state capitalism," proposal of, 138–140

Designer:	U.C. Press Staff
Compositor:	Asco Trade Typesetting Ltd.
Text:	10/13 Sabon
Display:	Sabon
Printer:	Braun-Brumfield, Inc.
Binder:	Braun-Brumfield, Inc.